THE LOST BIBLE

FORGOTTEN SCRIPTURES REVEALED

THE LOST BIBLE

FORGOTTEN SCRIPTURES REVEALED

J. R. PORTER

DUNCAN BAIRD PUBLISHERS

LONDON

The Lost Bible
J. R. Porter

First published in the United Kingdom and Ireland in 2001 by
Duncan Baird Publishers Ltd
Sixth Floor
Castle House
75–76 Wells Street
London W1T 3QH

Conceived, created and designed by Duncan Baird Publishers

Senior Editor: Peter Bently
Editors: Chris Westhorp, Hanne Bewernick and James Hodgson
Designers: Paul Reid and Lloyd Tilbury at Cobalt id
Picture Editor: Julia Ruxton
Commissioned Map: Sallie Alane Reason
Decorative Borders: Sally Taylor

Managing Editor: Diana Loxley

British Library Cataloguing-in-Publication Data:
A CIP record for this book is available from the British Library

ISBN: 1-903296-19-6

10 9 8 7 6 5 4 3

Typeset in Filosofia 11.5/16.5pt and Goudy Catalogue MT 10/15pt
Colour reproduction by Scanhouse, Malaysia
Printed and bound in China by Imago

Captions to illustrations on pages 1 (half-title) and 2 (title):
Page 1: *The Hand of God Presenting a Book to a Prophet or Saint*,
from the "Octateuch": Scenes from the Life of Christ and
the Apostles, an Ethiopic manuscript dated 1744.
Page 2: *Head of an Angel*, by Fra Angelico (1399/1400–1455).

CONTENTS

INTRODUCTION

The Lost Bible is an anthology of ancient scriptures which did not become part of the Jewish or Christian Bibles. They are drawn from the body of literature known as the Pseudepigrapha of the Hebrew Scriptures (Old Testament) and the New Testament Apocrypha, works which are of great interest for the light they shed on the history, religion, and culture of both Judaism and Christianity around the turn of the Common Era.

The "Lost Bible" and the Canons of Scripture

The Hebrew Bible, or Old Testament, is itself a selection from a large mass of ancient scriptures that included the Pseudepigrapha. Similarly, the New Testament was selected from a body of literature that included the apocryphal works considered here. The final selections became the Jewish and Christian canons of Scripture—books recognized as authoritative and divinely inspired. The Hebrew canon began to evolve sometime after the end of the Jewish exile in Babylon at the end of the sixth century BCE, but it was fixed only near the end of the first century CE or even later. The New Testament canon was settled only in the fourth century CE (see Timechart on pp.8–9). Before the canons were finalized, several of the works in *The Lost Bible* would probably have been widely accepted as authoritative. Certainly, on the grounds of character and content alone, it is not really possible to draw a sharp distinction between the non-canonical works on the one hand and the Hebrew Bible and the New Testament on the other.

With the closing of the canons, other writings inevitably became "lost" from the Bibles of Judaism and the mainstream Church, which denounced them as erroneous or heretical. But they were never completely suppressed, especially in more peripheral regions—to this day, the Bible of the Ethiopian church contains the First Book of Enoch and the Book of Jubilees—and many of these works remained influential in the West throughout the Middle Ages. It was the Reformation, with its emphasis on the sole authority of canonical Scripture, and the Enlightenment, with its rational and scientific outlook, that brought about their neglect. Only in the twentieth century were these works rediscovered and their true significance appreciated once more.

The Lost Bible aims to provide representative examples of the main literary genres of non-canonical scriptures, concentrating on texts attributed to, or concerned with, biblical figures. Excluded are the Old Testament Apocrypha (see Glossary)—which are not counted among the Pseudepigrapha, although they share many of the same characteristics—or the Dead Sea Scrolls. Translations of these works are already widely available. The book falls into two main parts, the first (The "Lost" Hebrew Scriptures) dealing with the Pseudepigrapha and the second (the "Lost" New Testament) with the New Testament Apocrypha. In each part, a commentary on the

The Presentation of Mary in the Temple, by Titian (ca. 1487–1576). It depicts an episode in the apocryphal
Protevangelium of James (see pp.130–131) in which the 3-year-old Mary enters the Temple of Jerusalem.

content, origins, and significance of each work is accompanied by one or more translated
extracts that give something of the flavor and character of the original texts. Basic information
for each work—title, date of composition, original language, provenance, and earliest extant
manuscript—is summarized in "data boxes," and special feature boxes highlight key themes.

Part 1: The "Lost" Hebrew Scriptures

"Pseudepigrapha" literally means works with a "false title," or attributed to someone other than
the real author. However, many other Jewish or early Christian writings fit this definition—
including some books of the Bible—and hence many scholars are unhappy with the term. But it

has proved difficult to find any alternative. The Pseudepigrapha include apocalypses ("revelations" of cosmic events); testaments (the last words of a great figure from Israel's past); expansions of Bible narratives; philosophical writings; poems; psalms; and prayers. They are unified by their recurring themes, notably the origin of evil; the end of the world; the Messiah; the transcendence of God; angels; resurrection; and paradise as the reward of the righteous. Most of these works were probably of Jewish origin, but they were of equal interest to Christians—it was only in the Church that they were preserved, and some may even be Christian compositions.

These writings are now recognized as essential for understanding the formative period of both Judaism and Christianity. They show the Judaism of this epoch to have been lively, diverse, and speculative, open to a range of influences from the surrounding world, yet concerned to preserve and reinterpret its traditions in the face of outside threats. The adoption of these works by the Church reveals how deeply the new religion remained rooted in the soil of Judaism.

Part 2: The "Lost" New Testament

The New Testament Apocrypha were written from the second to perhaps as late as the ninth century CE. In the main they imitate the New Testament genres—gospels, acts, letters, and

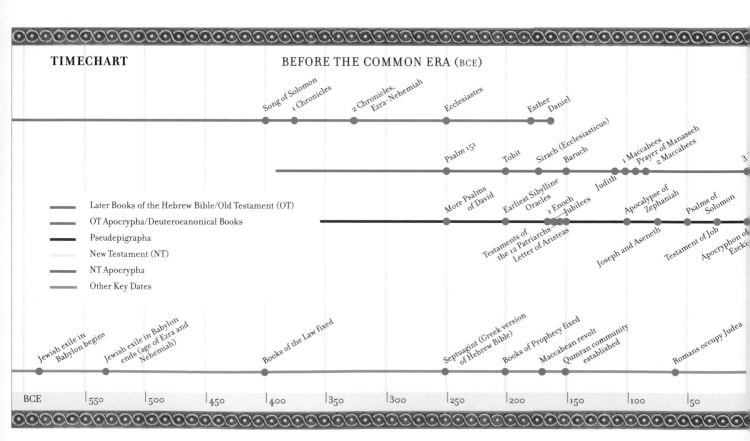

TIMECHART — BEFORE THE COMMON ERA (BCE)

Later Books of the Hebrew Bible/Old Testament (OT)
OT Apocrypha/Deuterocanonical Books
Pseudepigrapha
New Testament (NT)
NT Apocrypha
Other Key Dates

Song of Solomon · 1 Chronicles · 2 Chronicles, Ezra-Nehemiah · Ecclesiastes · Esther · Daniel

Psalm 151 · Tobit · Sirach (Ecclesiasticus) · Baruch · 1 Maccabees · Prayer of Manasseh · 2 Maccabees · 3

More Psalms of David · Earliest Sibylline Oracles · 1 Enoch · Jubilees · Judith · Apocalypse of Zephaniah · Psalms of Solomon · Testaments of the 12 Patriarchs · Letter of Aristeas · Joseph and Asenath · Testament of Job · Apocryphon of Ezeki

Jewish exile in Babylon begins · Jewish exile in Babylon ends (age of Ezra and Nehemiah) · Books of the Law fixed · Septuagint (Greek version of Hebrew Bible) · Books of Prophecy fixed · Maccabean revolt · Qumran community established · Romans occupy Judea

BCE | 550 | 500 | 450 | 400 | 350 | 300 | 250 | 200 | 150 | 100 | 50

apocalypses—and often appear under the names of the apostles. Responding to the desire of ordinary believers to know more about the great figures of the faith than was available in what became the New Testament, these works claim to present authentic memories of Jesus and his followers. While it is unlikely that they provide much, if any, reliable historical information, alongside the New Testament itself they witness to the vigor of literary activity in the early Church. They also throw light on the lifestyles and diverse outlooks of the early Christians. Particularly fascinating in this respect are the numerous gospels, acts, and apocalypses of Gnostic origin (see pp.156–9).

Although dismissed by the mainstream Church as heretical, the apocryphal Christian writings lost little of their popular appeal, while their ideas and legends have regularly been represented in literature and, especially, art.

The extracts are taken from the standard scholarly collections of the Pseudepigrapha by J.H. Charlesworth and of the New Testament Apocrypha by W. Schneemelcher (see Bibliography). These four volumes represent the most authoritative discussions of individual books by modern scholars and *The Lost Bible* largely, though not invariably, accepts their conclusions.

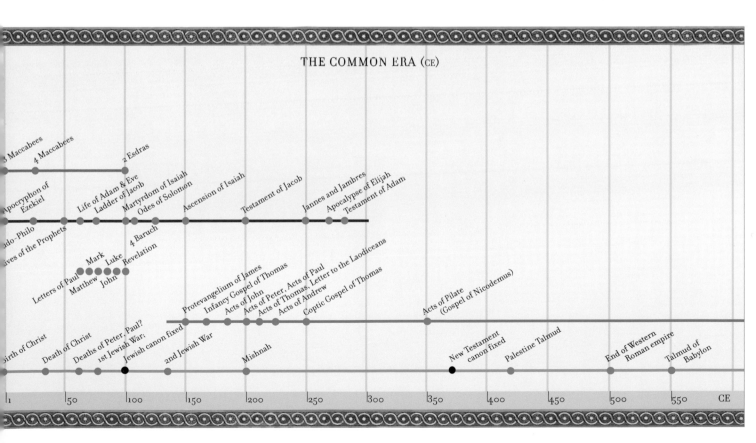

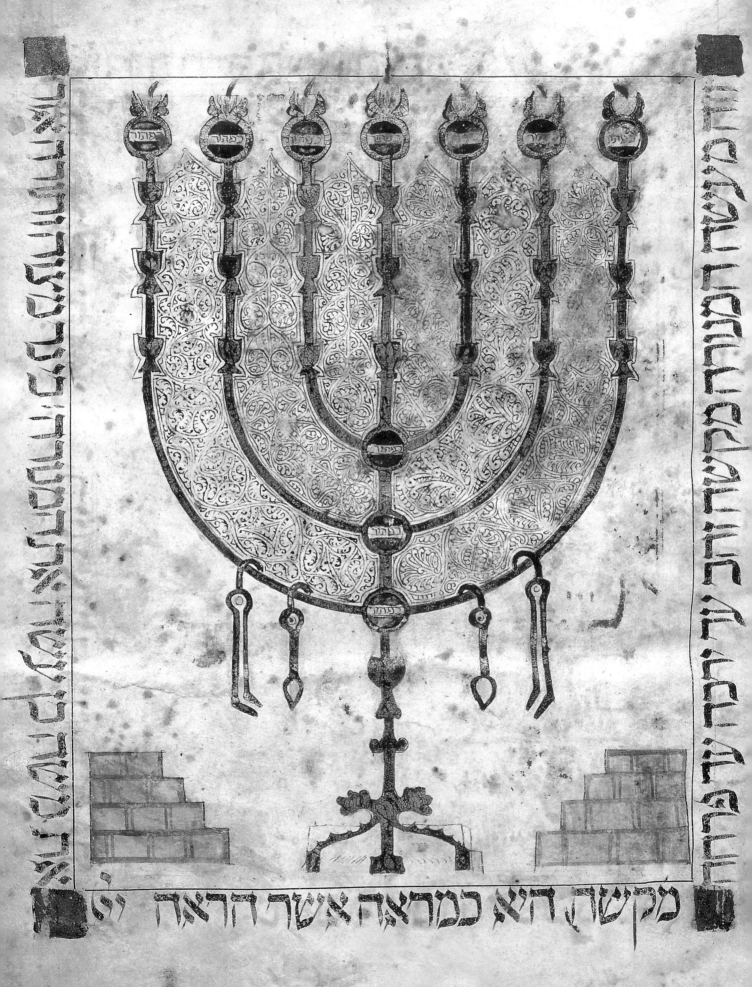

THE "LOST" HEBREW SCRIPTURES

OPPOSITE The Menorah (candelabrum) of the ancient Temple of
Jerusalem, from a manuscript of the Hebrew Bible copied by Jacob
ben Joseph of Ripoll in Solsona, Spain, and dated 1384CE.

CHAPTER 1

IN THE BEGINNING

◆

THE CREATION OF THE WORLD

The narrative of the creation of the universe in the first chapter of Genesis is comparatively brief and simple, and inevitably invited further writings about the nature of God's creative activity. The fullest and most remarkable example of such speculation is found in the work known as the Second Book of Enoch (2 Enoch), which may have been the sacred scripture of a Jewish sect, perhaps in Egypt.

This work claims to record the extraordinary visions of Enoch, a biblical figure who inspired a whole tradition of writings (see pp.30–35). Creation is central to the theology of 2 Enoch: it reaches its climax when, after Enoch's ascent to the divine throne room in the highest heaven, God reveals to him the secrets of the creative process in a long discourse. While the depiction of the creation is not wholly consistent, it is possible to discern a creative progression within it. God's account basically follows Genesis, but the author almost entirely transforms the biblical picture by presenting it in terms of ancient Greek physics, mingled with a range of ideas that seem to reflect Egyptian and Iranian mythology. It has been claimed that 2 Enoch may be one of the earliest known attempts to reconcile the Bible with science.

Adoil and Arkhas

In the beginning, according to 2 Enoch, God moved in a setting of "invisible things" and the act of creation primarily involved making the invisible visible or bringing the non-being into being. This was accomplished through two invisible agents, called Adoil and Arkhas. Adoil is an unknown name, but Arkhas may be connected with the Greek word *arkhe*, an important concept in early Greek physics.

At God's command, Adoil gives birth to the light and Arkhas to the darkness and these respectively constitute the upper and lower foundations of the world. Next, the mixing of these fundamental elements creates the other features of the universe: light and darkness together produce water (see extract, opposite), which in turn produces the seven heavenly spheres and the dry land of earth.

Finally, God creates the first man from various earthly and celestial components—human reason, for example, is said to come from "the mobility of angels and from clouds"—and gives him a name, Adam, derived from the names of the four directions in Greek (see extract on p.23).

The Creation: The Separation of Light from Darkness, from a mosaic in St Mark's basilica, Venice (12th–13th cent.).
It shows an angel as the agent of God's commands, an idea going back to 2 Enoch and other non-canonical texts.

From the Second Book of Enoch, chapters 24–27

Before anything existed at all, from the very beginning, whatever is, I [God] created from non-being into being, and from the invisible things into the visible.

And I commanded the lowest things: "Let one of the invisible things descend visibly!" And Adoil descended, extremely large. And I looked at him, and, behold, in his belly he had a great light. And I said to him, "Disintegrate yourself, Adoil, and let what is born from you become visible." And he disintegrated himself and there came out a very great light.

And then to the light I spoke: "You go up higher and be solidified and become the foundation for the highest things." And there is nothing higher than the light, except nothing itself.

And I called out a second time into the lowest things, and I said, "Let one of the invisible things come out solid and visible." And Arkhas came out, solid and heavy and very red. And I said, "Open yourself up, Arkhas, and let what is born from you become visible!" There came out an age, dark, very large, carrying the creation of all lower things.

And I gave the command: "Let there be taken some of the light and some of the darkness." And I said, "Become thickened, and be wrapped around with light!" And I spread it out, and it became water.

DATA

TITLE:
The Second Book
of Enoch

ORIGINAL DATE
OF COMPOSITION:
2nd cent. BCE–
1st cent. CE

ORIGINAL LANGUAGE:
Hebrew
or Aramaic?

PROVENANCE:
Egypt?

EARLIEST EXTANT
MANUSCRIPT:
14th cent. CE
(Old Slavonic)

THE CREATION OF THE ANGELS

A large number of writings give great prominence to the nature and work of angels. In the canonical Hebrew Bible, angels play a relatively restricted role in human history compared with the direct interventions of God. However, the centuries following the Jewish exile in Babylon in the sixth century BCE saw a marked change in Israel's concept of its deity, and the notion of the angels also underwent a significant development that found its fullest expression in the non-canonical scriptures.

Increasingly during this period, God came to be viewed as wholly transcendent, a majestic being dwelling in the further realm of the heavens above the created world, essentially invisible and unknowable. Only exceptional human beings who were transported to the heavens, such as Enoch, could come into direct contact with him. Since God was remote from the world, he communicated with creation and humanity through intermediaries, primarily the angels, who thus acquired great importance in Jewish religious thought. The universe came to be viewed as full of an incalculable number of angelic beings.

Genesis provides no information about the origin of the angels and so later writers undertook to describe how God had produced them as part of the divine creative activity. In these accounts, the angels' bodies are often said to be made from the element of fire, and a further novel feature not found in the Bible is that angels are viewed as controlling natural phenomena such as heavenly bodies, the weather, and the seasons. Hence, under the authority of God, the angels may be said to be the directing power of the whole universe.

OPPOSITE *The Host of Angels*, an Ethiopian painting of the 17th century. The important role of angels in the Ethiopian Orthodox church derives from the sacred status accorded to the books of Enoch in that culture.

From the Book of Jubilees, chapter 2

On the first day he created the heavens, which
are above, and the earth, and the waters and
all of the spirits which minister before him:
the angels of the presence,
and the angels of sanctification,
and the angels of the spirit of fire,
and the angels of the spirit of the winds,
and the angels of the spirit of the clouds and
darkness and snow and hail and frost,
and the angels of resoundings and thunder
and lightning,
and the angels of the spirits of cold and
heat and winter and springtime and harvest
and summer,
and all of the spirits of his creatures which
are in heaven and on earth.

From the First Book of Enoch, chapter 71

I, Enoch, was in the heaven of heavens. There I saw—in the midst of that light—a structure built of crystals; and between those crystals, tongues of living fire. ... And I saw countless angels—a hundred thousand times a hundred thousand, ten million times ten million—encircling that house. Michael, Raphael, Gabriel, Phanuel, and numerous other holy angels that are in heaven above, go in and out of that house. ... With them is the Antecedent of Time: his head is white and pure like wool and his garment is indescribable. I fell on my face, my whole body mollified and my spirit transformed. Then I cried with a great voice by the spirit of power, blessing, glorifying, and extolling.

THE ANGELS AND THEIR WORK

The non-canonical writings classify the angels into a large number of different groups, according to their areas of responsibility. So, in addition to angels who control natural phenomena, there are figures such as "the angel of peace" or "the angel of death." There is also a whole range of celestial beings whose primary function is to guard God's heavenly throne; these are not really distinguishable from the angels except that they have distinctive names, such as seraphim, cherubim, and ophannim.

Such names and classifications vary considerably from one author to another. One notable feature not found in the Bible is the concept of the angels as a hierarchy, headed by a group of

Tobias and the Archangels Michael, Raphael, and Gabriel, by Francesco Botticini (1446–97). In the Book of Tobit, Raphael (center), the angel of healing, helps Tobias cure his father Tobit's blindness with the gall of a fish.

The Names of the Angels

In the Pseudepigrapha, the angels, and particularly the archangels, are given specific names and functions. The exact significance of these is not always easy to determine and perhaps all that can be said is that they confer a wide-ranging sphere of authority. The origin of the angelic names is obscure, but several of them seem to refer to the angel's special role: thus the name of Raphael, who is associated with healing, comes from Hebrew *rapha* ("to heal") and that of Raguel, the angel who "takes vengeance," derives from Hebrew *raa*, "to shatter." All the names contain the element *el* ("divine being"), which suggests that they reflect older, and originally polytheistic, concepts—in particular, "the sons of God" who make up God's council in the Bible (Job 38.7, Ps. 29.1 and elsewhere).

senior angels who came to be described as "archangels" but are also called by other names. Most frequently there are said to be seven archangels (see extract, below), but some accounts list four or even three. Other writings present a different picture of the angelic hierarchy and its leaders. In the Book of Jubilees, for example, the highest ranks are "the angels of the presence" and "the angels of sanctification," whose special function is to keep the Sabbath.

In the Bible an angel is primarily a messenger (the meaning of the Greek *aggelos*), but in non-canonical writings the angels have much more varied and extensive roles. As well as being messengers from God to humanity they also actively intercede for people and convey their prayers to God. The angels usually reside close to the divine throne of God, where they conduct a kind of perpetual liturgy of praise to him. Another important function is to guard the righteous individual—and the Chosen People as a whole—against the wicked. Angels test men and women to prove their loyalty to God and bind up evil spirits that might lead people astray.

From the First Book of Enoch, chapter 20

And these are the names of the holy angels who watch:

Suruel [or Uriel], one of the holy angels—for he is of eternity and of trembling.

Raphael, one of the holy angels, for he is of the spirits of man.

Raguel, one of the holy angels who take vengeance for the world and for the luminaries [of heaven].

Michael, one of the holy angels, for he is obedient in his benevolence over the people and the nations.

Saraqael, one of the holy angels who are set over the spirits of humankind who sin in the spirit.

Gabriel, one of the holy angels who oversee the garden of Eden, and the serpents, and the cherubim.

Remiel, one of the holy angels, whom God set over those who rise.

THE FALL OF SATAN AND
THE REBEL ANGELS

Alongside the innumerable host of benevolent angels, the pseudepigraphical writings describe a superhuman realm of wicked spirits opposed to the rule of God. This dualistic view of the universe reflects the authors' preoccupation with the problem of evil and its origin, a concern that arose from the actual historical background against which they wrote. The high hopes among the Jews sparked by their return from the exile in Babylon in the late sixth century BCE had not been realized, and the Promised Land had come to be ruled by a succession of foreign oppressors. To devout followers of the Jewish law, it was the sinners who appeared to prosper in the world. But how could an all-powerful and all-righteous God apparently abandon his Chosen People to the grip of evil forces?

The most common view was that evil resulted not from God, whose creative works were wholly good, but from a group of angels who had rebelled and sinned against God. As a consequence they were expelled into the lower part of the universe, but they remained superhuman beings who used their power to afflict humans and to thwart God's plans for the world. The sin that caused the expulsion of the fallen angels is sometimes said to be their refusal to worship Adam as the image of God (see extract, below). Another common explanation is that

From the Life of Adam and Eve, chapters 13–16.

Gen. 2.7
Gen. 1.27

[The devil speaks to Adam:] "When God blew into you the *breath of life* and your countenance and likeness were made *in the image of God*, Michael ... called all the angels, saying, 'Worship the image of the Lord God, as the Lord God has instructed.' ... And when Michael kept forcing me to worship, I said to him, 'Why do you compel me? I will not worship one inferior and subsequent to me. I am prior to him in creation; before he was made, I was already made. He ought to worship me.'

When they heard this, other angels who were under me refused to worship him. ... God was angry with me and sent me with my angels out from our glory; and because of you, we were expelled into this world from our dwellings and have been cast onto the earth. And immediately we were made to grieve, since we had been deprived of such great glory. And we were pained to see you in such bliss of delights. So with deceit I assailed your wife and made you to be expelled through her from the joys of your bliss, just as I have been expelled from my glory."

OPPOSITE *The Archangel Michael Drives the Rebel Angels from Heaven*, by Domenico Beccafumi (1485–1551). The fall of Satan and his followers inspired many dramatic artistic depictions (see also p.20).

The Fall of Satan and the Rebel Angels, by Jakob Isaaks Swanenburgh (1571–1638). Michael drives the evil angels into "a chaotic and terrible place" (1 Enoch 21) in the depths of the earth.

these angels sought to exalt themselves by setting up a rival throne above that of God.

The view that God himself was not the cause of evil arose from a somewhat obscure passage of ancient Israelite folklore at the beginning of Genesis 6, which tells how the "sons of God" married human women. The offspring of these unions was a race of giants called Nephilim, which probably means "fallen ones" in Hebrew (Gen. 6.1–4). Following this story, but not very clearly linked to it, the Bible mentions God's displeasure and his determination to destroy all life on earth (Gen. 6.5–7). Later writers interpreted this tale as the descent of angels ("sons of God") from the heavens, while their monstrous offspring were the demons who became the source of all the world's evils. Sometimes the original sin of the angels is described as simply lust, provoked by the beauty of the human women or possibly by the wish of the angels to increase their number by reproducing themselves.

Like their heavenly counterparts, the fallen angels form a hierarchy. They have a ringleader called by several names including Satan, the devil, Belial, Mastema, Semyaz or Satanail. Also echoing a feature of the heavenly angels, a number of the evil angels are given names. A few of these, such as Azazel, probably derive from the Bible, where an Azazel

From the First Book of Enoch, chapter 8

And [of the fallen angels] Azazel taught the people the art of making swords and knives, and shields, and breastplates; and he showed to their chosen ones bracelets and decorations, shadowing of the eye with antimony … the beautifying of the eyelids, all kinds of precious stones and all coloring tinctures and alchemy. And there were many wicked ones and they committed adultery and erred, and all their conduct became corrupt. Amasras taught incantation and the cutting of roots; and Armaros the resolving of incantations; and Baraqiyal astrology, and Kokabel the knowledge of the signs, and Tamel taught the seeing of the stars, and Asderel taught the course of the moon.

appears as a kind of wilderness spirit (Lev. 16)—the desert is often viewed as the haunt of demons. It has been plausibly suggested that the titles originally represented personifications of celestial phenomena: thus the name Kokabel would derive from the Hebrew *kokab* ("star"). In the Pseudepigrapha, angels are often virtually identified with stars. Another parallel with the good angels is that these named beings are also assigned specific functions. In particular, they are said to lead Israel astray by teaching the people what were regarded as forbidden arts and sciences, such as alchemy and astrology (see extract, below).

The abode of the fallen angels is generally said to be either on or under the earth, but in 2 Enoch some dwell in different parts of the heavens. The most frequently mentioned group are the "Watchers," who were originally good angels: the seven archangels are described in 1 Enoch as "the holy angels who watch" (see extract on p.17). But they are also frequently identified with the "sons of God" who consorted with earthly women and so were cast out of heaven. Some accounts record that only some of the Watchers sinned—the others were greatly distressed at what their fellows had done, even pleading, in vain, for divine mercy on their behalf.

The story of the fall of the angels, probably first attested in 1 Enoch (see pp.31–3), exerted a profound and wide influence on subsequent belief and writings, especially on later pseudepigraphical texts, where it frequently occurs. The New Testament shows clearly that the legend of the fallen angels was well known to early Christians, as seen in Revelation and especially the Letter of Jude, which mentions the rebellion of the angels and their subsequent imprisonment (Jude 6), and even quotes 1 Enoch directly (Jude 14–15). The legend has figured prominently in Christian thought, literature, and art over many centuries.

The Fate of the Fallen Angels

Although evil is so pervasive in the world, it does not have the last word: the Lord, as the God of justice, must punish all sin, including that of the evil angels. Sometimes it is said that God killed off the evil angels (or at least the first generation of them); alternatively, it is often claimed that they were imprisoned until their final judgment, either below the earth in "a chaotic and terrible place" (1 Enoch 21) or in one of the seven heavens.

The Book of Jubilees includes an interesting attempt to explain how, in spite of the confinement of the demonic forces, evil still remains so active in the world. According to Jubilees, the chief of the evil spirits was allowed to retain a tenth of his followers as agents of punishment on humanity, while the remainder was imprisoned.

Although accounts of how God acts toward the fallen angels vary, the Pseudepigrapha are unanimous that they will meet their final fate at the Last Judgment, when their power will be utterly destroyed, and there are several vivid descriptions of the ultimate destiny that awaits them.

ADAM AND THE FALL

The figure of Adam, the first human, is greatly developed in the Pseudepigrapha as compared with his depiction in the Bible. He is made into a superhuman being and invested with great glory, and non-canonical Jewish and Gnostic writings lay particular emphasis on his creation in the image of God (Gen. 1.27). One work, the Life of Adam and Eve, states that the angels had a duty to worship Adam because he bore the divine image, and that it was because Satan and his followers failed to do so that they were expelled from heaven (see p.18).

In 2 Enoch, Adam is described as "a second angel," assigned to be a king and to possess wisdom, so that there was nothing comparable to him on earth. This book relates how Adam was made from the seven components of the universe, denoting him as a cosmic being (see extract, opposite). Other works claim that God intended Adam to be deified, or that he and Eve were derived not from earthly substance but from one of the "aeons," sublime celestial beings which, according to the Gnostics, were direct emanations of God (see p.157).

However, the fact that Adam had fallen from his original glorious state could not be ignored. Because of his sin, his deification has to be postponed for many years and his death must come first. Indeed, the more Adam's pristine perfection was emphasized, all the more tragic were the consequences of the Fall felt to be. Adam's sin in the garden of Eden came to

Original Sin

The Christian doctrine of original sin is based on the idea that evil resulted from Adam's transgression in Eden, which in the Pseudepigrapha is much less common than the view that it was caused by fallen angels (see p.18). But while the Christian teaching no doubt derives from chapter 5 of Paul's letter to the Romans, Paul may well have been influenced by the kind of speculations found in the Pseudepigrapha. Both depend on the biblical outlook that Adam contained all future humanity within himself and determined its character. Adam's disobedience changed his original happy state of immortality and harmonious communion with his Maker into a state of inevitable death and alienation from God. All human beings share this state, not through any act of their own but simply by being Adam's descendants.

Christianity has usually taught that human beings all share in Adam's sin itself and not just in its consequences. Certainly, the Pseudepigrapha imply that living in a broken relationship with God results in a propensity to sin, but they also teach that humans still have genuine free will and can choose between the "Two Ways" of righteousness—with its reward of a blessed afterlife—and evil (see p.81).

be viewed as the source of all human ills, especially death, but it also disrupted the whole of nature: the Book of Jubilees (see p.26) recounts that when Adam was driven from Eden, animals lost the power of speech and all the creatures which had lived in unity in paradise were scattered and divided over the earth.

But even after the Fall, according to the Life of Adam and Eve, Adam was granted an ascent to the throne of God, who accepted his repentance, promised him ultimate resurrection and restoration, and revealed the course of future history to him. At his death, Adam's soul was taken up to the heavenly Paradise, the counterpart of the earthly Eden, and the Testament of Abraham pictures him there as a "wondrous man" adorned in glory and sitting on a golden throne (see p.41), from where he observes the righteous and the sinners as they enter through either the narrow gate of eternal paradise or the broad gate leading to eternal punishment.

From the Second Book of Enoch, chapter 30

On the sixth day I commanded my wisdom to create man out of the seven components:
first, his flesh from earth;
second, his blood from dew and from the sun;
third, his eyes from the bottomless sea;
fourth, his bones from stone;
fifth, his reason from the mobility of angels and from clouds;
sixth, his veins and hair from the grass of the earth;
seventh, his spirit from my spirit and from the wind. ...
And on the earth I assigned him to be a second angel, honored and great and glorious ...
And I assigned to him a name from the four components:

from East [*Anatolé*] – A
from West [*Dusmé*] – D
from North [*Arktos*] – A
from South [*Mesémbria*] – M

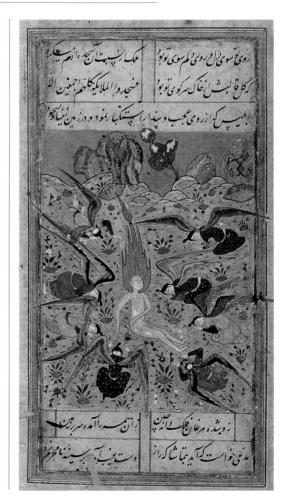

The Angels Adoring Adam, a 17th-century Persian miniature. In the background, Iblis (as Satan is known in Islam) refuses to bow (see pp.18–21).

EVE'S ACCOUNT OF THE FALL

As Adam gained in stature (see pp.22–3), there was a repeated attempt to put the blame for the Fall entirely upon Eve, the first woman: as 2 Enoch bluntly says, when the devil entered Paradise he corrupted Eve, "but Adam he did not contact" (2 Enoch 31). It was natural to speculate as to how and why Eve had succumbed to temptation and to find answers by expanding the laconic narrative in Genesis. An especially interesting section in the Life of Adam and Eve consists of Eve's own account, related to her children and grandchildren, of the events surrounding the Fall. She emerges as a considerable figure in her own right, in charge of half of the garden of Eden and all the female animals—in contrast to the Bible, where Adam is in sole control.

The Life of Adam and Eve introduces a more explicit religious and moral tone into the biblical story. Eve is misled by covetousness, which is described as the origin of all sin—an idea also found in the New Testament (Romans 7.7)—and her nakedness is not primarily physical but rather the loss of righteousness, a common rabbinic interpretation (see extract, below). To lend authority to the narrative, the author adds concrete details: thus the tree of knowledge is said to be a fig tree, and the serpent possesses hands and feet before he is reduced to crawling on the ground. The serpent acts at the instigation of Satan, reflecting the increasing prominence of Satan as the force of evil. He approaches Eve in the guise of one of the angels, who play a notable role throughout and are depicted as participating in regular acts of divine worship.

From the Life of Adam and Eve, chapters 17–20 (Greek version)

DATA

TITLE:
The Life of
Adam and Eve

ORIGINAL DATE
OF COMPOSITION:
1st cent. CE

ORIGINAL LANGUAGE:
probably Hebrew

PROVENANCE:
Palestine?

EARLIEST EXTANT
MANUSCRIPT:
9th cent. CE
(Latin)

[Satan] said to me, "Are you Eve?" And I said to him, "I am." And he said to me, "What are you doing in Paradise?" I replied, "God placed us to guard it and eat from it." The devil answered me through the mouth of the serpent, "You do well, but you do not eat of every plant." And I said to him, "Yes we eat from every plant except one only, which is in the midst of Paradise, concerning which God commanded us not to eat of it, else *you shall most surely die.*[1]"

Then the serpent said to me, "May God live! For I am grieved over you, that you are like animals. For I do not want you to be ignorant; but rise, come and eat, and observe the glory of the tree." And I said to him, "I fear lest God be angry with me, just as he told us." He said to me, "Fear not". ...

He went, climbed the tree, and sprinkled his evil poison on the fruit which he gave me to eat, which is his covetousness. For covetousness is the origin of every sin. And I bent the branch toward the earth, took of the fruit, and ate. And at that very moment my eyes were opened and I knew I was naked of the righteousness with which I had been clothed.

[1] Gen. 2.17

24

The Fall from Grace, by Hugo van der Goes (ca. 1440–82). Here the serpent is depicted with limbs, a tradition first recorded in the non-canonical work known as the Life of Adam and Eve.

THE RHYTHMS OF TIME

Embellishments of the early part of the Bible are also found in an important work called the Book of Jubilees. In form, Jubilees is a retelling of the narratives in Genesis and the first chapters of Exodus, which are presented as a secret revelation from an angel to Moses on Mount Sinai. The work is so called because the author uses the biblical "jubilee," a period of forty-nine (seven times seven) years, as the basic unit of time (see Lev. 25.8ff.). The course of history is divided into a succession of jubilees, and events are dated to a particular jubilee or to one of its "weeks" of seven years.

The Book of Jubilees adds some interesting details to the familiar Genesis stories. In chapter 3 it is said that the beasts and birds could all speak in Eden, communicating "with one language" (see extract, opposite)—presumably Hebrew, which Jubilees later describes as "the tongue of creation." But they were silenced after the Fall, perhaps because Eve had "listened to the voice of the serpent." In the section on the descendants of Adam (Jubilees 4.9–11, expanding on Gen. 5), the author explains how it was possible for the sons of Adam and Eve to beget offspring: they took their sisters as wives (see genealogy on p.29). It is intriguing that Jubilees does not appear to object to incest between brother and sister, unlike that between father and daughter or mother and son, which is strongly condemned elsewhere. According to Jubilees, Adam's famous descendant, Enoch (see pp.30–37), was transported to Eden—from which both humans and animals had been expelled after the Fall—where he wrote "condemnation and judgment of the world, and all of the evils of the children of men." According to Jubilees, because of Enoch's presence, Eden was spared from the great Flood (Jubilees 4.24).

An issue of central importance in Jubilees is the calendar, and indeed it is a matter of crucial significance in Judaism, since it regulates the observance of the various festivals that are at the heart of the nation's religious life. Any disagreement over the calendar would have been a serious issue, because it meant that a feast day for some Jews would have been an ordinary working day for others. There is evidence of bitter calendrical disputes in the later centuries BCE, which are reflected in a number of writings, especially Jubilees and 1 Enoch, which advocate a solar calendar that diverges markedly from the lunar calendar adopted by mainstream Judaism after the Babylonian exile.

In the lunar calendar, the beginning of each month was marked by the appearance of the new moon: each lunar month consisted of twenty-nine or thirty days and the year was made up of 354 days. In contrast, the solar calendar actively promoted by Jubilees and other works was marked by perfect regularity, with four seasons of three months, each month consisting of exactly thirty days. However, because twelve months of thirty days totaled only 360 days, an extra

DATA

TITLE:
The Book of
Jubilees

ORIGINAL DATE
OF COMPOSITION:
2nd cent. BCE

ORIGINAL LANGUAGE:
Hebrew

PROVENANCE:
Palestine

EARLIEST EXTANT
MANUSCRIPT:
16th cent.
(Ethiopic)

The caves at Qumran near the Dead Sea, where the Dead Sea Scrolls were found in 1947. The earliest known fragments of the Book of Jubilees were among the scrolls, which were probably the library of a Jewish sect that lived at Qumran until 70CE. The sect observed the 364-day solar calendar advocated in Jubilees.

day was added after each season but not counted as part of a month. The whole year therefore consisted of 364 days, which was divided by the sacred number seven into precisely fifty-two weeks. In practice, of course, this calendar lagged behind the annual movements of the sun (the actual solar year is 365.25 days), but it is not apparent that Jubilees is aware of the problem.

The author of Jubilees roundly condemns those who observed the official Jewish lunar calendar, describing them as apostates who keep the "feasts of the Gentiles"—perhaps hinting at the fact that after the exile, Judaism increasingly employed the Babylonian names for the months of the year. For Jubilees, the solar calendar was an original and essential part of the

From the Book of Jubilees, chapter 3

Gen. 3.21,23 | *And God made for them garments of skin and he dressed them and sent them from the garden of Eden. ... On that day the mouth of all the beasts and cattle and birds and whatever walked or moved was stopped from speaking because all of them used to speak with one another with one speech and one language.* | And he sent from the garden of Eden all of the flesh which was in the garden of Eden and all of the flesh was scattered, each according to its kind and each according to its family, into the place which was created for them. But from all the beasts and all the cattle he granted to Adam alone that he might cover his shame.

framework of the universe and had been recorded at the creation on celestial tablets. The main Jewish festivals had been celebrated from the beginning of time by the angels in heaven before being revealed to the Israelites. The weekly Sabbath, marking the day on which God rested from the work of creation, was understandably viewed as especially sacred and it is pictured in glowing terms (see extract, below). In Jubilees the most important annual celebration is the Feast of Weeks, which plays a comparatively minor role in the Bible. It is a double festival, celebrating the first fruits of the harvest and also the renewal of God's covenant with Israel.

Jubilees is of special significance in that it is among the earliest works to deal with issues that would come to dominate Judaism in the succeeding centuries, such as the growing importance of Scripture and its interpretation, and speculation about spirits and angels. The primary purpose of Jubilees is to expand on the Jewish law and to ensure its strict observance: the author appears in fact to claim that the work is a second law book given to Moses, the first being the first five books of the Bible (the Torah, or Pentateuch). It is most likely that Jubilees originated among a group of pious Jews who resisted the policies of Antiochus IV Epiphanes (ruled 175–164BCE), king of the Seleucid empire, which was founded in 312BCE by one of Alexander the Great's generals and included Palestine. Antiochus sought to harmonize all the religions of his empire—to this aim, in 167BCE, he erected an altar to Zeus in the Jewish Temple in Jerusalem and banned distinctive Jewish customs such as circumcision and Sabbath observance. The ensuing Jewish revolt, led by the Maccabee family under Judas Maccabeus, culminated in the creation of the last independent Jewish state before modern times.

From the Book of Jubilees, chapters 2 and 6

He gave us a great sign, the Sabbath day, and he told us—all of the angels of the presence and all of the angels of sanctification, these two great kinds—that we might keep the Sabbath with him in heaven and on earth. ... That day is more holy and more blessed than any day of the jubilee of jubilees. On this day we kept the Sabbath in heaven before it was made known to any human being to keep the Sabbath thereon upon the earth.

The Creator of all blessed it, but he did not sanctify any people or nations to keep the Sabbath thereon with the sole exception of Israel. ... And the Creator of all, who cre-

ated this day for a blessing and sanctification and glory, blessed it more than all days. ...

It is ordained and written in the heavenly tablets that they should observe the Feast of Weeks ... once a year, in order to renew the covenant in all respects, year by year. And all of this feast was celebrated in heaven from the day of creation until the days of Noah, twenty-six jubilees and five weeks of years. ...

And you [Moses], command the children of Israel so that they shall guard the years in this number, 364 days, and it will be a complete year.

THE DESCENDANTS OF ADAM AND EVE

according to the Bible and the Book of Jubilees

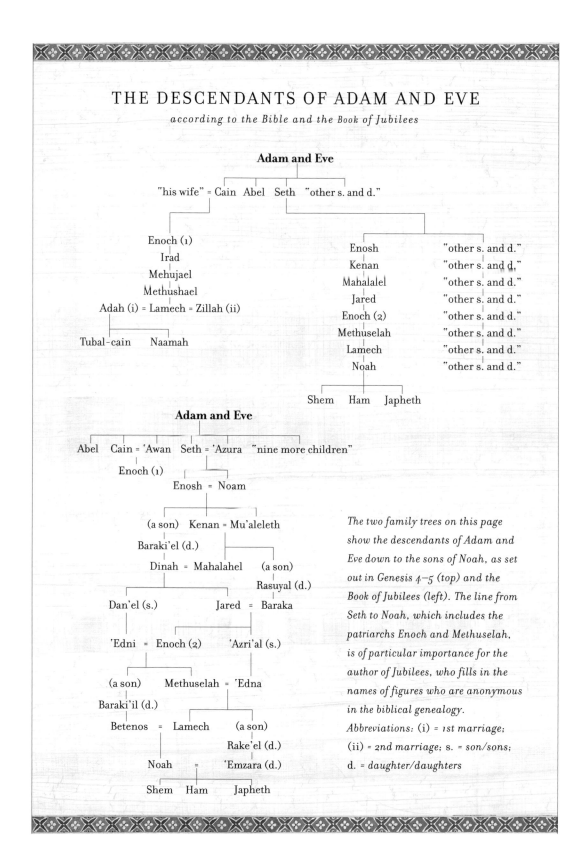

The two family trees on this page show the descendants of Adam and Eve down to the sons of Noah, as set out in Genesis 4–5 (top) and the Book of Jubilees (left). The line from Seth to Noah, which includes the patriarchs Enoch and Methuselah, is of particular importance for the author of Jubilees, who fills in the names of figures who are anonymous in the biblical genealogy.

Abbreviations: (i) = 1st marriage; (ii) = 2nd marriage; s. = son/sons; d. = daughter/daughters

ENOCH THE WISE

DATA

TITLE:
The First Book
of Enoch

ORIGINAL DATE
OF COMPOSITION:
2nd cent. BCE—1st
cent. CE

ORIGINAL LANGUAGE:
Aramaic and/or
Hebrew

PROVENANCE:
Palestine (Judea)

EARLIEST EXTANT
MANUSCRIPT:
14th–15th cent. CE
(Ethiopic)

Perhaps the most intriguing and prominent figure in the Pseudepigrapha is Enoch, who is referred to in numerous texts. He is mentioned in the Hebrew Bible only briefly as the seventh descendant of Adam in the genealogy of Genesis 5, where, in addition to some stock information about his age and children, all that is recorded of him is the enigmatic verse: "Enoch walked with God; then he was no more, because God took him" (Gen. 5.24). From this cryptic statement ancient authors were able to present Enoch as a prophet and patriarch and the channel of a large amount of revelatory writing.

The phrase "walked with God" could be understood in the sense that Enoch was a righteous man living in an evil age, which was how the authors viewed their own time. "God took him" was interpreted to mean that Enoch had been admitted to God's dwelling place in heaven, where he had received secret revelations about the cosmos and the final age, which he had written down for the benefit of pious Jews who would be living in those last years.

Many of the writings about Enoch were eventually collected together in a work now known as the First Book of Enoch (1 Enoch), which includes some of the earliest of the Pseudepigrapha (see box, below). The book had a great influence on later Jewish and Christian literature, including the New Testament (see p.21), and it was highly valued in the early Church before generally falling out of favor from the fourth century CE. However, 1 Enoch is revered as Scripture in the Ethiopian church and the complete text exists only in Ethiopic. Fragments in Aramaic discovered among the Dead Sea Scrolls suggest that the work's original language was Aramaic or

The "Pentateuch" of Enoch

It is generally agreed that 1 Enoch is made up of five originally independent texts: the Book of the Watchers (chapters 1–36); the Book of the Parables, or Similitudes (chapters 37–71); the Astronomical Treatise (chapters 72–82); the Book of Dream Visions (chapters 83–90); and the Letter of Enoch to his children (chapters 91–107).

This fivefold arrangement invites comparison with the Pentateuch, the first five books of the Bible (Genesis to Deuteronomy, also referred to as the Torah or the Books of the Law), and was perhaps intended as a kind of "Enochian Pentateuch." It represents a variety of traditions dating from different periods in the last centuries BCE.

In general, the complete work reflects the circumstances of the Maccabean revolt against the Hellenizing policies of the Seleucid empire in the second century BCE (see p.28). It is therefore another example of the reaction of one devout Jewish group to that particular crisis for Judaism.

possibly Hebrew or, as with the biblical Book of Daniel, a combination of the two. Fragments of versions in Greek—of which the Ethiopic text is a translation—and Latin are also extant.

The first part of 1 Enoch, the Book of the Watchers, opens with eleven chapters which depict Enoch as standing in the line of the biblical prophets and summarize the theme of the whole work: the coming judgment, when God will reward the righteous and condemn the evil. Chapters 6–11 give what is probably the earliest account of the fall of the angels (see pp.18-21) and were originally an independent writing, as shown by the fact that they do not mention Enoch at all. The remainder of the Book of the Watchers is more characteristic of the distinctive Enoch

From the First Book of Enoch, chapter 1

Enoch, the blessed and righteous man of the Lord, took up his parable while his eyes were open and he saw, and said, "This is a holy vision from the heavens which the angels showed me: and I heard from them every-thing and I understood. I look not for this generation but for the distant one that is coming. I speak about the elect ones and con-cerning them. ...

"The God of the universe, the Holy Great One, will come forth from his dwelling. And from there he will march upon Mount Sinai and appear in his camp emerging from heaven with a mighty power. And everyone shall be afraid, and the Watch-ers shall quiver. ... And there shall be a judg-ment upon all, including the righteous. And to all the righteous he will grant peace. He will preserve the elect, and kindness shall be upon them. They shall all belong to God and they shall prosper and be blessed; and the light of God shall shine unto them. Behold, he will arrive with ten million of the holy ones in order to execute judgment upon all. He will destroy the wicked ones and censure all flesh on account of everything that they have done, that which the sinners and the wicked ones committed against him."

Enoch and Angels, a 16th-century Turkish miniature. Enoch is identifed in Islam with a prophet called Idris, "a true man," whom Allah raised up "to a high place" (Quran, *sura* 19, "Mary," trans. A. J. Arberry).

The Prophet Enoch and his Writings. Part of a fresco of the biblical prophets by Theophanes the Greek (ca. 1330–1410) in the Russian Orthodox Cathedral of the Transfiguration in Novgorod, Russia.

tradition. Enoch makes a series of journeys to the highest heaven and the remoter parts of the universe, and acquires an unparalleled knowledge of God's creation, which he in turn passes on to humankind. As a whole these chapters develop the earlier theme of the fallen angels, the "Watchers" (see p.21), including detailed and gruesome depictions of their confinement and punishment. Enoch recounts to the Watchers a vision in which he is taken up to God's heavenly temple and throne and hears the divine judgment on them. The narrative seems to be indebted to the biblical books of Ezekiel and Isaiah (Ezek. 1–2, Isa. 6), and stands at the beginning of a long line of Jewish mystical speculation about the throne of God (the "Merkabah tradition").

Next, angels take Enoch on a westward tour of the cosmos, during which he learns the nature and functions of the winds and is shown the place of the Watchers' punishment, which has many features of Sheol, the Hebrew realm of the dead. In the succeeding chapters, Enoch moves to seven mountains in the far northwest, where he sees the tree of life (see extract). From there he goes eastward to the holy city of Jerusalem, described as the center of the earth, and at this point there is another description of the place of punishment of the evil angels. Then Enoch journeys east, north, west, and south to the extreme ends of the world, at each of which stand three heavenly gates from which issue the winds and the stars. He also sees the garden of Eden with the tree of knowledge, and further visions of the heavenly throne. The description of Enoch's tours may be influenced by ancient Greek mythology: thus "the river of fire which flows like water" recalls Puriphlegethon, one of the rivers of Hades.

From the First Book of Enoch, chapters 24–25

I went to another place of the earth, and [the angel] showed me a mountain of fire which was flaming day and night. And I went in its direction and saw seven dignified mountains—all different one from another, of precious and beautiful stones. ... And among them, there was one tree such as I have never at all smelled; there was not a single one among the other trees which was like it; among all the fragrances nothing could be so fragrant; its leaves, its flowers, and its wood would never wither forever. ... Then Michael, one of the holy and revered angels—he is their chief—who was with me, responded to me.

And he said to me, Enoch, "What is it that you are asking concerning the fragrance of this tree and why are you so inquisitive about it?" At that moment, I answered, "I want to know everything, but specially about this tree." He replied, "This tall mountain ... whose summit resembles the throne of God is indeed his throne, on which the Holy and Great Lord of Glory, the Eternal King, will sit when he descends to visit the earth with goodness. And as for this fragrant tree, not a single human being has the authority to touch it until the great judgment. ... It shall be given to the righteous and the pious, and from its fruit life will be given to the elect. He will plant it in the direction of the northeast, upon the holy place—in the direction of the house of the Lord, the Eternal King."

THE COMING OF THE SON OF MAN

Chapters 37–71 of 1 Enoch were originally a separate work known as the Book of Parables (or Book of Similitudes), so called because each of its three sections is given the title "parable." This does not have the same sense as the term found in the New Testament but denotes a message announcing a revelation, as in the Balaam oracles in the Bible (Num. 23–24). This section of 1 Enoch repeats many of the themes in the earlier part of the book, such as Enoch's journeys to heaven and various parts of the cosmos, and the judgment of the fallen angels, and also has elements only loosely connected with the main topics—for example, a little poem about wisdom and passages dealing with Noah and the Flood. However, the dominant theme of the Book of Parables is the announcement of the arrival of the Last Judgment, which is described in great detail in a succession of scenes set in heaven.

The Last Judgment is not so much on the evil angels, as in earlier chapters, but rather on the kings and the powerful, who are seen as the enemies of God's Chosen People. The latter are vindicated by the overthrow of their oppressors and by the gift of resurrection and eternal life for those who have died. This reflects the opposition of devout Jews both to the foreign imperial powers of the Near East and to the exploitative upper classes within their own society.

Great attention has been focused on the "messianic" teaching of the Book of Parables. In it,

The "Son of Man" in Enoch and the Gospels

There has been much discussion about the possible influence of the figure of the Son of Man in 1 Enoch on the New Testament, and especially whether it is the origin of the expression "Son of Man" found in the gospels. The early Christians were certainly familiar with 1 Enoch (see p.21), but it is uncertain whether the work they knew included the Book of Parables, where the term "Son of Man" appears.

Unfortunately it is very difficult to date the Parables. Most scholars have tended to opt for the late first century BCE or the early first century CE, in which case it would predate the New Testament. On the other hand, the Parables only exists in the comparatively late Ethiopic version so it is possible that it is a Christian work, based on the New Testament. But perhaps the strongest argument against this hypothesis is that, in its present form, the final chapter of the Book of Parables apparently identifies the Son of Man with Enoch himself ("an angel…said to me, 'You are the Son of Man who was born in righteousness' "). If this passage is original, it is highly unlikely that it was written by a Christian author, for whom Jesus, and no other, would have been the Son of Man. But the issue remains open.

the agent of the judgment is not solely God (called here "the Lord of the Spirits") as in the earlier chapters of 1 Enoch, but a heavenly figure who appears alongside him and takes over many of his attributes and functions. This being has three names, all derived from biblical prototypes: the "Elect One" (or "Chosen One"); the "Son of Man"; and the "Anointed One" (or "Messiah"). The name "Anointed One" occurs only twice and nothing is said about his function. "Son of Man," a phrase derived from the Book of Daniel, is not really a title but means only "human being": in 1 Enoch it indicates someone with the appearance of a human, either an angel or a man transformed into angelic form in heaven. This mysterious figure existed before the creation and will, in the last days of the world, sit on God's throne to execute judgment on all the forces of evil and usher in a kingdom of everlasting peace and blessedness (see box, opposite).

From the First Book of Enoch, chapter 46

I saw the One to whom belongs the time before time. And his head was white like wool, and there was with him another individual, whose face was like that of a human being. His countenance was full of grace like that of one among the holy angels. And I asked the one—from among the angels—who was going with me … "Who is this, and [why] does he go with him who precedes time?" And he answered me … "This is the Son of Man, to whom belongs righteousness. … the Lord of the Spirits has chosen him and he is destined to be victorious before the Lord of the Spirits in eternal uprightness. This Son of Man whom you have seen is the One who would remove the kings and the mighty ones from their comfortable seats and the strong ones from their thrones … and kingdoms. For they do not extol and glorify him, and neither do they obey him, the source of their power."

The Son of Man Enthroned, from the Commentary on the Apocalypse by the Spanish abbot Beatus of Liébana (died 798 CE). This manuscript was produced ca. 1100 at San Domingo de Silos.

COSMIC VISIONS

The remaining three books that make up 1 Enoch differ considerably from one another in form and content. The Astronomical Treatise, which deals with the solar calendar, is one of the earliest of the Pseudepigrapha and was originally an independent work that was longer than the version in 1 Enoch. The Book of Dream Visions contains two visions of Enoch about cataclysmic future events. The concluding section is presented as a letter written by Enoch to his descendants, a type of work known as a testament.

In the Astronomical Treatise, Enoch again traverses the heavens and is instructed in the workings of the cosmos by his guide, the angel Uriel. The result is an indigestible mass of detailed calculations and conclusions which provide a quasi-scientific justification for the 364-day solar calendar (see pp.26–8). The work was highly valued by those who adopted this calendar, such as the community of Qumran—the Dead Sea Scrolls include four fragmentary Aramaic copies of the Treatise, apparently dating from as early as the third century BCE.

The Book of Dream Visions was composed during the Maccabean revolt (see p.28), most probably before the death of Judas Maccabeus in 160BCE. The first vision is a detailed description of the biblical Flood, which was of great significance as evidence of God's past verdict on sin and as a pattern for his future final judgment. The vision concludes with a moving prayer to God for mercy. The much longer second vision is an example of a literary genre called "apocalyptic"—a revelation of the end of time. For the most part the vision is a summary of the history of Israel down to the time of the Maccabees, rounded off by a prophecy of the coming messianic kingdom. Such reviews of the past and future are characteristic of apocalyptic, the Book of Daniel being perhaps the most famous example. Typically, past events are presented as predictions by an ancient prophet who lived before they occurred, the point being to demonstrate that because the seer was accurate about the known past he can be trusted when he predicts the unknown future. Another feature of this vision, also characteristic of apocalyptic, is its bizarre imagery, whereby protagonists are not named but represented as animals such as oxen (the patriarchs), sheep (the faithful Israelites), and wild beasts (Israel's enemies). Such imagery is biblical in origin and acts as a sort of code, understood only by those who know the Bible.

The final section of 1 Enoch reflects a number of literary forms drawn from the Bible, including ethical teaching about the "Two Ways" (see pp.22 and 81) and a series of "woes" prophesying doom to the wicked (see extract, opposite). Two sections contain the so-called "Apocalypse of Weeks," which sets out, in rather mysterious terms, future events up to the end of time, a period divided into ten eras ("weeks") of varying lengths. The book concludes with what appear to be fragments of independent materials, including a section concerned with Noah and the Flood.

The Ascension of Enoch. An angel leads Enoch to the heavens on this panel from an altar of *cloisonné* enamel on gilded copper made in 1181 by Nicholas of Verdun for Klosterneuburg monastery, Austria.

From the First Book of Enoch, chapter 94

Woe unto those who build oppression and injustice! Who lay foundations for deceit. They shall soon be demolished; and they shall have no peace. Woe unto those who build their houses with sin! For they shall all be demolished from their foundations; and they shall fall by the sword.

Those who amass gold and silver; they shall quickly be destroyed. Woe unto you, O rich people! For you have put your trust in your wealth. You shall depart from your riches, for you do not remember the Most High. In the days of your affluence, you committed oppression, you have become ready for death, and for the day of darkness and for the day of great judgment.

Thus I speak and let you know: For he who has created you, he will also throw you down! Upon your fall there shall be no mercy for you.

METHUSELAH, NOAH, AND MELCHIZEDEK

Enoch is by far the most important of the pre-Flood heroes to feature in the non-canonical scriptures, but these works also contain traditions about other famous characters from the Book of Genesis who are linked with Enoch, notably his son Methuselah and, most significantly, his great-grandson Noah.

Enoch recounts his revelations in 1 Enoch to his eldest son, Methuselah, and writes them down in a book which he entrusts to Methuselah to transmit to all future generations. Thus Methuselah—whose lifespan of 969 years (Gen. 5.25) is the longest in the Bible—represents continuity, the channel through which Enoch's teaching is preserved and handed on. Methuselah appears in the same light in 2 Enoch, but in the context of the origins of priesthood. There, Enoch seems to have priestly functions, but after his death it is Methuselah who is the agent of priestly succession. God explicitly designates him as priest and instructs him to invest his grandson Nir, who is described as the younger brother of Noah, to succeed him.

Noah is important as the one who was spared from the great Flood, God's punishment on the consequences of the fall of the angels (see p.20) and a cataclysm that came to be seen as a sort of prototype of the Last Judgment. In 1 Enoch there is a lengthy narrative—also found in one of the Dead Sea Scrolls—of Noah's birth, where he appears as a superhuman child, able to speak from the moment he is born. His father Lamech believes Noah to be the offspring of the angels and asks his own father, Methuselah, to go to Enoch to discover the truth. Enoch reassures Lamech that the boy is his and that Noah's amazing physical characteristics mark him out as an extraordinary individual chosen by God for a great future. Noah, like Enoch, "walked with God" (Gen. 6.9).

The birth story of Melchizedek shares many of the same features and is

This 6th-century CE mosaic in the church of San Apollinare in Classe, Ravenna, Italy, presents Melchizedek (center) as a Christ-like priest-king whose sacrifice (Gen. 14.18–20) prefigured the Eucharist.

Enoch and the Letter to the Hebrews

In the Letter to the Hebrews in the New Testament, Melchizedek is described as a priest whose priesthood prefigures that of Jesus, and as one "without father, without mother, without genealogy." It has been suggested that 2 Enoch is dependent on Hebrews and that the former is therefore most probably a Christian text, or at least that this section of 2 Enoch is by a Christian author.

However, the correspondence between the picture of Melchizedek in Hebrews and the narrative in 2 Enoch is not particularly close: in 2 Enoch, he does, after all, have a mother and a genealogy. Among the Dead Sea Scrolls is a manuscript in which Melchizedek appears as a heavenly savior, identified with the archangel Michael, and this indicates that he was the object of speculation in Jewish circles. So it is probably best to think of Melchizedek as a figure who was of interest to both Jews and Christians, with 2 Enoch and Hebrews representing independent developments of the same theme.

related in 2 Enoch. Here, Melchizedek is described as Noah's nephew and also has resemblances with Methuselah. However, it is emphasized that the child is not of human conception, since his putative father, Nir, had not had intercourse with his wife, Sopanim, at the time. Following the common pattern of birth stories in the Bible, Nir's wife is described as barren and hence Melchizedek's birth is to be seen as the result of direct divine intervention. In the Bible, Melchizedek appears after the Flood in connection with the patriarch Abraham (Gen. 14), but 2 Enoch places his birth in the period before the deluge, and, like Noah, he is chosen by God to survive the cataclysm. The Melchizedek whom Abraham met was a priest, and in 2 Enoch he is invested with the insignia of priesthood from the moment of his birth.

From the First Book of Enoch, chapter 106

Methuselah took a wife for his son Lamech, and she bore him a son. And his body was as white as snow and as red as a rose; the hair of his head as white as wool and beautiful ... and as for his eyes, when he opened them the whole house glowed like the sun ... and when he arose from the hands of the midwife, he opened his mouth and spoke to the Lord with righteousness. And Lamech was afraid of him and fled ... to Methuselah his father; and said to him, "I have begotten a strange son. He is not like a human being, but he looks like the children of the angels of heaven; his form is different, and he is not like us. His eyes are like the rays of the sun, and his face glorious. It does not seem to me that he is of me, but of angels; and I fear that a wondrous phenomenon may take place upon the earth in his days." ... [Methuselah went to Enoch, who answered:] "Make known to Lamech that the one who has been born is in truth his son; and call his name Noah."

CHAPTER 2

WORDS OF THE PATRIARCHS

◆

THE TESTAMENT OF ABRAHAM

The Testament of Abraham, which purports to be the words of Israel's first patriarch, belongs to a genre of non-canonical writings in which a great biblical figure utters his "testament," or legacy, to his descendants on his deathbed. The prototype for these works is the scene in Genesis 49 where the dying Jacob summons his twelve sons and utters a series of predictions about them; a similar pattern is found in the account of the death of Moses (Deut. 33–34). The writers of testaments also included ethical teachings as well as prophecies about Israel, universal events, and the end of the world.

The Testament of Abraham is not strictly a testament, because in it Abraham bequeaths no message. However, death and the fate of the dead form a central theme of the work. "The common and inexorable bitter cup of death" is inevitable for all human beings, even Abraham—a tragic note recalling other ancient writings such as the Mesopotamian Epic of Gilgamesh and the biblical Ecclesiastes. In spite of his blameless life, Abraham is presented as a far from idealized figure who endeavors to put off his death, asking God that he may first "see all the inhabited world and all the created things." The request is granted and Abraham soars over the earth on a chariot of cherubim. In the central and most dramatic part of the work, he reaches heaven's first gate,

The Unity of Humankind

A striking characteristic of the Testament of Abraham is its universalism. As the children of Adam, all humans are to be judged by God on the same basis: there is no distinction between Jew and Gentile and, apart from a single reference to the twelve tribes, there is no special role for Israel. Equally striking is the work's emphasis on God's merciful intentions toward humanity. In language reminiscent of Ezekiel 18, he is said not to desire the death of sinners, but rather he seeks to give them space to repent. Premature death, which allows no time for repentance, fully atones for past sins, and no further punishment follows.

God can also respond to intercession from the righteous on behalf of sinners. During his journey, Abraham sees people engaged in various evil activities and calls down the punishment of death upon them. But later, when he realizes that this contradicts the divine purpose, he intercedes with God for them and they are restored to life.

Weighing the Soul of the Departed, from an Egyptian manuscript of ca.1285 BCE. The Testament of Abraham employs this common Egyptian funerary motif, suggesting it originates among the Greek-speaking Jews of Egypt.

where he sees the souls of the dead being judged by the record of their deeds in a heavenly book; by being weighed in a balance (an Egyptian motif—see illustration); or by fire (see extract). Pronouncing judgment are Abel, the twelve tribes of Israel, and finally God. In the presence of Adam, the souls of the righteous pass through a narrow gate (see p.23), while the souls of sinners—much the more numerous—pass through a wide one, an image found also in Matthew 7.13–14.

Abraham returns home and God sends the personified figure of Death for his soul. The patriarch continues to resist the summons, but eventually his soul is captured by a trick. Abraham's body receives an honorable burial and his soul is borne to paradise by angels.

From the Testament of Abraham, chapters 12–13

Between the two gates there stood a terrifying throne. ... And upon it sat a wondrous man, bright as the sun, like a son of God. Before him stood a table, all of gold and covered with finest linen. On the table lay a book whose thickness was six cubits, while its breadth was ten cubits. On its right and on its left stood two angels holding papyrus and ink and pen. In front of the table sat a light-bearing angel, holding a balance in his hand. On his left sat a fiery angel, merciless and relentless, holding a trumpet in his hand, which contained within it an all-consuming fire for testing the sinner.

... The [angel] on the right recorded righteous deeds, the one on the left the sins. And the one in front of the table, holding the balance, weighed the souls. And the fiery angel, holding the fire, tested the souls. ...

[And Michael said to Abraham,] "Do you see, all-pious Abraham, the frightful man who is seated on the throne? This is the son of Adam, the first-formed, who is called Abel. ... And he sits here to judge the entire creation, examining both righteous and sinners. For God said, 'I do not judge you, but every man is judged by man.'"

DATA

TITLE:
The Testament of Abraham

ORIGINAL DATE
OF COMPOSITION:
1st–2nd cent. CE

ORIGINAL
LANGUAGE:
Greek

PROVENANCE:
Egypt?

EARLIEST EXTANT
MANUSCRIPT:
ca. 1100 CE
(Greek)

THE APOCALYPSE OF ABRAHAM

Another work claiming Israel's first patriarch as its author is the Apocalypse of Abraham. The book was written in response to the Roman destruction of Jerusalem and the Jewish Temple in 70CE and may date from soon after that catastrophe. It is therefore roughly contemporaneous with the Christian gospels, which offer their own understanding of the same event. A central theme of the Apocalypse is the total division between Jew and Gentile, a very different approach from the Testament of Abraham (see p.40). The author sees this division as a fundamental aspect of the created world, which is divided into right and left sides, peopled respectively by the Jews and the Gentiles.

In common with many apocalypses, the starting point of the work is various biblical passages that the author develops and interprets in his own way. As with other apocalyptic writings, it consists of a narrative followed by a series of revelations of future history. Informing the narrative section (chapters 1–8) is Genesis 12.1, which is almost quoted at the end of chapter 8, where God commands Abraham to leave his homeland in Mesopotamia. The Bible (Joshua 24.2) records a tradition that in Mesopotamia the ancestors of the Jewish nation, in particular Terah, Abraham's father, worshiped deities other than God. Hence it was easy to interpret Abraham's departure from this pagan environment at God's command as his conversion from idolatry to the worship of the one true God. The Apocalypse describes how Abraham rejected Terah's idols, a topic that was already well known (it also occurs in the earlier Book of Jubilees).

A second influence on these earlier chapters is the polemic against idolatry which

Abraham in the Fire, from the Golden Haggadah, a Jewish manuscript from Spain, ca. 1320CE. It depicts a legend not found in the Bible in which Abraham, after smashing his father's idols, is thrown into a fire by King Nimrod (right), but is rescued by an angel.

became characteristic of Judaism after the Babylonian exile, as seen very clearly in, for example, Isaiah 44.9–20. Idols are mocked with broad humor as lifeless, manufactured objects, without even the power to help themselves: when Abraham accidentally leaves a wooden idol too close to a fire it just burns to ashes. The theme of true worship, and the need to preserve it from a relapse into idolatry, is one which runs through the whole work.

The starting point of the apocalyptic section proper (chapters 9–32) is another biblical passage, Genesis 15, in which Abraham has a vision of God and offers a sacrifice to him. In the Apocalypse, he is aided and directed by the angel Iaoel. In Genesis, Abraham drives away birds of prey that come down on the sacrificial carcasses, but in the Apocalypse there is just one bird, which is revealed as the demon Azazel. Iaoel consigns the demon to the underworld, and as the ceremony is consummated, Abraham and the angel are transported to heaven.

In heaven, Abraham recites the song of the angels of the divine throne, which Iaoel has taught him (see p.116). Then he is shown the mysteries of the cosmos and various future events, but the climax of the vision is concerned with the Jerusalem Temple. Abraham first sees the Temple as it should be, but it is profaned by a relapse into idol worship and as a result God permits the Gentiles to destroy it. However, in the final age, the children of Israel will return to offer true worship in a restored Temple and the Gentiles will be annihilated. Finally, Abraham returns to the earth, where God repeats his promise to destroy the Gentiles and announces the coming of the "Elect One" to restore Israel. At its close, the book reverts to Genesis 15, reproducing the prophecy of Israel's enslavement in Egypt (Gen. 15.13).

DATA

TITLE:
The Apocalypse
of Abraham

ORIGINAL DATE OF
COMPOSITION:
70CE–ca. 150CE

ORIGINAL LANGUAGE:
Semitic (probably
Hebrew)

PROVENANCE:
Palestine?

EARLIEST EXTANT
MANUSCRIPT:
14th cent. CE
(Old Slavonic)

From the Apocalypse of Abraham, chapter 7

[Abraham said:] "Father Terah, fire is more venerable than your gods, the gold and the silver ones, and the stone and the wooden ones, because the fire burns your gods. And your gods being burned obey the fire, and the fire mocks them while it is consuming your gods. But neither will I call the fire god, because it is subjugated to water. Water is more venerable than it, because it overcomes fire and sweetens the earth with fruits. But I will not call it god either, for water subsides under the earth. But I will not call earth a goddess either, for it is dried by the sun and subordinated to humans for their work. The sun I call more venerable than the earth, for with its rays it illuminates the whole universe. But I will not call it a god because when night comes it becomes murky with darkness. Nor again shall I call the moon or the stars gods, because they too at times during the night dim their light.

"But hear this, Terah my father, let me proclaim to you the God who created all things. But this is the true God who has made the heavens crimson and the sun golden, who has given light to the moon and the stars with it, who has dried the earth in the midst of the many waters, who set you yourself among all these things and who has sought me out now in the perplexity of my thoughts."

THE TESTAMENT OF ISAAC

The Testament of Abraham (see pp.40–41) forms a distinct trilogy with the Testament of Isaac and the Testament of Jacob (see pp.46–7), and such are their similarities that they are grouped together as a unit in the Coptic, Arabic, and Ethiopic manuscripts of these writings. The three patriarchs appear in all three texts—in the Testament of Isaac, Abraham is almost more significant than Isaac himself. The testament is read in the Coptic church on September 4, the feast day of Abraham, Isaac, and Jacob.

In its present form, the Testament of Isaac is a Christian work, but the Christian elements seem to be later additions, so it is possible that the original work, like its prototype, the Testament of Abraham, was by a Jewish author and written in Greek. The distinctive characteristic of the whole text, especially as compared with the Testament of Abraham, is the moral and ethical teaching put into the mouth of Isaac, which has a markedly universalistic note.

The Three Patriarchs: Abraham, Isaac, and Jacob. A ceiling painting in the Ethiopian Orthodox church of Abune Yemata, Gheralta, Tigray.

The work begins with the archangel Michael announcing to Isaac that his death is imminent. Isaac's son, Jacob, is very disturbed by this, but Isaac reassures him, reminding him of his distinguished ancestry and promising him a glorious future as the ancestor both of the twelve tribes of Israel and—at this point the Christian influence is clear—of Jesus Christ. Next, a crowd assembles, which Isaac addresses in a long sermon centering on the virtues of neighborliness and harmony. It includes a model of confession to be recited by those offering sacrifice and ends with the special obligations of priests, among whom Isaac himself is numbered.

The angel returns and takes Isaac up into the heavens, where he first witnesses the tortures of departed sinners, particularly those who have been at odds with their neighbors. He ascends even higher to the divine throne (which is hidden by a curtain) and meets his father Abraham. Through Abraham, God orders every man to follow Isaac's example and leave behind a written testament or will at his death, and commends the observance of a festival day in Isaac's honor. The book ends with Isaac's soul being taken to heaven in a chariot flanked by cherubim, and a final paean of praise to the Holy Trinity.

DATA

TITLE:
The Testament
of Isaac

ORIGINAL DATE OF
COMPOSITION:
2nd cent. CE

ORIGINAL LANGUAGE:
Greek?

PROVENANCE:
Egypt?

EARLIEST EXTANT
MANUSCRIPT:
9th cent. CE
(Coptic)

From the Testament of Isaac, chapter 4

Isaac said ... "If you speak in anger, guard yourself from slander and beware of empty boasting. ... Be careful that an evil word does not come forth from your mouth. ... Beware of stretching out your hand to what you do not own. ... Do not mingle your thoughts with the thoughts of the world, as you stand at the altar before the presence of God. As you are about to present your offering to God ... you shall pray to him a hundred times without ceasing. At the beginning you shall voice this thanksgiving as follows, 'O God the incomprehensible, who cannot be searched out, the possessor of power, the source of purity, cleanse me by your mercy, a free gift from you. ... For behold, my cause is in your hands and my recourse is to you. ... Pardon me, that am a sinner. And pardon all your creatures whom you have fashioned, but who have not heard and learned of you.' ...

The work of the priesthood is not easy, since it is incumbent upon every priest, from today until the completion of the last of the generations and the end of the world, that he should not be filled by the drinking of wine nor be satisfied by the eating of bread; and that he should not talk about the concerns of the world nor listen to one who does talk about them. But priests must expend all of their efforts and their lives in prayer and watchfulness ... in order that each one may petition the Lord successfully. And now continue to supplicate God with repentance for your past sins, and do not commit more sin. Accordingly, do not kill with the sword, do not kill with the tongue, do not fornicate with your body, and do not remain angry until sunset. Do not let yourself receive unjustified praise, and do not rejoice at the fall of your enemies or of your brothers. Do not blaspheme; beware of slander. Do not look at a woman with a lustful eye."

THE TESTAMENT OF JACOB

A number of non-canonical writings focus on Jacob, the ancestor of the twelve tribes of Israel. One of the most interesting is the Testament of Jacob, which is closely linked to the Testament of Isaac—both writings are read in the Coptic church on the feast of the Three Patriarchs (see p.44). It begins with the archangel Michael announcing to Jacob that his death is imminent, but before it happens Jacob is taken up into the heavens, where he witnesses the tortures of the damned and then meets Abraham and Isaac in a place of light. Finally, God and his angels transport Jacob's soul to heaven, while his corpse is buried in the ancestral tomb at Hebron.

However, the Testament of Jacob is not simply an imitation of the Testament of Isaac. It is much more closely dependent on the Book of Genesis, recording most of the events in the biblical story of Jacob and commending the Genesis account—which is much fuller than that of Isaac. Also, the Testament of Jacob is far more obviously Christian than the earlier Testament of Isaac, although it still employs Jewish legendary matter. A third feature of this work is the prominent presence of the actual author: the two concluding chapters are wholly taken up with the narrator's own counsel and teaching, which make it plain that he is a Christian. Finally, there is a marked absence of apocalyptic predictions of history and the end of the world. A single reference to "the last days" in chapter 5 is limited to the future of the twelve tribes of Israel and adds little to the Genesis account of their descent into Egypt and subsequent possession of the land of Canaan. The work's real concern is to set out the religious, liturgical, and moral requirements for the proper conduct of life in the present.

The Ladder of Jacob

With their marked interest in angels and the celestial realm, non-canonical writers were naturally attracted to the biblical episode in which Jacob dreams of a ladder or staircase to heaven, upon which angels ascend and descend (Gen. 28.11–22). In one work, the Ladder of Jacob, the ladder has twelve steps, each flanked by a bust or statue in human form. Jacob prays to God to interpret his mysterious vision and in response he is visited by the angel Sariel (see extract 2, opposite). This recalls chapter 7 of the Book of Daniel, which may be the author's model. In the usual apocalyptic manner, the angel goes on to prophesy the fate of Jacob's descendants and their triumph in the final age, when the leader of the powers of evil—here called by the strange name Falkon—will be forever destroyed. The final chapter seems to be an originally separate Christian work, foretelling the birth and crucifixion of Jesus.

From the Testament of Jacob, ch. 2

DATA

TITLE:
The Testament of
Jacob

ORIGINAL DATE OF
COMPOSITION:
2nd cent. CE

ORIGINAL LANGUAGE:
Greek?

PROVENANCE:
Egypt?

EARLIEST EXTANT
MANUSCRIPT:
9th cent. CE
(Coptic)

[An angel said to Jacob:] "Blessed be the nation which will strive for your purity and will see your good works. Blessed be the man who will remember you on the day of your noble festival. Blessed be the one who will perform acts of mercy in honor of your several names, and will give someone a cup of water to drink, or will come with an offering to the sanctuary, or will take in strangers, or visit the sick and console their children, or will clothe a naked one in honor of your several names. Such a one shall neither lack any of the good things of this world, nor life everlasting in the world to come. Moreover, whoever shall have caused to be written the stories of your several lives and sufferings at his own expense or shall have written them by his own hand, or shall have read them soberly, or shall hear them in faith, or shall remember your deeds, such persons will have their sins forgiven and their trespasses pardoned."

From the Ladder of Jacob, chs. 5–6

DATA

TITLE:
The Ladder of
Jacob

ORIGINAL DATE OF
COMPOSITION:
Unknown

ORIGINAL LANGUAGE:
Probably Greek

PROVENANCE:
Unknown

EARLIEST EXTANT
MANUSCRIPT:
14th–15th cent. CE
(Old Slavonic)

[Sariel, the angel of dreams] said to me, "You have seen a ladder with twelve steps, each step having two human faces which keep changing appearance. The ladder is this age, and the twelve steps are the periods of this age. But the twenty-four faces are the kings of the ungodly nations of this age. Under these kings the children of your children and the generations of your sons will be tried. ... Know, Jacob, that your descendants shall be exiles in a strange land, and they will afflict them with slavery and inflict wounds on them every day. But the Lord will judge the people for whom they slave. ... For the

Jacob's Dream, a detail of a painting in Torcello cathedral, Venice. Jacob dreams of the heavenly ladder, upon which angels ascend and descend.

angels and archangels will hurl their bolts of lightning before them for the sake of the salvation of your tribe. ... There will be earthquakes and much destruction. And the Lord will pour out his wrath against Leviathan the sea-dragon; he will kill the lawless Falkon with the sword, because he will raise the wrath of the God of gods by his pride."

THE TESTAMENTS OF THE TWELVE PATRIARCHS

The Testaments of the Twelve Patriarchs are the most important witnesses to the popularity of the "testament" genre among the non-canonical writers. The basic model is the account of Jacob's last words to his sons in Genesis 49, and it was obviously felt that his sons, as the progenitors of the twelve Israelite tribes, should have left similar testaments to their descendants.

It is generally agreed that the Testaments of the Twelve Patriarchs are the products of a single author (who may have drawn on earlier material), because almost all the testaments follow the same basic pattern. With the exception of the short Testament of Asher, each begins with the patriarch summoning his family to his deathbed in Egypt and recounting to them exemplary episodes from his past life. There follows a section of ethical instruction, concentrating on a specific virtue to be adhered to or a specific vice to be avoided: a common theme in the texts is the doctrine of the two spirits active in the world, the one of truth and the other of error, and the consequent choice for humanity between two ways of conduct, one directed by the angels of God, the other by the angels of the evil power, called Beliar or Satan. The right choice, as the texts frequently exhort, is to be made by keeping the divine law and obeying the commandments of the Most High. Next come predictions of the future, warnings of the disaster that will befall the Israelites because of their wicked conduct, but also a promise that, in the end-time, the nation will be restored and its defiled Temple rebuilt and the Gentiles also will be saved. Finally, the patriarch dies, expressing a desire to be buried in the ancestral tomb at Hebron in the Promised Land, which is duly carried out. The Testaments thus exemplify a range of motifs characteristic of many of the Pseudepigrapha as a whole, and they have particularly close links with the Book of Jubilees (see pp.26–8).

Ten or so passages in the texts are undoubtedly Christian in character, but there is some debate as to whether these are integral to the work—in which case a Christian author must be assumed—or interpolations in a Jewish document aimed at making it more acceptable to the Church, where it was known and read certainly by the early fourth century CE. The evidence either way is not conclusive and it is perhaps unnecessary to decide the issue, because it is increasingly recognized that the distinction between "Jewish" and "Christian" in the early centuries CE cannot always be sharply drawn and that "Jewish Christianity" long remained significant (see p.140).

In one group of manuscripts, each testament has a heading that states the particular virtue or vice with which it is concerned. This feature seems to reflect the influence of Hellenistic writings on philosophy and ethics, which can be detected throughout the twelve testaments.

DATA

TITLE:
The Testaments
of the Twelve
Patriarchs

ORIGINAL DATE OF
COMPOSITION:
ca. 250BCE–ca.
150CE?

ORIGINAL LANGUAGE:
Semitic?

PROVENANCE:
Palestine?

EARLIEST EXTANT
MANUSCRIPT:
10th cent. CE
(Greek)

The Story of Joseph and his Brothers, a panel from the bronze doors made by Lorenzo Ghiberti (1378–1455) for the Baptistery of Florence cathedral, Italy.

From the Testament of Asher, chapters 7–8

[Asher said:] "Do not become like Sodom, which did not recognize the Lord's angels and perished for ever. For I know that you will sin and be delivered into the hands of your enemies; your land shall be made desolate and your sanctuary wholly polluted. You will be scattered to the four corners of the earth; in the dispersion you shall be regarded as worthless, like useless water, until such time as the Most High visits the earth. He shall come as a man eating and drinking with human beings, crushing the dragon's head in the water. He will save Israel and all the nations, God speaking like a man. ... For I know that you will be thoroughly disobedient ... heeding not God's Law but human commandments, being corrupted by evil. For this reason, you will be scattered like Dan and Gad my brothers, you shall not know your own lands, tribe, or language. But he will gather you in faith through his compassion and on account of Abraham, Isaac, and Jacob."

After he had said these things he gave instructions, saying, "Bury me in Hebron." And he died, having fallen into a beautiful sleep. And his sons did as he commanded them: they took him up to Hebron and buried him with his fathers.

THE TESTAMENT OF REUBEN

In some manuscripts of the Testament of Reuben, which claims to be by Jacob's eldest son, it is described as being "about thoughts," but these thoughts are very largely lustful ones, for the work mainly consists of a series of warnings against fornication. At the beginning of the work, Reuben reminisces about his past life, in particular his sin in having had sexual intercourse with his father's concubine Bilhah, which the Bible mentions briefly (Gen. 35.22) and for which he was cursed by the dying Jacob (Gen. 49.4). As a result, he lost his status as Jacob's first-born (1 Chron. 5.1–5).

The author fills out the laconic biblical references with various salacious details, such as Reuben's sight of Bilhah bathing, which also appears in the Book of Jubilees and is probably borrowed from the story of King David and Bathsheba (2 Sam. 11.2) or from the story of Susanna in the Apocrypha (Sus. 15-16). Bilhah was drunk on the occasion of the seduction, a detail very

likely derived from the stories of the drunkenness of Noah (Gen. 9.20) and Lot (Gen. 19.32–36). By contrast, Reuben cites the example of his brother Joseph, who resisted Potiphar's wife in Egypt (Gen. 39). Joseph is regularly held up in the Testament as the ideal man of virtue.

Reuben then moves to a diatribe against women in general, accusing them of seeking to control men by using their wiles to seduce them. He repeats a traditional motif that fornication leads to idolatry, and refers to the story of the Watchers, the evil angels, whose downfall he blames on the earthly women (see p.20). This low view of women is found in other Jewish writings of the period but it is expressed with special force in the Testament of Reuben.

The last section of the work introduces a concept which is further developed elsewhere in the Twelve Testaments: the supremacy of the tribes of Levi and Judah, from which sprang Israel's high priests and kings respectively. This diarchy of priest and king may be compared to the two messianic figures appearing in some Dead Sea Scrolls, the "Messiah of Aaron" and the "Messiah of Israel." The priestly figure is much the more important of the two, since he is responsible for the nation's welfare as the one who interprets the law and offers sacrifice.

Another sin to which fornication leads is jealousy, a theme further developed in the Testament of Simeon. Fornication will cause Reuben's children to become jealous of the sons of Levi, but if they succumb to their jealousy they will incur divine vengeance.

From the Testament of Reuben, chapters 3 and 5

Give heed to the words of Reuben, your father: Do not devote your attention to a woman's looks, nor live with a woman who is already married, nor become involved in affairs with women.

For if I had not seen Bilhah bathing in a sheltered place, I would not have fallen into this great lawless act. For so absorbed were my senses by her nakedness that I could not sleep. ... At Gader near ... Bethlehem, Bilhah became drunk and was sound asleep, naked in her bedchamber. So when I came in and saw her nakedness, I performed the impious deed without her being aware of it. ...

Women are evil, my children, and by reason of their lacking authority or power over man, they scheme treacherously how they might entice him to themselves by means of their looks. ... For it was thus that they charmed the Watchers, who were before the Flood. As they continued looking at the women, they were filled with desire for them and perpetrated the act in their minds. Then they were transformed into human males, and while the women were living with their husbands they appeared to them. Since the women's minds were filled with lust for these apparitions, they gave birth to giants.

OPPOSITE *Susanna and the Elders*, by Pompeo Batoni (1708–87). In this story in the biblical Apocrypha, two lecherous elders spy on the virtuous Susanna and, thwarted in their sexual advances, have her tried on false adultery charges. In the end, Daniel intervenes to save her and the elders are put to death.

THE TESTAMENT OF SIMEON

The title of this document includes the words "about envy" and its setting is the biblical narrative of the jealousy felt for Joseph by his brothers. In the Genesis account of the episode there is no explicit mention of Simeon, but the author has here chosen him as a typical example of the ravages wrought by envy: Simeon is said to have wished to kill Joseph—a view found elsewhere in the twelve testaments—and only to have been foiled in the attempt by divine intervention.

Simeon may have been singled out because, in Genesis 42.24, when his brothers met Joseph in Egypt, Joseph is said to have had Simeon put in fetters, which may have been understood as indicating that he had a particular reason for punishing him. The testament refers to this event and Simeon says that he realized he was suffering justly and did not complain. Another biblical reference may have motivated some of Simeon's opening words: "I became extraordinarily strong; I did not hold back from any exploit, nor did I fear anything." This may be hinting at Genesis 34, where Simeon, along with Levi, appears as a fierce warrior, who takes a brutal revenge on the inhabitants of Shechem for the rape of his sister, a deed which brings his father's deathbed curse on him. However, the author is not greatly concerned with the actual biblical narrative or with providing a consistent account of historical events: so, in chapter 1, Judah is said to have sold Joseph into Egypt but, in chapter 4, Simeon admits to being the one responsible. The author's main concern is with ethical instruction, of a quasi-philosophical kind, describing the nature of envy and its baleful effects.

Other themes are found in the work, most of which recur elsewhere in the twelve testaments. Levi and Judah are lauded as the founts of the high priesthood and kingship respectively, but Levi will meet with opposition from Simeon's descendants, who will be unable to prevail because of Jacob's enduring curse on them. The figure of Joseph is emphasized as the ideal of virtue and generosity.

Chapters 6 and 7 contain prophecies of the triumph of God in the final age, which have been adapted in the existing text to refer to the advent of Christ as Savior. The prophecy in chapter 6 includes the names of the traditional enemies of Israel, as found in the Bible, and also the "Cappadocians" and "Hittites," who appear to be peoples contemporary with the period of the writer. Finally, Joseph is again specially honored, by means of an embellishment of the brief biblical account of his burial in Egypt (Genesis 50.26).

Joseph Ordering Simeon to be Bound in Fetters, ca. 1785, by William Blake (1757–1827). According to the Testaments of the Twelve Patriarchs, Simeon was bound because he had wanted to kill Joseph.

From the Testament of Simeon, chapter 2

In the time of my youth I was jealous of Joseph, because my father loved him more than all the rest of us. I determined inwardly to destroy him, because the Prince of Error blinded my mind, so that I did not consider him as a brother nor did I spare Jacob, my father. But his God and the God of our fathers sent his messenger and delivered him from my hands. ... I was furious with Judah because he had let Joseph go away alive. For five months I was angry with him. The Lord bound my hands and feet, however, and thus prevented my hands from performing their deeds, because for seven days my right hand became partly withered. I knew, children, that this had happened to me because of Joseph. Then I prayed to the Lord God that my hand might be restored and that I might refrain from every defilement and grudge and from all folly, for I knew that I had contemplated an evil deed ... on account of Joseph, my brother, because of my envying him.

THE TESTAMENT OF LEVI

As might be expected, the longest and most significant of the Testaments of the Twelve Patriarchs are those concerned with Levi, Judah, and Joseph, the most important of the brothers in the biblical account. The Testament of Levi is described as "about the priesthood and arrogance": it relates how the priesthood is conferred on Levi and his descendants and also how these descendants corrupt the priesthood by arrogantly disobeying the divine regulations of their office.

The opening section describes two visions of Levi. In the first, following the pattern of 1 Enoch 14–16, an angel leads Levi to the divine throne in heaven, where God promises him the priesthood until the end of time. He is also instructed about the geography of the heavens. In the second vision, the high priest's insignia, as listed in Exodus 28, are actually conferred on Levi by seven angelic beings.

After the second vision, Levi visits Isaac, who warns him that his descendants will pollute the sanctuary and instructs him how to preserve purity. Subsequently, a lengthy section details the sins which will be committed by Levi's successors in the priesthood, which will bring about the destruction of the Jerusalem Temple: here there is clear evidence of a Christian editor who knew of the catastrophe of 70CE, when the Romans razed the Temple. All this appears to indicate that the work is a product of Jewish circles, such as the sect of Qumran, which viewed the Temple and its official rites as defiled and illegitimate and looked for a new Temple and priesthood. The Testament of Levi reaches a climax with the promise of a new priest at the end of time, a glorious being described in terms which, in the Bible, denote a royal figure. Some scholars have seen here an allusion to the ruler John Hyrcanus (135–105BCE), of the Maccabean dynasty (see p.28), whom Jewish tradition viewed as combining the roles of priest, king, and prophet.

The ruins of what may be the Samaritan temple on Mount Gerizim, near the ancient city of Shechem and modern Nablus. To this day, the tiny Samaritan community (see box) gathers here to celebrate Passover.

54

From the Testament of Levi, chapters 5–6

[The angel said to Levi:] "Perform vengeance on Shechem for the sake of Dinah, your sister, and I shall be with you, for the Lord sent me." At that time I put an end to the sons of Hamor, as is written in the tablets of the fathers. ... When my father heard of this he was angry and sorrowful, and so he passed us [Levi and Simeon] by in his blessings. ... But I saw God's sentence was "guilty," because they had wanted to do the same thing to Sarah and Rebekah as they did to Dinah, our sister. They persecuted Abraham when he was a nomad, and harassed his flocks when they were pregnant, and grossly mistreated Eblaen, who had been born in this house. ... But the wrath of God ultimately came upon them.

From the Testament of Levi, chapter 8

I again saw the vision as formerly. And I saw seven men in white clothing who were saying to me, "Arise, put on the vestments of the priesthood, the crown of righteousness, the oracle of understanding, the robe of truth, the breastplate of faith, the mitre for the head and the apron for prophetic power." ... And they said to me, "Levi, your posterity shall be divided into three offices as a sign of the glory of the Lord who is coming. The first lot shall be great. ... The second shall be the priestly role. But the third shall be granted a new name, because from Judah a king will arise and shall found a new priesthood in accord with the Gentile model and for all nations. His presence is beloved, as a prophet of the Most High, a descendant of Abraham."

The Samaritans

In between the two visions of Levi there is a passage, apparently from a different tradition, which narrates how Levi came to earn his endowment with the priesthood in the second vision. The angel-guide, named as the angel of intercession for Israel, returns Levi to earth and commands him to wreak vengeance on the Shechemites because of their rape of his sister Dinah, as recounted in Genesis 34. Levi duly slaughters the male Shechemites.

The author is aware that, in Genesis, Levi's action is condemned by his father Jacob, but he seeks to justify it on the grounds that God had pronounced judgment on the inhabitants of Shechem as a result of their persistent wrongdoing. Behind the Shechemites there lie the Samaritans of the author's own day, who are denounced as "the foolish people that live in Shechem" in the apocryphal Book of Sirach (Sir. 50.26), which is probably from much the same period. The Samaritans, who regard only the Pentateuch (the first five books of the Bible) as Scripture, claimed descent from the northern Israelite tribes of Ephraim and Manasseh, but by the time of The Twelve Testaments they were regarded by the Jews as a foreign people.

THE TESTAMENT OF JUDAH

The Testament of Judah is the longest of the twelve testaments and, as part of its title states, it deals with "courage and love of money and fornication." The first nine chapters, in which Judah portrays his ideal character in the days of his youth, exemplify the theme of courage. But the following chapters present a sharply contrasting picture of the degeneration of the patriarch through sexual desire and greed.

In chapters 1–9, Jacob designates Judah as a king and he proves his fitness for office by a series of brave acts both in the face of wild animals and above all by a succession of successful military exploits (such as the expansion of the brief notice of Jacob's defeat of the Amorites at Genesis 48.22). In the following chapters, the narrative focuses on his relations with his wife Bathshua (that is, the daughter of Shua) and his daughter-in-law Tamar. Both were non-Israelites and marriage outside the Chosen People was a grave sin in the author's eyes. He fills

Landscape with Judah and Tamar (detail), by Lucas Cassel (before 1500–ca. 1570). The painting depicts the scene in Genesis 34 where Judah woos his widowed daughter-in-law Tamar, who is disguised as a prostitute.

out the accounts of these events in Genesis 38 with picturesque details, such as the claim that strong drink led Judah to have sexual intercourse with both Bathshua and Tamar, and that his marriage to Bathshua was achieved by means of a large bribe from her father.

Next, there are two sections of ethical exhortation, one a warning against excessive drinking, the other against excessive love of money—such sins are said to be unworthy of a king like Judah. The supreme error into which drink leads Judah is his revealing of divine mysteries to a heathen woman (this suggests that the testament's origin was in an esoteric Jewish group which had its own secret teachings). As elsewhere in the twelve testaments, there is a forecast of the doom that awaits Judah's descendants should they follow his bad example, culminating in what seems to be a reference to the national disaster of 70CE (see p.42). Another section commands Judah's children to be obedient to the tribe of Levi, since the priesthood is superior to kingship. However, in spite of the calamities which await the nation, it is emphasized that God's promise of an everlasting kingdom for Judah will not be abrogated. In the usual concluding eschatological section, there appears the figure of the messianic king, described in poetic imagery close to that used of the ideal priest in the Testament of Levi. His coming will be followed by the resurrection and all nations will speak the same language, reversing the curse of the Tower of Babel in Genesis 11.

From the Testament of Judah, chapters 1–2

My father declared to me, "You shall be king, achieving success in every way." And the Lord bestowed on me grace in all my undertakings, in the field and at home. ... I killed a lion and removed a kid from its mouth. Seizing a bear by the paw, I dropped it over a cliff and it was crushed. I raced a wild boar and, as I ran, overtook it and dismembered it. I found a wild ox grazing in the country; grasping it by the horns and brandishing it in a circle until it was blind, I hurled it down and destroyed it.

From the Testament of Judah, chapter 13

Since I had boasted that during a war not even a beautifully formed woman's face would entice me, and I had scolded Reuben my brother about Bilhah, my father's wife, the spirit of envy and fornication plotted against me until I lay with Bathshua, the Canaanite woman, and with Tamar. For I said to my father-in-law, "I will confer with my father and then I will take your daughter." But since he was unwilling to delay, he showed me a measureless mass of gold which was in his daughter's name. He decked her in gold and pearls, and made her pour out wine for us in a feast. The wine perverted my eyes; pleasure darkened my heart. I longed for her and lay with her; thus I transgressed the Lord's command.

THE TESTAMENT OF ISSACHAR

This short work consists largely of ethical instruction, and is indebted both to biblical teaching and to Hellenistic morality. In its title it is described as "about simplicity," a Greek term, but a virtue also commended in Israel's wisdom literature.

The narrative sections of the book depend on two passages from Genesis. One is what Jacob says of Issachar in his last words (Gen. 49.14–15). The Hebrew text emphasizes the fertility of the territory occupied by Issachar, yet he is apparently condemned to forced labor, probably to serve Canaanite overlords. However, in the Septuagint (the Greek translation of the Hebrew Scriptures), which the author is clearly employing, Issachar is described much more positively as a farmer, putting hard labor into the working of his land—and this is how he appears throughout the testament, leading a simple agricultural existence (see box).

The other biblical passage, Genesis 30.1–24, forms the basis of the two opening chapters, which are a retelling of a dispute about the possession of the mandrakes—a plant considered to induce pregnancy—between Jacob's two wives, Leah, the mother of Issachar, and Rachel. The version in the testament is somewhat confused but its main point is clear. The heroine here is Rachel, who is divinely commended for her sexual abstinence, declining sex for pleasure and seeking it only so as to acquire offspring.

The final eschatological section in Issachar is much briefer than in the other testaments. It predicts the moral decline of Issachar's descendants and their resulting oppression by the Gentiles, and the promise of restoration if they repent. The last chapter repeats the description of Issachar's virtues and closes with the typical notice of his death and burial at Hebron.

A Vision of Society

In the third chapter of the Testament of Issachar, the patriarch describes himself as a simple hard-working farmer, who keeps himself to himself and who first dedicates the fruits of his labor in gratitude to God and then bestows them for the relief of the poor and downtrodden. Here Issachar represents the Hebrew Bible's basic vision of a pastoral and agricultural society, exemplified by the simple life of Adam and Eve after the Fall, and centered on the family and its possession of house and land to provide its livelihood. Issachar exhorts his children to imitate the pattern of his life. They are to eschew the pursuit of riches and sexual temptation and devote themselves to their daily labors, which will enable them to enjoy the blessings of the good land which God has granted to Israel. Again this is a fundamental biblical ideal of the good life, with its stress on the virtue of hard work.

Adam and Eve, from the Moutier-Grandval Bible, produced ca. 840CE at Tours, France, illustrating Gen. 3.23 and 3.16. Jewish and Christian tradition views the simple life of Adam and Eve after the Fall as exemplary.

From the Testament of Issachar, chapter 2

If Leah, my mother, had not given up the two [mandrake] fruits in exchange for sexual intercourse, she would have borne eight sons. But accordingly, she bore six and Rachel two, because through the use of mandrakes the Lord had regard for her. For he perceived that she wanted to lie with Jacob for the sake of children and not merely for sexual gratification. ... Thus it was through the mandrakes that the Lord listened to Rachel. Even though she longed for them passionately, she did not eat them, but presented them in the house of the Lord, offering them up to the priest of the Most High.

From the Testament of Issachar, chapter 3

I lived my life in rectitude of heart; I became a farmer for the benefit of my father and my brothers. ... I was no meddler in my dealings, nor was I evil or slanderous to my neighbor. ... when I was thirty-five I took myself a wife because hard work consumed my energy, and pleasure with a woman never came to my mind; rather sleep overtook me because of my labor. ... Whatever I labored over at every harvest and whenever there was a firstborn, I first made an offering to the Lord through the priest, then for my father, and then for myself. And the Lord doubled the good things in my hands. ... In the integrity of my heart, I supplied everything from the good things of the earth to all the poor and the oppressed.

THE TESTAMENT OF JOSEPH

As an exemplary figure, Joseph is prominent throughout the Testaments of the Twelve Patriarchs, but the fullest treatment of him occurs in the testament which bears his name. The work's title includes the words "about chastity" and the depiction of him as the model of sexual purity is certainly the main theme of the book. However, the second half of the testament primarily emphasizes Joseph as one who demonstrates the importance of brotherly love and upholds family harmony. The material is predominantly narrative and, although the reader is exhorted to imitate Joseph in both his aspects, there is notably less ethical instruction than in the other eleven testaments.

The first chapter consists of a poem in which Joseph praises God for the numerous times he was delivered from danger during his career: its form corresponds to the pattern of the individual thanksgiving psalms in the Bible. Its main feature appears to be a list of ten such deliverances, although others are mentioned. In the next chapter, Joseph says that "in ten testings God showed that I was approved, and in all of them I persevered."

There follows a lengthy series of episodes detailing the history of Joseph's relations with Potiphar's wife, and expanding on the narrative in Genesis 39.6–23, in which God's concern and support for Joseph is underlined. Potiphar's wife, here called "the Egyptian woman," embarks on a succession of wiles to win his favor—the author was perhaps inspired by the brief statement in Genesis 39.10 that "although she spoke to Joseph day after day, he would not consent to lie beside her or be with her." She first employs threats and torture, then flattery, asking Joseph to instruct her in the worship of the true God. Afterwards, she offers to kill her husband and marry Joseph, then she tries a magical potion, which Joseph neutralizes, then threatens suicide if Joseph will not succumb. Finally, as in Genesis, she falsely denounces him to her husband for attempting to seduce her, and Joseph is thrown into prison.

The next section introduces the theme of brotherly love, by means of an extended narrative of Joseph's harsh life as a slave in Egypt before being taken into Potiphar's household. Here, Potiphar's wife is called the "Memphian woman," but the purpose of the story is to show how Joseph kept silence through all his troubles so as not to disgrace his brothers.

The final apocalyptic prediction points to the biblical motif of Joseph the dreamer. He has a dream, the imagery of which is unfortunately obscure (see extract, opposite). However, he sees the advent of a redeemer figure, who in the present christianized text is plainly Jesus, the lamb of God and son of the Virgin Mary. He is said to descend from Levi and Judah and will inaugurate an everlasting kingdom to supersede that of Joseph. After this the patriarch dies and his sons transport his bones to Hebron.

Joseph's Dreams, by Bartolo di Fredi (1330–1410), illustrating Gen. 37.5–9. The biblical theme of
Joseph as a dreamer and dream interpreter features prominently in the Testament of Joseph.

From the Testament of Joseph, chapter 1

Listen to Joseph, the beloved one of Israel.
Give ear to the words of my mouth.
In my life I have seen envy and death.
But I have not gone astray: I continued
    in the truth of the Lord.
These, my brothers, hated me, but the
    Lord loved me.
They wanted to kill me, but the God of
    my fathers preserved me. ...
They sold me into slavery; the Lord of all
set me free.
I was taken into captivity; the strength of
    his hand came to my aid.
I was overtaken by hunger; the Lord
    himself fed me generously.
I was alone, and God came to help me.
I was in weakness, and the Lord showed
    his concern for me.
I was in prison, and the Savior acted
    graciously on my behalf.

JOSEPH AND ASENETH

In Genesis 41.45, Joseph is recorded as marrying Aseneth (or Asenath), the daughter of the Egyptian priest of On or Heliopolis. Aseneth subsequently bore him two sons, Manasseh and Ephraim. These brief statements caught the imagination of later writers, who expanded the story with details intended to give artistic verisimilitude to the narrative. The fullest and most influential example is the work called Joseph and Aseneth.

The book falls into two distinct sections. The first records the events leading up to the marriage of the two protagonists. Aseneth lives a life of secluded virginity as a priestess to the Egyptian deities (her name may mean "Belonging to Neith," an important Egyptian goddess). She has refused numerous suitors, even the Pharaoh's eldest son, but one day her father announces that he is going to wed her to Joseph. Aseneth refuses because Joseph is a foreigner, a fugitive, a former slave, and a convicted adulterer. However, when he arrives Aseneth falls in love with him, only to be rejected in her turn, since he will not contemplate marrying a heathen.

According to the author, Joseph's subsequent marriage to Aseneth was justified on the grounds that she renounced her idolatry and turned to the one true God, and the work devotes considerable attention to the story of Aseneth's conversion. When Joseph and Aseneth first meet, Joseph prays to God to bring about Aseneth's conversion. In his prayer, conversion is defined as a passage from darkness to light, from error to truth, and from death to life, following the pattern of the creation of the universe, with particular emphasis on the theme of new life, and this language recurs more than once in the subsequent narrative. Inspired by Joseph's blessing, Aseneth repents in sackcloth and ashes, a

An Egyptian limestone votive tablet of ca. 150 BCE showing the powerful mother goddess Neith, whose worship was centered on Sais in the Nile Delta.

The Rite of the Sacred Bees

After Aseneth's final plea for deliverance from the power of the devil (see main text, below), she is visited by an angelic being in human form who grants her request, conferring upon her the gift of immortality. Aseneth acquires this by eating a miraculous honeycomb made by bees of paradise. The angel marks the honeycomb with a cross—this may, though not necessarily, indicate Christian influence at this point—after which the comb produces a huge swarm of bees which surrounds Aseneth.

Some of the bees return to heaven while others die, but are restored to life by the angel: perhaps here there is a symbol of resurrection.

It is not easy to interpret all of this strange episode. It is likely that behind it there lies an actual esoteric rite, of the kind represented by the initiation rituals of Hellenistic mystery cults, which were also believed to confer immortality. If this is so, the account is to be seen as deliberately mystifying, its symbolism understood only by initiates.

sign of mourning, indicating that she is still in the realm of death, and destroys her idols. There follow three soliloquies by Aseneth in poetical form, in which she throws herself upon the mercy of the God of Jacob and, in a long final lament, confesses her sins and prays for deliverance from the attacks of the devil, "the father of the gods of the Egyptians." Finally, she expresses her love for Joseph and promises to cherish and obey him as a good wife. These poems are moving and it is perhaps not too fanciful to see in them the personal reflection of an actual conversion experience. Aseneth subsequently takes part in a mysterious ritual that may reflect the practice of an

From Joseph and Aseneth, chapters 1–2

Pentephres, [the] priest of Heliopolis ... had a daughter [Aseneth] of eighteen years, very tall and handsome and beautiful to look at beyond all virgins on the earth. And this girl had nothing similar to the virgins of the Egyptians, but was in every respect similar to the daughters of the Hebrews, tall as Sarah and handsome as Rebekah and beautiful as Rachel. ...

Aseneth was despising and scorning every man. ... And no man had ever seen her, because Pentephres had a tower adjoining his house, very big and high, and on top of this tower was an upper floor including ten chambers. And the first chamber was big and splendid, paved with purple stones, and its walls were faced with colored and precious stones, and the ceiling of that chamber was of gold. And within the chamber the gods of the Egyptians in gold and silver, who were without number, were fixed to the walls. And Aseneth worshiped them all and feared them and performed sacrifices to them every day. ... seven virgins occupied ... seven chambers, one each, and these were waiting on Aseneth, and they were all of the same age, born in one night with Aseneth. And they were very beautiful.

DATA

TITLE:
Joseph and
Aseneth

ORIGINAL DATE
OF COMPOSITION:
ca. 150BCE–
ca. 150CE

ORIGINAL LANGUAGE:
Greek

PROVENANCE:
Egypt

EARLIEST EXTANT
MANUSCRIPT:
6th cent. CE
(Syriac)

The Influence of Joseph and Aseneth

Joseph and Aseneth became one of the most popular and widely read works of all the non-canonical writings. It was completely neglected by Judaism but was taken over by the Church, where it was certainly well known in the early centuries CE, both in the West and East, particularly in Armenia and Ethiopia. In Europe, its popularity was largely due to Vincent of Beauvais (ca. 1190–1264CE) who published a condensed version of the work in his Mirror of History, an encyclopedia of world history. His abridgment was frequently copied separately and then printed, and found its way into numerous collections in a wide variety of languages, which continued to be published up to the eighteenth century. The figure of the beautiful and pious Aseneth naturally attracted the attention of artists, and representations of her are common in biblical and other medieval manuscripts.

esoteric Jewish sect (see box on p.63) and is admitted, as one reborn, into the company of the elect (Israel). She is promised that she will marry Joseph and the wedding duly takes place in a splendid ceremony conducted by Pharaoh himself.

The second section of the book is set eight years later. Pharaoh's eldest son is still in love with Aseneth and tries to suborn Joseph's brothers to kidnap her and kill Joseph. Dan and Gad agree to assist him, but their ambush is foiled by another brother, Benjamin. Magnanimously, Aseneth forgives Dan and Gad, but three days later Pharaoh's son dies of wounds received in the attack, and his father dies of grief. In a final happy ending, Joseph becomes king in his place.

The narrative seeks to resolve the problem of how Joseph, the perfect Israelite hero, could have married a foreigner, the daughter of a heathen priest—the conversion of Aseneth provides the answer, and the author appears to be defending Gentile converts to Judaism, who were becoming numerous in his day, against his stricter contemporaries. Aseneth is the prototype of all succeeding proselytes. She is also a model of virginity and chastity, virtues highly prized by many non-canonical writers, and the moral superiority of those who follow Judaism is emphasized, as when Levi stops Benjamin from killing the Pharaoh's son.

However, the work should be seen primarily as a romance, written for enjoyment as much as for edification. The author piles up a succession of vivid and picturesque scenes, such as the description of Aseneth's house (see extract, p.63) or the account of the attack on Aseneth, which is mainly an adventure story with comparatively little religious content. Throughout there are many folklore features, including the common theme of the central character who endures many trials but eventually triumphs. The work may be compared to biblical or apocryphal books that also center on a heroine, such as Ruth, Esther, and Judith. It also bears many resemblances to Greco-Roman romances such as the well-known Golden Ass by Apuleius.

From Joseph and Aseneth, chapter 8

Pentephres said to his daughter Aseneth, "Greet your brother [Joseph], because he, too, is a virgin like you and hates every strange woman, as you, too, every strange man." ... And as Aseneth went up to kiss Joseph, he stretched out his right hand and laid it ... between her breasts, and her breasts were already standing upright like two handsome apples. And Joseph said, "It is not fitting for a man who worships God, who will bless with his mouth the living God and eat blessed bread of life and drink a blessed cup of immortality and anoint himself with blessed ointment of incorruptibility to kiss a strange woman who will bless with her mouth dead and dumb idols and eat from their table food of strangulation and drink from their libation a cup of insidiousness and anoint herself with ointment of destruction. But a man who worships God will kiss ... his mother and his sister who is born of his clan and family and the wife who shares his bed, all of whom bless with their mouths the living God." ... When Aseneth heard these words ... she was cut to the heart.

Jacob Blessing the Sons of Joseph, by Rembrandt (1606-69). From early Christian times, Aseneth (right) is often shown in this scene from Genesis 48, although neither the Bible nor Joseph and Aseneth mention her presence.

THE TESTAMENT OF MOSES

Although there are many references to Moses in the non-canonical texts, this is the only work in which he appears as the subject of the regular testament form and the consequent revealer of apocalyptic predictions of future history and the end-time. In contrast, for example, the Book of Jubilees says nothing of the end of Moses' life and its main concern is with the institution of Passover and the Sabbath.

As it stands, the Testament of Moses is structured as a retelling and expansion of Deuteronomy 31–34. The first chapter is a farewell speech of Moses to Joshua, nominating him as his successor and handing over some books which Joshua is to anoint with cedar oil and store in earthenware jars. The idea of sacred writings being kept hidden until they are revealed at the

The Testament and Death of Moses, by Luca Signorelli (1441–1523). In the foreground, Moses commissions Joshua as his successor (left), before delivering his testament (right). In the background, he is buried on Mount Nebo.

due time is common in Judaism (beginning with Daniel 12.4), while the storage of documents in jars was an actual practice, as shown by the discoveries of the Dead Sea Scrolls. Moses describes himself as the one "prepared from the beginning of the world to be the mediator of the covenant." There follows the typical apocalyptic device of a review of past events presented as prediction, in this case a recounting of biblical history down to the fall of Jerusalem in 586BCE and the return from the Babylonian exile, in a form reflecting Deuteronomy 33.

The author then turns to his own day, in which he sees the pattern of Israel's history being repeated, whereby the nation's sins bring down divine judgment. This judgment now takes the shape of Antiochus IV Epiphanes and the author appears to be writing not long after the beginning of the king's persecution of Judaism in 167BCE (see p.28). The details of this attack are paralleled in Daniel, and particularly in 1 and 2 Maccabees in the biblical Apocrypha. The account reaches its climax in the story of the Levite Taxo and his seven sons, who hide themselves in a cave, resolving to die rather than disobey God's commands. The Taxo episode ends with the assurance that God will avenge their deaths (see extract). Strikingly, it is said that Israel will be lifted up into heaven, while the earth is given over to the punishment of its enemies.

The testament was later revised by an editor who speaks of the wickedness into which the Hasmonean king-priests, the successors to the Maccabean liberators, had fallen. There follows an account of the reigns of Herod the Great (ruled 37–4BCE) and his sons. The author says that the sons would have shorter reigns than Herod, so the latest date of the revision must be 30CE, since two sons actually ruled for longer than their father's thirty-four years. Another clearly identifiable episode is the suppression of a Jewish revolt by the Romans after Herod's death in 4BCE. As in the original work, all these events are seen as the immediate prelude to the final age.

DATA

TITLE:
The Testament of Moses

ORIGINAL DATE OF COMPOSITION:
2nd cent. BCE–
1st cent. CE

ORIGINAL LANGUAGE:
Semitic

PROVENANCE:
Palestine

EARLIEST EXTANT MANUSCRIPT:
6th cent. CE
(Latin)

From the Testament of Moses, chapter 10

And the earth will tremble, even to its ends
    shall it be shaken.
And the high mountains will be made low. ...
The sun will not give light.
And in darkness the horns of the moon
    will flee.
Yea, they will be broken in pieces. ...
And the sea all the way to the abyss will
    retire, to the sources of water which fail.
Yea, the rivers will vanish away.
For God Most High will surge forth, the
    Eternal One alone.

In full view, he will come to work vengeance
    on the nations.
Yea, all their idols will he destroy.
Then you will be happy, O Israel!
And you will mount up above the necks
    and the wings of an eagle.
Yea, all things will be fulfilled.
And God will raise you to the heights.
Yea, he will fix you firmly in the heaven of
    the stars in the place of their habitations.
And you will behold from on high.
Yea, you will see your enemies on the earth.

PSEUDO-PHILO

The book known as Pseudo-Philo ("the False Philo") recounts the biblical history of Israel from the descendants of Adam to the death of King Saul. It is difficult to know just how the work—traditionally entitled "The Book of Biblical Antiquities"—came to be ascribed to Philo of Alexandria (ca.15BCE-ca. 150CE), a famous Jewish philosopher and scholar. It was included among the Latin translations of his writings, although its method of treating the biblical text is very different from that of Philo.

Saul's death may seem a curious place at which to end and some scholars therefore conclude that part of the original has been lost. However, the present ending may represent a kind of comment on the sad condition of the Jewish nation in the writer's own day, probably sometime in the first century CE, following the Roman conquest. The author's method is to quote verses from the Bible and then elaborate on them with a mass of legendary and moralizing material. In some cases Pseudo-Philo may draw on older traditions, but his work is distinguished by a large number of legends and images not found elsewhere, which may well be the products of his own considerable imagination (see box, below). His style is similar to the rabbinical method known as *haggadah*, whereby the text is interpreted and embellished by the extensive use of legends, parables, popular stories, and folklore, and his work provides the earliest evidence for many such features that became common in later Jewish writings. The passages of the Bible containing the Jewish law employed a different method of interpretation (*halakah*), and Pseudo-Philo omits almost all the legal sections from Exodus to

Embellishments of Scripture

Pseudo-Philo treats the biblical text with considerable freedom. Thus the patriarch Abraham appears as the leader of a group of men who refuse to provide bricks to build the Tower of Babel. As a result, in a clear echo of Daniel 3, he is thrown into a fiery furnace, from which God saves him (see also p.42). The work is the earliest record of a Jewish tradition that Moses was born circumcised, and attributes songs to Deborah, Jephthah's daughter, and Hannah (the mother of Samuel) which are quite different from

their songs in Judges and 1 Samuel. The work shows a marked interest in its heroines: Deborah calls herself "woman of God," reworking the common biblical phrase "man of God," and, even more strikingly, Jephthah's daughter goes at her death to the "bosom of her mothers," rather than "fathers."

The author is also concerned to satisfy his readers' curiosity about figures who are no more than a name in the Bible, such as Moses' father Amram, and Kenaz, the father of the first judge (see main text).

This mural from the 2nd-century CE synagogue of ancient Dura Europos, Syria, illustrates the kind of popular embellishments of the Bible that are found in Pseudo-Philo. Here, it is Pharaoh's daughter herself who retrieves Moses from the river, rather than one of her servants, as in the Bible (Exod. 2.5).

From Pseudo-Philo, chapter 9

Exod. 2.1 *And* Amram *of the tribe of Levi went out and took a wife* from his own tribe. ... And this man had one son and one daughter; their names were Aaron and Miriam. And the spirit of God came upon Miriam one night, and she saw a dream and told it to her parents in the morning, saying, "I have seen this night, and behold a man in a linen garment stood and said to me, 'Go and say to your parents: Behold, he who will be born from Exod. 2.3 you will be cast forth into the water; likewise through him the water will be dried up. And I will work signs through him and save my people, and he will exercise leadership always.'" And when Miriam told of her dream, her parents did not believe her. ...

Now Jochebed *conceived* from Amram [and bore a son]. ... The king of Egypt appointed local chiefs who, when the Hebrew women gave birth, would immediately throw their male children into the river. *And she took* her child and *made for him an ark* from the bark of a pine tree *and placed the ark at the bank of the river.* Now that child was born in the covenant of God and the covenant of the flesh [circumcised].

DATA

TITLE:
Pseudo-Philo
(The Book of
Biblical Antiquities)

ORIGINAL DATE OF
COMPOSITION:
1st cent. CE

ORIGINAL LANGUAGE:
Hebrew or Aramaic

PROVENANCE:
Palestine

EARLIEST EXTANT
MANUSCRIPT:
11th cent. CE
(Latin)

David Plays Before Saul, by Salomon Konink (1609–56), illustrating 1 Sam. 16.23 and also 1 Sam. 19.9–10, which describes how Saul attempted to kill David with a spear.

Deuteronomy. He is also highly selective in what he covers from the narrative sections—for example, he gives only a brief summary of the ancestors from Abraham to Joseph and entirely leaves out the account of the conquest of Canaan. Another notable feature is his habit of giving speeches to his characters, in the manner of Hellenistic historians.

At least one third of the work is taken up by the author's treatment of the Book of Judges, which records the exploits of the great leaders of Israel. It has been suggested that this may reflect Pseudo-Philo's special concern for good leadership in his own day, which may therefore have been the time of the first Jewish revolt against Rome (66—70CE). However, this may be laying too great emphasis on just one aspect of the work. More probably, the book is to be seen as an example of how the scriptures might have been conveyed to synagogue congregations in first-century CE Palestine. It may not be too fanciful even to see Pseudo-Philo as originating in a series of lively illustrations for use in synagogue sermons or in teaching.

The material on Judges and the First Book of Samuel well illustrates the author's methods. The first judge of Israel is named in the Bible as "Othniel son of Kenaz" (Judg. 3.9). The Bible says little else about Kenaz, but Pseudo-Philo devotes four entire chapters to him. Pseudo-Philo knows the tradition of King David as a psalmist, but the psalm he ascribes to him is quite different from any in the Bible. David also utters a mysterious song of exorcism to drive away the evil spirit from Saul, the language of which may reflect the usage of contemporary exorcists (see extract below).

From Pseudo-Philo, chapter 60

The song that David played for Saul in order that *the evil spirit might depart from him.* [1 Sam. 16.23]
"Darkness and silence were before the world was made,
and silence spoke a word and the darkness became light.
Then your name [O spirit] was pronounced in the drawing together of that which had been spread out,
the upper of which was called heaven and the lower was called earth.
And the upper part was commanded to bring down rain according to its season,
and the lower part was commanded to produce food for all created things.

And after these was the tribe of [evil] spirits made.
And now do not be troublesome as one created on the second day.
But if not, remember Tartarus where you walk.
Or is it not enough for you to hear that, through what resounds before you, I sing to many?
Or have you forgotten that you were created from a resounding echo in the chaos?
But let the new womb from which I was born rebuke you,
from which after a time one born from my loins will rule over you."

CHAPTER 3

LOST WRITINGS OF THE PROPHETS

◆

THE LIVES OF THE PROPHETS

This short work is summed up in its opening sentence: "The names of the prophets, and where they are from, and where they died and how, and where they lie." In most cases the accounts of the prophets also include legends, prophecies, and miracles not found in the Bible. The work covers the "major prophets" (Isaiah, Jeremiah, Ezekiel), Daniel, the twelve "minor prophets," and seven others whose names are recorded in Scripture.

By the 1st century CE there was a Jewish tradition—recorded in Luke 11.47 and Hebrews 11.37—that some of the ancient prophets had met violent ends. The Bible relates nothing about how the major prophets died, but the Lives says that Isaiah was sawn in two (see p.83), Jeremiah stoned, and Ezekiel executed (Paul lists these fates in Hebrews, without naming the prophets). In the popular Judaism of the time there was apparently a great reverence for such holy figures, their powers of intercession, and also for their tombs (see box, below). Such devotion can be seen as one source for the later Christian veneration of saints and the custom of pilgrimages to their burial sites. The author displays a good knowledge of Judea and Jerusalem and his work could be compared with the famous travel diary of Egeria, a fourth-century Christian nun. The work exists only in Christian manuscripts and it has clear Christian interpolations; the sections on Elijah and Elisha, which do little but reproduce the biblical narratives, also look like additions.

The Tombs of the Prophets

The Lives shows considerable interest in the tombs of the prophets, which are described in some detail, especially those of the major prophets. There is evidence of an increasing veneration of the burial places of Israel's heroes around the time of Jesus, and miracles and healings were believed to be granted to pilgrims who visited them. Perhaps, in its original form, the Lives was intended as a kind of manual for Jewish pilgrims, providing information about the holy people they were going to honor and what they could expect to find at their tombs. Herod the Great (ruled 37–4 BCE) is said to have adorned the tomb of David with a new marble entrance, and in Matthew's gospel Jesus speaks of the scribes and Pharisees who "build the tombs of the prophets and decorate the graves of the righteous" (Matt. 23.29).

From The Lives of the Prophets, chapter 1–2

DATA

TITLE:
The Lives of the Prophets

ORIGINAL DATE OF
COMPOSITION:
1st cent. CE

ORIGINAL LANGUAGE:
Probably Greek

PROVENANCE:
Probably Palestine

EARLIEST EXTANT
MANUSCRIPT:
6th cent. CE
(Greek)

Isaiah, from Jerusalem, died under Manasseh by being sawn in two, and was buried underneath the Oak of Rogel, near the place where the path crosses the aqueduct whose water Hezekiah shut off by blocking its source. And God worked the miracle of Siloam for the prophet's sake, for, being faint before he died, he prayed for water to drink, and immediately it was sent to him from it; therefore it is called Siloam, which means "sent." … If the Jews … were coming, water would come out, but if foreigners approached, it would not. Wherefore to this day it comes out intermittently, in order that the mystery may be manifested. And since this happened through Isaiah, as a memorial of it the nation also buried him nearby with care and in great honor, so that through his prayer even after his death they might enjoy the benefit of the water, for an oracle was also given to them concerning him.

His tomb is near the tomb of the kings, west of the tomb of the priests in the southern part of the city. For Solomon made the tombs, in accordance with David's design, east of Zion, which has an entrance from Gabaon, twenty stadia distant from the city. And he made a secret construction with winding passages; and it is to this day unknown to most people. There the king kept the gold from Ethiopia and the spices.

Jeremiah was from Anathoth, and he died in Taphnai of Egypt, having been stoned by his people. He was buried in the environs of Pharaoh's palace, because the Egyptians held him in high esteem, having benefited through him. For he prayed, and the asps left them, and the monsters of the waters, which the Egyptians call *Nephoth* and the Greeks crocodiles. And those who are God's faithful pray at the place to this very day, and taking the dust of the place they heal asps' bites.

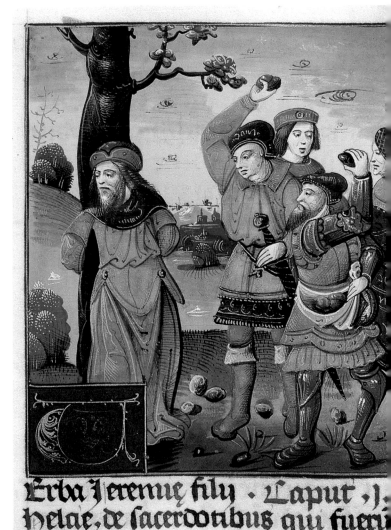

The Stoning of Jeremiah, from a French Bible of 1526. It depicts the non-biblical legend that Jeremiah was stoned to death in Egypt.

THE HISTORY OF THE RECHABITES

This remarkable document displays concerns and interests that set it apart from the rest of the Pseudepigrapha. As in other cases, its present form is explicitly Christian, but there can be little doubt that its earliest sections represent an originally Jewish work. It describes the community of the Rechabites, the "Blessed Ones," who live a blissful life on an island far across the sea. The work was popular in Europe and the Near East in the Middle Ages and versions exist in several languages.

In the Bible, Jeremiah 35 describes a group led by "Jonadab son of Rechab"—hence the name "Rechabites"—which preserves the lifestyle of Israel's earlier nomadic existence, abstaining from wine and the practice of agriculture, and living only in tents. Jeremiah commends their piety and promises that, although God will shortly wipe out the kingdom of Judah, he will preserve the Rechabites, so that Jonadab "shall not lack a descendant to stand before me for all time" (Jer. 35.19). The History of the Rechabites is a kind of *midrash* (interpretative embellishment) on Jeremiah, to explain how the Rechabites were able to escape the destruction decreed for the rest of Israel.

The work begins with Zosimus, a hermit in the desert, who for many years begs God to show him the land of the Rechabites. Finally an angel appears and leads Zosimus on a long and wearisome journey, at the end of which he is miraculously transported to a remote island paradise which he describes as "pleasant and beautiful and filled with luxuriant trees bearing pleasant and fragrant fruits … adorned with flowers and filled with many and delightful pleasures." There Zosimus meets the Blessed Ones, who write an account of their life

The Age of Gold, by Jacopo Zucchi (1541–90). The History of the Rechabites draws on Greek and Roman traditions of the Four Ages of the World, of which the first, the idyllic Age of Gold, came to be linked in Christianity with Eden and the blessed abode where the righteous live until the Last Judgment.

on stone tablets for him to take with him back to the ordinary human world (see extract, below). The Blessed Ones are like Adam and Eve before the Fall, enjoying the fellowship of angels. They lead an ascetic existence, eat no bread and drink no wine and—again like Adam and Eve before the Fall—they go about naked but without any suspicion of impurity. Although sinless, the Blessed Ones are mortals who marry and have children and await the end of the age. After seven days, Zosimus departs in the same miraculous way by which he had arrived.

The work clearly draws on the legend of the Island of the Blessed Ones, widely current in the ancient Mediterranean world and found in the works of famous Greek and Latin writers including Hesiod, Homer, Herodotus, and Lucian. The author may also know of Jewish ascetic movements around the turn of the Common Era, especially the Therapeutae in Egypt (see p.98). Descriptions of this contemplative sect by contemporary Jewish authors have many points of resemblance with the Rechabites, although it is perhaps going too far to claim that the latter are actually to be identified with the Therapeutae. The Christian historian Eusebius (died 339CE) viewed the Therapeutae as Christian monks, and it may well be that the later, Christian-ized, form of the History of the Rechabites aims to portray an idealized picture of monasticism.

From the History of the Rechabites, chapters 10–12

Angels of God in glorious form appeared to us. And they led all of us out from prison, and placed us in the air that is above the land, and brought us to this place in which you now see us. ... And we are without sins and evil and abominable thoughts. And we are mortals; however, we are purified and spot-less ... and our sight is fixed continuously and unceasingly on the light of the future life. ...

There are not among us vineyards, grain, husbandry, wood, iron, houses, buildings, gold, or silver; and neither stormy weather nor rain with us; neither snow nor ice. ... And the land in which we are is filled with a glorious light so darkness and night do not enter it. And we possess a shining appear-ance and dwell in light.

And there are among us men who take wives and once only the man has intercourse with his wife. And then they are set apart from each other and they remain in purity for the remainder of their lives. ... But the wife conceives and bears two children; one of them is for marriage and the other grows up in virginity. ...

[And] we are naked not as you suppose, for we are covered with a covering of glory; and we do not show each other the private parts of our bodies. But we are covered with a stole of glory similar to that which clothed Adam and Eve before they sinned.

We have knowledge about you people who inhabit the world. ... And the angels of God dwell with us and they announce to us those things which happen among you; and we rejoice at the good deeds which the upright who are among you do. And we grieve over the sinners and pagans who are in the world; and petition God constantly to restrain his anger concerning you.

DATA

TITLE:
The History of the Rechabites

ORIGINAL DATE OF COMPOSITION:
1st–6th cent. CE

ORIGINAL LANGUAGE:
Uncertain

PROVENANCE:
Palestine?

EARLIEST EXTANT MANUSCRIPT:
12th cent. CE
(Syriac)

THE TESTAMENT OF SOLOMON

DATA

TITLE:
The Testament
of Solomon

ORIGINAL DATE OF
COMPOSITION:
1st–3rd cent. CE

ORIGINAL LANGUAGE:
Greek

PROVENANCE:
Egypt

EARLIEST EXTANT
MANUSCRIPT:
4th cent. CE
(Coptic)

As it stands, the Testament of Solomon is probably by a Greek-speaking Christian. However, it is based on older Jewish traditions, along with Hellenistic magic and other concepts and beliefs with a long history in the civilizations of the ancient Near East.

Although it is described as a "testament," the regular testament pattern is not prominent and the usual feature of a prediction of future history is virtually absent. Rather, Solomon's book is said to be "a testament to the sons of Israel that they might know the powers of the demons and their forms." This places the work among the large number of texts used by Jewish exorcists to combat the effects of evil spirits, especially disease (compare Acts 19.19).

In the Bible, Solomon's wisdom is said to consist primarily of knowledge about natural phenomena, plants, and animals (1 Kings 4.29–34). Extrapolating from this passage, the rabbis credited Solomon with a vast store of astrological, magical, medical, and especially demonological lore, which enabled him to compel evil spirits to work on the Temple. Hence the testament begins with a narrative of how Solomon harnesses a succession of demons to help build the Temple. A charming story tells of a little boy working on the Temple, who is attacked by a demon. The boy complains to Solomon, and God gives the king a ring with a seal, which enables the boy to subdue the demon. Solomon's magical ring is first mentioned by the Jewish historian Josephus (1st century CE) and plays a large part in subsequent Jewish writings and legends. There follows a string of encounters between Solomon and various demons, who reveal their names, and the name of the angels who thwart them, before being put to work on the Temple.

Other episodes are dependent on the Bible, such as brief references to the visit of the queen of Sheba, who is labeled a witch, as she regularly appears in later Jewish legend.

Demons, Astrology, and Healing

The Testament of Solomon is notable for linking demonology and astrology: in the work, each spirit explains that he resides in a particular star or constellation or zodiac sign. A later chapter lists thirty-six heavenly bodies, who are the decans of the zodiac, an astrological notion well known in the ancient world. Each of these spirits is the cause of a particular human disease, for which charms and remedies are prescribed, and the section has been likened to "an ancient medical encyclopedia." Underlying this part of the book are similar lists in Babylonian texts which name demons and the illness for which each is responsible. One passage tells how Solomon seals a demon inside a broad flat bowl with his magic ring—this recalls Aramaic incantation bowls designed to trap evil spirits.

The Tempest, by Giorgione (1477–1510). The two broken pillars refer, in esoteric traditions, to the Temple of Solomon, pointing to a deeper mystical significance than is evident from the apparent simple charm of this scene.

From the Testament of Solomon, chapter 18

There came to me thirty-six heavenly bodies. … I, Solomon, asked them, saying: "Well, who are you?" All at once, with one voice, they said, "We are thirty-six heavenly bodies, the world rulers of the darkness of this age."… Then I summoned the first spirit and said to him, "Who are you?" He replied, "I am the first decan of the zodiac and I am called Ruax. I cause heads of men to suffer pain and … their temples to throb. Should I hear only, 'Michael, imprison Ruax,' I retreat immediately." The second spirit said, "I am called Barsafael. I cause those who reside in my time period to have pains on the sides of their heads. Should I hear, 'Gabriel, imprison Barsafael,' I retreat immediately."

THE APOCALYPSE OF ELIJAH

This obscure document contains many historical allusions and references which, at the present state of knowledge, largely defy interpretation. Its form is not really that of an apocalypse—essentially a secret revelation by an angel to a seer concerning the events of the last days of the world—although the work does contain apocalyptic-type material, especially about the end-time.

In spite of the title, nothing in the text attributes the work to Elijah, but he is mentioned twice in the work and one can only presume that this led to its being ascribed to him. It begins with a prophetic formula: "The word of the Lord came to me, saying, 'Son of man, say to this people...' " without giving the prophet's name. The term "son of man" might more probably point to the prophet Ezekiel, of whom it is regularly used in the Bible. The work as a whole would appear to be a collection of originally separate sources, loosely strung together. As it stands, this is undoubtedly a Christian text, but it is possible to discover distinctively Jewish strata within it, which have been expanded or modified. Thus the core of the first chapter is a Jewish treatise on the virtues of fasting and of perseverance in prayer, but this is preceded by a Christian apocalyptic passage about the deliverance to be wrought by the son of God and the ultimate destiny of the righteous and sinners, based on various New Testament verses.

The next chapter—"Concerning the Kings of Assyria and the Dissolution of the Heaven and the Earth and the Things Beneath the Earth"—reproduces the typical apocalypse pattern whereby the past is presented as prediction, culminating in a prophecy of the end-time. The kings listed cannot be identified with certainty, but Egypt features prominently and it is likely that this was the home of the original apocalypse, and of the Christian reworking of the text.

The third chapter is concerned with the advent of the Antichrist, "the son of lawlessness," who is pictured in Christian terminology, although the strange account of his physical appearance betrays the Jewish origin of the passage (see extract, opposite). The following chapter deals with martyrdom and names three martyrs: Elijah, Enoch, and Tabitha. The martyrdom of Enoch and Elijah recalls the deaths of the "two witnesses" in Revelation 11.1–12, while Tabitha is the woman restored to life by Peter in Acts 9.36–41. Thus they are clearly Christian figures, but there follows a more straightforward account of the martyrdom of sixty men that probably belongs to the genre of Jewish martyr legends also found in the books of the Maccabees.

Finally, the author returns to the Antichrist. He recounts his death after a cosmic struggle and the Last Judgment and concludes with the inauguration of the millennial age through the second coming of Christ. The description is predominantly Christian, but there are again indications that it represents a reworking of a Jewish source.

DATA

TITLE:
The Apocalypse
of Elijah

ORIGINAL DATE OF
COMPOSITION:
1st–3rd cent. CE

ORIGINAL LANGUAGE:
Greek

PROVENANCE:
Probably Egypt

EARLIEST EXTANT
MANUSCRIPT:
ca. 400CE
(Coptic)

The Preaching and Deeds of the Antichrist, by Luca Signorelli (1441–1523). The painting reflects a Christian tradition that the Antichrist (right foreground, on pedestal) will take the physical form of Christ himself.

From the Apocalypse of Elijah, chapters 3 and 5

Behold, I will tell you [the signs of the son of lawlessness] so that you might know him. He is [text lost] a skinny-legged young lad, having a tuft of grey hair at the front of his bald head. His eyebrows will reach to his ears. There is a leprous bare spot on the front of his hands. He will transform himself in the presence of those who see him. He will become a young child. He will become old. … But the signs of his head will not be able to change. Therein you will know that he is the son of lawlessness. … After these things, Elijah and Enoch will come down. They will lay down the flesh of the world, and they will receive their spiritual flesh. They will pursue the son of lawlessness and kill him since he is not able to speak. On that day he will dissolve in their presence like ice which was dissolved by fire.

THE APOCALYPSE OF ZEPHANIAH

The Apocalypse of Zephaniah is attributed to one of the "minor prophets," who is known only from the short book of the Bible that bears his name. The work, of which large portions are lost, is found in the same Coptic manuscripts as the Apocalypse of Elijah, although both texts were most probably originally written in Greek.

Certain features suggest why the author chose to ascribe the work to Zephaniah. The biblical Book of Zephaniah contains much apocalyptic material, especially the announcement of the coming Last Judgment. This is pictured in similar terms at the close of the extant text of the Apocalypse, where it may originally have been more prominent. The biblical Zephaniah fulminates against some renegade priests and the Apocalypse condemns a similar group. The Book of Zephaniah and the Apocalypse also share a marked interest in the city of Jerusalem.

Although the work survived only in Christian circles, it shows remarkably few signs of Christian influence. There are no indisputably Christian passages and, while parts of chapter two seem related to verses in the New Testament, the resemblances are not sufficiently close to be dependent.

The work takes the form of a prophet's journey to the heavens and what he sees there. However, as compared with other accounts of such journeys, the work is not interested in cosmology or celestial geography or the angelic hierarchy (although inevitably angels figure prominently). The author is almost entirely concerned with the fate of souls in the afterlife. The seven scenes that make up Zephaniah's journey are followed by four scenes which each begin with an angel blowing a trumpet: originally there may have been

An Angel Weighing Souls, a Catalan fresco of the 13th century. This motif, which occurs in the Apocalypse of Zephaniah, is ultimately of ancient Egyptian origin (see also p.41).

more trumpet scenes, perhaps corresponding to the seven angels of the Book of Revelation. Subsequently Zephaniah is taken to the underworld, where he sees two great angels, a terrifying accusing angel and the angel Eremiel, the guardian of the souls in Hades. The accusing angel presents him with a scroll listing all his sins, but the seer is proclaimed innocent and a second scroll is presented that almost certainly recorded his far more numerous good deeds (there is a gap in the text at this point). The seer is absolved and, like Enoch, is transformed into an angel. There are several mythological features in the description of the underworld, such as the account of good and evil souls being weighed in a balance, as in ancient Egyptian tradition. The vindicated Zephaniah crosses from the underworld in a boat, recalling the picture of Hades in Greek mythology—which in turn reflects older Near Eastern concepts.

From the Apocalypse of Zephaniah, chapters 6–7

I saw a great angel before me. ... His teeth were outside his mouth like a bear. His hair was spread out like women's hair. His body was like a serpent's when he wished to swallow me. And when I saw him, I was afraid of him. ... and I saw [another] great angel standing before me with his face shining like the rays of the sun in its glory. ... I fell upon my face and I worshiped him. He said to me ... "Do not worship me. I am not the Lord Almighty, but I am the great angel Eremiel, who is over the abyss and Hades, the one in which all of the souls are imprisoned from the end of the flood, which came upon the earth, until this day." ... Then I asked him, "Who is the great angel ... whom I saw?" He said, "This is the one who accuses men in the presence of the Lord."

Then I looked, and saw him with a manuscript in his hand. He began to unroll it. ... I found that all my sins which I had committed were written into it.

DATA

TITLE:
The Apocalypse of Zephaniah

ORIGINAL DATE OF COMPOSITION:
ca. 100 BCE– ca. 175 CE

ORIGINAL LANGUAGE:
Greek

PROVENANCE:
Egypt?

EARLIEST EXTANT MANUSCRIPT:
ca. 400 CE (Coptic)

The Two Ways

Underlying the whole Apocalypse of Zephaniah is the motif of the "Two Ways"—of good or sin, of life or destruction—between which human beings are free to choose. They are judged according to the actions they have performed while on earth, and the angels appear to Zephaniah in pairs, one who records the deeds of the righteous and one who inflicts eternal punishment on the wicked. In Hades there are also a fearful accusing angel and a benevolent rewarding angel (see main text). Yet God is merciful, and has "compassion on behalf of the world and the souls which are in punishment," and he is open to the prayers of the patriarchs Abraham, Isaac, and Jacob on behalf of the souls in torment. God wills human beings to repent of their misdeeds and if they do so they will escape judgment. A call for repentance is sounded powerfully several times in the course of the work.

THE MARTYRDOM AND ASCENSION OF ISAIAH

DATA

TITLE:
The Martyrdom
and Ascension
of Isaiah

ORIGINAL DATE OF
COMPOSITION:
2nd cent. BCE–
4th cent. CE

ORIGINAL
LANGUAGES:
Hebrew
(Martyrdom);
Greek
(Ascension)

PROVENANCE:
Palestine
(Martyrdom)
Unknown
(Ascension)

EARLIEST EXTANT
MANUSCRIPT:
15th cent.
(Ethiopic)

The Martyrdom and Ascension of Isaiah is a composite work with two distinct sections of widely different dates. The first five chapters narrate the events leading up to the execution of the prophet Isaiah by King Manasseh of Judah. In the Bible, nothing is said about the death of Isaiah but the author of the Martyrdom is clearly aware of the account of the reigns of Hezekiah and Manasseh in 2 Kings.

A legend that Isaiah had been martyred was widespread in ancient times, its source perhaps the statement that Manasseh, who is depicted in the Bible as the worst of rulers, "shed very much innocent blood, until he had filled Jerusalem from one end to another" (2 Kings 21.16). In the Martyrdom, Isaiah's murder is given a cosmological and supernatural dimension. The agent of his death is not so much Manasseh as Beliar, "the angel of iniquity who rules the world," who is said to dwell in Manasseh's heart.

The text begins with a testament-type scene, in which Hezekiah gives his last instructions to his son Manasseh. Isaiah warns the king that Manasseh will pay no heed to his words, and so it proves. As a consequence of the evil policies of Manasseh, Isaiah and a group of prophets withdraw from Jerusalem to live an austere existence in the desert. At this point, a false prophet, Belkira, emerges to accuse Isaiah of treason, inspired by Beliar. Belkira is a Samaritan who escaped to Judah on the capture of Samaria by the Assyrians. When the king condemns Isaiah to death, Belkira plays the leading part in his execution (see extract, opposite).

The theme of martyrdom assumed great significance in Judaism as a result of the persecutions of Antiochus IV Epiphanes (see p.28), and the Martyrdom section of this work may be linked—for example, with the account of the martyrdom of the scribe Eleazar in 2 Maccabees. The flight of Isaiah and his companions to the desert is paralleled by the numbers of pious Jews who sought refuge there from Antiochus' attacks. Also, the hostility expressed toward the Samaritans reflects the regular outlook of Palestinian Jews in that period and the following years (see p.55). Hence the original form of the Martyrdom is to be dated in the late second century BCE, which makes it one of the oldest of the Pseudepigrapha and perhaps the earliest witness for the legend of Isaiah's martyrdom.

The present work contains two obvious Christian additions, with common apocalyptic elements. The longer, which interrupts the narrative at the point where Belkira appears, is an account of a vision of Isaiah, in which he learns of the life and death of "the Beloved" (Jesus), the subsequent corruption of the Church, the reign of Beliar and the second coming of Christ. It refers to the belief that the emperor Nero would return as the Antichrist and what is said about the evils in the Church finds parallels in Christian writings of the later first century CE,

From the Martyrdom of Isaiah, chapters 3 and 5

Belkira discovered and saw the place of Isaiah and of the prophets who were with him, for he himself dwelt in the district of Bethlehem, and he was a follower of Manasseh. And he prophesied lies in Jerusalem. ... but he himself was from Samaria. And it came about, when Shalmaneser the king of Assyria came and captured Samaria, ... this youth escaped and came to Jerusalem in the days of Hezekiah. ... And Belkira accused Isaiah and the prophets with him, saying, "Isaiah and the prophets with him prophesy against Jerusalem and against the cities of Judah that they will be laid waste ... and also against you, O lord king, that you will go bound with locks and chains of iron. ... And Isaiah himself has said, 'I see more than Moses the prophet.' Moses said, 'There is no man who can see the Lord and live.' But Isaiah has said, 'I have seen the Lord and behold I am alive.' Know therefore, O king, that they are false prophets." ... And he brought many accusations against Isaiah and the prophets before Manasseh. ... And the words of Belkira pleased him very much, and he sent and seized Isaiah.

[Then] Beliar was angry with Isaiah, and he dwelt in the heart of Manasseh, and he sawed Isaiah in half with a wood saw. And while Isaiah was being sawn in half, his accuser, Belkira ... and all the false prophets stood by, laughing and joyful because of Isaiah.

The Death of Isaiah, from a French Bible of 1526. In one version of the legend, Isaiah was sawn in half (compare Heb. 11.37) while hiding in a tree.

which gives a likely date for these sections. The second, shorter, Christian interpolation deals with aspects of the heavenly world, which is the theme of the originally separate Ascension of Isaiah. The new passage was probably composed to link the Ascension with the Martyrdom at the time when the two texts were brought together, perhaps as late as the fourth century CE.

In most manuscripts, the title of the Ascension is "The Vision of Isaiah," which indicates its character. It is essentially an apocalyptic text, giving an account of the seer's journey to the heavens, experienced in a vision. This work is much more obviously Christian than the Martyrdom, although it is based on older and well-known Jewish traditions. It concentrates almost entirely on the being of Christ and his incarnation, life, death, resurrection, and, above all, on the significance of his ascension. It might be described as reflecting a fairly early Christian theology, in which the doctrine of the Trinity had begun to develop. Set during an earlier period of Isaiah's life, the Ascension begins with a visit from Isaiah to Hezekiah, in the course of which the prophet is granted a vision by an angel, and there is a very interesting description of prophetic ecstasy (see extract, opposite). Isaiah recounts his vision to Hezekiah and, at the end of the work, this account becomes the testament which Hezekiah transmits to Manasseh.

A 1st-century CE fresco from Pompeii depicting an initiation into a Greco-Roman mystery religion. Such pagan cults were widely popular and may have influenced the Ascension of Isaiah and other scriptures (see box).

The Descent of the Beloved

During his tour of the heavens (see main text, below), Isaiah notices that although the righteous dead in the seventh heaven have been given their robes and become like the angels, they are not sitting on their thrones or wearing their crowns. He is told that they will not receive crowns and thrones "until the Beloved descends." There follows a narrative of the descent of Jesus into the human world. He passes through each of the heavens in descending order, but in each he transforms himself into the angelic appearance appropriate to that particular sphere, so that the angels do not recognize him.

In several cases, he gives a password to the gate-keepers, a feature which recalls the Greco-Roman mystery religions, where initiates received a magical formula which enabled them to pass through the various heavens to the final height.

Next, the author narrates the birth of Jesus and, very briefly, his life, death, and resurrection. The climax is a description of Christ's final triumphant ascension through the seven heavens (compare Eph. 4.9–10), where he is no longer transformed and hidden, but appears in his true nature to receive universal adoration from the angels.

The rest of the work describes Isaiah's celestial journey, in which he is borne by the angel through the seven heavens. Each heaven has its own particular angels, but the function of all the angels is to sing praises to the One who sits in the seventh heaven. There, Isaiah sees the Lord Christ and the Holy Spirit, who have the appearance of angels, but, unlike angels, are the objects of worship. These in turn are subordinate to the "Great Glory," the supreme deity, equivalent to the Father. The seventh heaven is the final home of the righteous, where they will receive clothing which will transform them into angelic beings, and crowns and thrones which symbolize their sharing in Christ's kingship (see box, above): they alone will see the glory of the true God—a privilege to which not even the angels can aspire.

From the Ascension of Isaiah, chapter 6

Isaiah came to Hezekiah in Jerusalem. ... And when Isaiah spoke with Hezekiah the words of righteousness and faith, they all heard a door being opened and the voice of the Spirit. ... And while he was speaking with the Holy Spirit in the hearing of them all, he became silent, and his mind was taken up from him, and he did not see the men who were standing before him. His eyes indeed were open, but his mouth was silent, and the mind in his body was taken up from him. But his breath was still in him, for he was seeing a vision. And the angel who was sent to show him the vision was not of this firmament, nor was he from the angels of glory of this world, but he came from the seventh heaven. ... And after Isaiah had seen this vision he recounted it to Hezekiah.

THE SECOND BOOK OF BARUCH

Baruch appears in the Bible only as the secretary of the prophet Jeremiah and there is no indication that he himself enjoyed prophetic powers. But the Bible relates that Jeremiah dictated his prophecies to Baruch and that "many similar words were added to them" (Jer. 36.32). It was assumed that these additions were Baruch's own words and, since they were similar to Jeremiah's, that they were also prophecies.

Several ancient texts sought to provide the words that Baruch might have written, the prototype for which is the Book of Baruch, or the First Book of Baruch (1 Baruch), in the apocryphal or deuterocanonical books of the Bible. Perhaps dating no later than ca. 150BCE, it contains a lament over the fall of Jerusalem in 587BCE, a hymn in praise of wisdom, and predictions of hope for the future. There is also a letter of Jeremiah to the Jewish exiles in Babylon, probably written as early as the fourth century BCE.

The Second Book of Baruch also includes a letter to the exiles, but this time from Baruch, who throughout this later work is depicted not only as a prophet in his own right but even as superior to Jeremiah. This work consists of lamentations, prayers, and apocalypses, much of it using traditional material. It begins with an account of the Babylonian destruction of Jerusalem in 587BCE, which in fact reflects the Roman capture of the city in 70CE, not long before the book was written. The book as a whole is to be seen as the reaction of one pious Jew to the tragedy of 70CE, written to encourage his people in the face of national disaster and to lay the foundation for their recovery. It shows parallels with rabbinic writings, especially 2 Esdras (see p.94) and Pseudo-Philo (see pp.68–71), which reflect the same background and general period. It is notable that 2 Baruch shows no trace of Christian influence.

The author of 2 Baruch displays a particular concern for the Jewish Temple, destroyed in 70CE. The text states that, although the earthly building has gone, it will be preserved in heaven. Angels remove its sacred objects for a future restoration—a variant on the tradition that Jeremiah had hidden them (2 Macc. 2.4–8). Baruch then undertakes three seven-day fasts. After the first fast, he utters a moving lament for Jerusalem (see extract, opposite); after the second, he has a dialogue with God which raises the issue of theodicy ("divine justice," specifically why God tolerates the existence of evil); and the third is followed by a typical apocalyptic vision of twelve disasters before the coming of the Messiah, the resurrection of the dead, and the Last Judgment. Next, Baruch warns the people about the coming disasters, the divine judgment, and God's immutable purposes. The seer receives two more visions and an explanation of the mysterious things that he has seen, following the pattern of the Book of Daniel. There follow further teachings to the people before the work ends with Baruch's lengthy letter. This was probably once a

DATA

TITLE:
The Second Book
of Baruch (The
Syriac Apocalypse
of Baruch)

ORIGINAL DATE OF
COMPOSITION:
Early 2nd cent. CE

ORIGINAL LANGUAGE:
Hebrew

PROVENANCE:
Probably Palestine

EARLIEST EXTANT
MANUSCRIPT:
6th or 7th cent. CE
(Syriac)

A late 1st-century CE Roman relief showing troops with objects looted from the Temple of Jerusalem in 70CE.

From the Second Book of Baruch, chapter 10

Blessed is he who was not born,
or he who was born and died.
But we, the living, woe to us,
because we have seen the afflictions of Zion,
and that which has befallen Jerusalem.
I shall call the Sirens from the sea,
and you night-demons, come from the desert,
and you demons and dragons, from the woods.
Awake and gird up your loins to mourn,
and raise lamentations with me,
and mourn with me.
You farmers, sow not again.
And you, O earth, why do you give the fruit
of your harvest? ...
And you, heaven, keep your dew within you,
and do not open the treasuries of rain.
And you, sun, keep the light of your rays
within you.
And you, moon, extinguish the multitude of
your light.
For why should the light rise again,
where the light of Zion is darkened? ...
Henceforth, do not speak any more of beauty,
and do not talk about gracefulness.
You, priests, take the keys of the sanctuary,
and cast them to the highest heaven,
and give them to the Lord and say,
"Guard your house yourself,
because, behold, we have been found to be
false stewards."

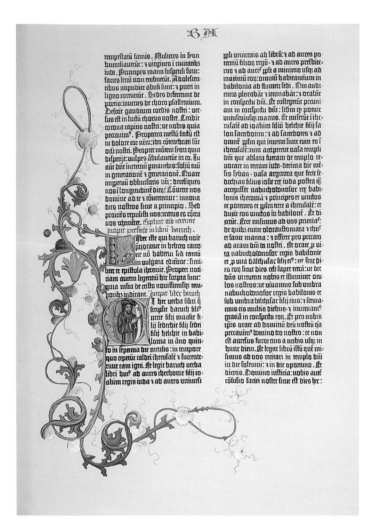

The prophet Baruch is depicted in the decorative initial "E" that adorns the opening of the Book of Baruch in the first printed Bible, produced by Johannes Gutenberg in 1455 or 1456.

separate document, but its contents show a second focal concern of the author: the primacy of the Jewish law, which the exiles are urged to obey.

The work displays signs of a triadic structure: Baruch has three visions, addresses the people three times, and embarks on three fasts. Of particular interest are the three sections consisting of a dialogue between Baruch and God. They are dominated by the author's profound awareness of the power of evil, the corruptibility of the world, and human mortality. The first dialogue concerns the problem of theodicy as it presented itself to the survivors of the Roman destruction. Had all God's promises to Israel come to nothing? A heavenly voice tells Baruch that Israel has been punished because of its sins, but that God will forgive his people. The Gentiles will ultimately meet with judgment, because they do not recognize that their present prosperity is a sign of God's blessing. But this answer does not satisfy Baruch, who, perhaps echoing Genesis 18, points out that Jerusalem should have been spared for the good deeds of the righteous and not destroyed on account of the evil deeds of the wicked, implying that God has acted unjustly. Baruch recognizes that mere mortals cannot understand God's judgments, but he still goes on to complain that, although the righteous who die can do so in the hope of eternal life, those still alive are suffering. He reaches the gloomy conclusion that, while the world as it is remains, Israel, for whom the world was created, has vanished. In reply, God denies that the divine decrees are unknowable: they have been revealed in the Books of the Law, so people have no excuse for disobedience and fully deserve their punishment. Second, the righteous who struggle in the present world can be assured of a glorious reward in the new world which is to come.

The issue of this new age is taken up in the second dialogue. Baruch meditates on the misery and brevity of present existence and asks how long this sorry state will continue, pleading with God to hasten the time of the end. God replies that he cannot change the end-time, which must wait until all those whom he has foreordained to exist have been born. But God promises that the end is very near, because Baruch and his companions will see it.

The third dialogue focuses on the question of the resurrection of the dead, a doctrine which had developed in Judaism in the late period BCE. Baruch asks whether the resurrected would retain their mortal bodies, with all their imperfections. God says that there will first be a general resurrection in the earthly body of all the departed, but then he will divide the wicked from the righteous. The wicked will be sent back to the realm of death, but the righteous—those who have lived by the law and its teachings—will be transformed into angelic beings and be made like the stars. This concept is found in a number of other writings.

From the Second Book of Baruch, chapters 21–23

[Baruch prayed:] How long will corruption remain, and until when will the time of mortals be happy, and until when will those who pass away be polluted by the great wickedness in this world? Therefore, command mercifully and confirm all that you have said that you would do, so that your power will be recognized by those who believe that your long-suffering means weakness. ...

A voice was heard from on high which said to me: "Baruch, Baruch, why are you disturbed? Who starts on a journey and does not complete it? ... when Adam sinned and death was decreed against those who were to be born, the multitude of those who would be born was numbered. And for that number a place was prepared where the living ones might live and where the dead might be preserved. No creature will live again unless the number that has been appointed is completed. ... truly, my salvation ... has drawn near and is not as far away as before."

Baruch and the Survival of Judaism

The importance of the law is repeatedly stressed throughout 2 Baruch, but it is most fully developed in the letter to the exiles, which forms a program for the survival of the Jewish people after the calamity of 70CE. Baruch assures his audience that ultimate vindication is certain but only at the time God wills. Until then, the people must live in perfect obedience to the law, not neglecting it as their ancestors did. This anticipates the situation after 70CE, when, under the direction of the rabbis, the law became the heart of Jewish religious life, replacing the Temple and its sacrificial system. As Baruch writes: "We have nothing now apart from the Mighty One and his Law." The author is clearly in touch with rabbinic Judaism and it has been suggested that he was one of the rabbis who assembled at Jamnia (Yavneh), west of Jerusalem, in the early second century CE to rebuild the foundations of Jewish national existence.

THE THIRD BOOK OF BARUCH

The Third Book of Baruch (3 Baruch) has the same setting—the fall of Jerusalem—as the other works in the Baruch tradition, and it confronts the same problem as 2 Baruch: what channel of communication can there be between God and humankind when the Temple and its sacrifices no longer function?

According to 2 Baruch, a heavenly Temple will be revealed in the last days to replace the former sanctuary, but in 3 Baruch this Temple in heaven is a present reality: the angels report there with the intercessions of human beings and their good or evil deeds, which the archangel Michael presents before the throne of God. The wicked then receive punishment while the righteous are rewarded with baskets of oil, which probably means that they are endowed with the divine glory (2 Enoch refers to "the ointment of the Lord's glory"). However, the crucial point is that there is no need for a rebuilt Temple in Jerusalem, either now or in the future.

The work is an apocalypse in the sense that an angel reveals to Baruch "all the mysteries of God," but unlike other apocalypses it contains no predictions of future history, no messianic figure, and no prophecies about the events of the end-time. The work is structured around the common motif of a journey through the heavens, during which Baruch discovers the mysteries of creation. He learns about the natural phenomena of the universe, the operations of the sun and moon, the origin of the rains, and the great serpent which drinks from the cosmic sea to prevent it overflowing.

There are also revelations in the form of legendary expansions of the early part of Genesis. Thus in the first and second heavens Baruch witnesses the punishments respectively of the builders and planners of the Tower of Babel described in Genesis 11. Then he is shown the serpent who deceived Adam and Eve and also

A 13th-century mosaic of the phoenix from the old basilica of St. Peter's, Rome. It is depicted with a fiery solar halo.

From the Third Book of Baruch, chapter 6

There was ... a bird flying, large as a mountain. And I said to the angel, "What is this bird?" And he said to me, "This is the guardian of the world." And I said, "Lord, how is it the guardian of the world? Teach me." And the angel said, "This bird accompanies the sun and, spreading its wings, absorbs its burning rays. For if it did not absorb them, none of the race of men would survive, nor anything else that lives, so God appointed this bird." And he unfolded his wings, and I saw on his right wing very large letters ... and the letters were gold. And the angel said to me, "Read them." ... and they said thus, "Neither earth nor heaven bear me, but the wings of fire bear me." And I said, "Lord, what is this bird, and what is its name?" And the angel told me, "His name is Phoenix." I said, "And what does he eat?" And he told me, "The manna of heaven and the dew of earth." ... The bird spread his wings and covered the rays of the sun and it flapped its wings and there was a noise like thunder and the bird cried out, saying, "O giver of light, give splendor to the world."

DATA

TITLE:
The Third Book of Baruch (The Greek Apocalypse of Baruch)

ORIGINAL DATE OF COMPOSITION:
1st–3rd cent. CE

ORIGINAL LANGUAGE:
Greek

PROVENANCE:
Uncertain

EARLIEST EXTANT MANUSCRIPT:
9th cent. CE (Old Slavonic)

the tree that led Adam astray: here it is said to have been a vine, which Noah replanted after the Flood, an embellishment of the biblical statement that he planted a vineyard (Gen. 9.20). Finally, Baruch is taken to the fifth heaven, where he faces a locked gate and can go no further. Here he encounters the archangel Michael, who alone can open the gate to pass through on his mission to the throne of God.

The work is extant in Greek and Old Slavonic. As it stands, the Greek version is doubtless a Christian production, as a number of New Testament echoes clearly indicate, but the Slavonic text lacks many of the obviously Christian features, which suggests that it is an extensive reworking of an older Jewish writing.

Mythology and Folklore in the Third Book of Baruch

The narrative of Baruch's journey to the heavens is enriched with many elements of Near Eastern mythology and folklore, notably the story of the phoenix, which in 3 Baruch is represented uniquely as the guardian of the world, shielding humanity from the harmful rays of the sun. There is no trace of the famous legend of the phoenix emerging from the ashes of its forebear, although the creature is clearly associated with fire and the sun (see extract, above). Those who planned and built the Tower of Babel (see main text) appear as strange hybrid animals that are reminiscent of ancient Mesopotamian demons ("men ... with faces of cattle and horns of deer and feet of goats and loins of sheep ... their appearance was like that of dogs, and their feet like those of deer").

THE FOURTH BOOK OF BARUCH

DATA

TITLE:
The Fourth Book
of Baruch ("The
Things Omitted
from Jeremiah the
Prophet")

ORIGINAL DATE OF
COMPOSITION:
1st–2nd cent. CE

ORIGINAL LANGUAGE:
Probably Hebrew

PROVENANCE:
Probably Palestine

EARLIEST EXTANT
MANUSCRIPT:
10th cent. CE
(Greek)

The title of the Fourth Book of Baruch (4 Baruch) in the Greek manuscripts is "The Things Omitted from Jeremiah the Prophet" and its original hero was Jeremiah, who dominates the opening chapters and the final narrative. But in between there are sections in which Baruch is set above the prophet, to the extent that he is portrayed as the mediator between Jeremiah and God (see extract, below).

This predominance of scribe over prophet may reflect the situation after 70 CE, when Palestinian Judaism largely turned its back on apocalyptic hopes in favor of the scholarly study and exposition of the Jewish law. The setting of the book—the Babylonian sack of Jerusalem and the exiling of many of its inhabitants—is the same as other books in the Baruch tradition, but while in the latter the restoration of the city is to take place only in an apocalyptic future, here the return of the exiles and the resumption of sacrificial worship are related as events that have already occurred.

The book's structure suggests that it began as a Jewish composition that later underwent Christian editing—clearly seen in the final chapter, in which Jeremiah is stoned to death after prophesying the coming of Christ. Some scholars have proposed that 4 Baruch was Christian writing from the outset, but the whole tenor of the work suggests that the author saw the future in terms of a revitalized Judaism. He shows a particular concern for national purity, as exemplified in the reforms of the biblical Ezra and Nehemiah: before the exiles can return to Jerusalem, they must put away their foreign wives. Those who insist on bringing them back are exiled to a desert place, where they build the city of Samaria, a reflection of the common Jewish view that the Samaritans were a mixed and unclean race. It is best, therefore, to see the original version of 4 Baruch as a call to Jews, in the face of all their disasters, to realize the abiding significance of the fundamental beliefs and institutions of their faith.

From the Fourth Book of Baruch, chapter 6

Baruch sent [for] papyrus and ink, and he wrote the following letter: "Baruch, the servant of God, writes to Jeremiah in the captivity of Babylon. Hail and rejoice! For God … has taken pity on our tears and has remembered the covenant that he established with our fathers Abraham, Isaac, and Jacob. And he sent his angel to me and told me these words which I have sent to you. Now, these are the words that the Lord God of Israel, who led us from the land of Egypt, out of the great furnace, spoke: 'Because you did not keep my commandments, but your heart was lifted up and you stiffened your neck before me, in wrath and anger I delivered you to the furnace of Babylon.' "

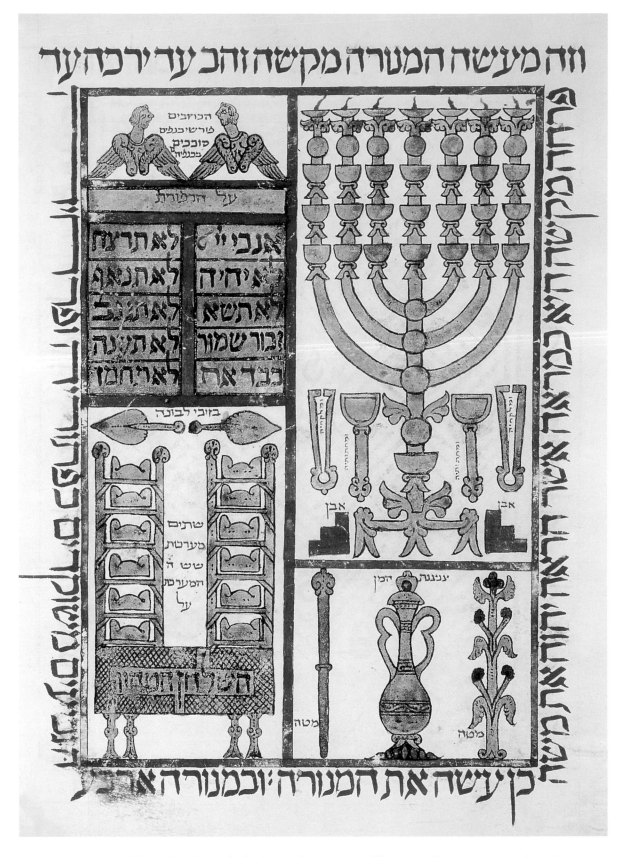

A page from a Bible produced in the Sephardic Jewish community of Perpignan, France, in 1299. It shows the lampstand (*menorah*) and other sacred objects traditionally held to have formed part of the Temple furnishings.

VISIONS OF EZRA

The Apocalypse of Ezra and the Vision of Ezra belong to a number of writings centered on the biblical figure of Ezra, who restored Judaism after the return of the exiles from Babylon in the late sixth century BCE. All these works depend on the Fourth Book of Ezra (the Second Book of Esdras), one of the biblical Apocrypha.

In a way that at times recalls the Book of Job, both works focus on the issue of divine justice. Ezra is conveyed to heaven and also to Tartarus (hell), where he sees the torments of sinners (see extract, opposite). In heaven, he asks God why he created humans with the capacity to sin, so that they would inevitably incur divine punishment. God replies that Adam was created perfect but also with free will, which enabled him—and all humans after him—to disobey God. If people sin, therefore, it is their own fault. But Ezra dares to say that Adam's Fall was really the fault of God, whose justice is arbitrary—a charge to which God makes no answer (see extract, below).

These gloomy speculations are balanced by the description of God as merciful and long-suffering, at least toward those who repent of their sins, and the works also depict the paradise that is the reward of the righteous. Above all, Ezra represents the concept that the righteous can intercede on behalf of sinners. He persistently prays to God to show mercy to the wicked and it is hinted that his petitions do not go wholly unregarded.

In their present forms, the Apocalypse and Vision are clearly Christian compositions, but they reflect a period when the Church was still in close contact with its Jewish heritage and the distinctively Christian or Jewish elements are not always easy to discern. The Christian contribution is clearest in the long description of the Antichrist in Tartarus, while the residents of the heavenly paradise include Peter, Paul, Luke, and Matthew from the New Testament.

DATA

TITLE:
The (Greek) Apocalypse of Ezra

ORIGINAL DATE OF COMPOSITION:
2nd–9th cents. CE

ORIGINAL LANGUAGE:
Greek

PROVENANCE:
Unknown

EARLIEST EXTANT MANUSCRIPT:
15th cent. CE (Greek)

From the Apocalypse of Ezra, chapter 2

"Where are your former mercies, O Lord? Where your long-suffering?" And God said, "As I made night and day I made the righteous and the sinner and it were fitting to conduct yourself like the righteous man." And the prophet said, "Who made Adam, the protoplast, the first one?" And God said, "My immaculate hands, and I placed him in Paradise to guard the region of the tree of life." [And the prophet said, "Why are we now separated from it?" And God said,] "Since he who established disobedience made this man sin." And the prophet said, "Was he not guarded by an angel? … And how was he deceived who was guarded by angels whom you commanded to be present whatever happened? Attend also to what I say! If you had not given him Eve, the serpent would never have deceived her. If you save whom you wish you will also destroy whom you wish."

From the Vision of Ezra, verses 1–11

Ezra prayed to the Lord, saying, "Grant me courage, O Lord, that I might not fear when I see the judgments of the sinners." And there were granted to him seven angels of hell who carried him beyond the seventieth grade in the infernal regions. And he saw fiery gates, and at these gates he saw two lions lying there from whose mouth and nostrils and eyes proceeded the most powerful flames. The most powerful men were entering and passing through the fire and it did not touch them. And Ezra said, "Who are they, who advance so safely?" The angels said to him, "They are the just whose repute has ascended to heaven, who gave alms generously, clothed the naked, and desired a good desire."

And others were entering that they might pass throught the gates, and dogs were ripping them apart and fire was consuming them. And Ezra said, "Who are they?" The angels said, "They denied the Lord and sinned with women on the Lord's Day." And Ezra said, "Lord, have mercy on the sinners!"

DATA

TITLE:
The Vision of Ezra

ORIGINAL DATE OF
COMPOSITION:
4th–7th cents. CE

ORIGINAL LANGUAGE:
Greek

PROVENANCE:
Unknown

EARLIEST EXTANT
MANUSCRIPT:
11th cent. CE
(Latin)

The Dream of Dante Being Killed by an Eagle, from a manuscript of the Divine Comedy by Dante (1265-1321), whose descriptions of hell, purgatory, and paradise were indirectly influenced by the Vision of Ezra.

THE APOCALYPSE OF SEDRACH

The Apocalypse of Sedrach really belongs within the Ezra tradition, and the name "Sedrach" is something of a puzzle. It is the Greek form of Shadrach, who in the Bible is one of the three young Jewish men thrown into the fiery furnace for refusing to worship an idol (Dan. 3). An angel saved them from the flames, and this may have led the author to think of Sedrach as someone with access to the angelic world. But perhaps "Sedrach" is simply a corruption of "Esdras," the Greek for Ezra. The book certainly has many similarities with the Apocalypse and Vision of Ezra (see pp.94–5) and shares all their main motifs: for example, Sedrach ascends to heaven, questions God, and discusses the creation of Adam.

However, the Apocalypse of Sedrach also has its own distinctive character. As they have survived, Sedrach and the two Ezra writings are all Christian in character, but in the case of Sedrach it is only at the beginning and the end of the work that Christian ideas and language are unquestionably present and even here they often do not penetrate very deeply. Christ appears only as the one who is sent to take Sedrach's soul to Paradise, but it looks very much as though his name has simply replaced that of the archangel Michael, who performs this function in other works and features elsewhere in the book.

The opening chapter of Sedrach is a homily on the primacy of love, largely modeled on the famous passage in 1 Corinthians 13. It was probably an originally quite separate work, added because God's love is a prominent theme in Sedrach. Elsewhere there seems to be a reference to Jesus' parable of the Prodigal Son in Luke 15, but the lesson drawn from it in Sedrach is so opposed to that of the gospel that it is likely to be a Jewish version of the same story (see extract, opposite).

Shadrach and his companions in the fire (right) and the parable of the Prodigal Son (left) are depicted in this window by John Piper (1903–92) in Aldeburgh church, Suffolk, England.

96

The Ethics of Sedrach

The main concern of the Apocalypse of Sedrach is ethical and religious teaching. There is one remarkable passage where Sedrach, faced with death, utters a long lament for the beauty of the human body, which must now be confined to the grave (see second extract, below). Above all, the author stresses God's mercy and compassion and his wish to do everything possible to allow sinners to repent (although, if they do not, they must face judgment).

There is also a pronounced universalistic note: God grants salvation even to good Gentiles. Unlike other works, such as the Vision and Apocalypse of Ezra, the Apocalypse of Sedrach does not deplore God's gift to humanity of free will, which brings with it the capacity to sin. For Sedrach, free will springs from God's love for human beings: he is patient and long-suffering with them and sends angels to guide them in making the right choices in life.

From the Apocalypse of Sedrach, chapter 6

God said to [Sedrach], "Be it known to you, that everything which I commanded man to do was within his reach. I made him wise and the heir of heaven and earth, and I subordinated everything under him and every living thing flees from him and from his face. Having received my gifts, however, he became an alien, an adulterer and sinner. Tell me, what sort of a father would give an inheritance to his son, and having received the money the son goes away leaving his father, and becomes an alien and in the service of aliens. The father then, seeing that the son has forsaken him and gone away, darkens his heart and, going away, he retrieves his wealth and banishes his son from his glory, because he forsook his father. How is it that I, the wondrous and jealous God, have given everything to him, but he, having received them, became an adulterer and a sinner?"

From the Apocalypse of Sedrach, chapter 11

[Sedrach said:] "O wondrous head, ornamented like heaven; O sunlight upon heaven and earth; your hair is known from Theman, your eyes from Bosra ... but as soon as it falls in the earth it is unrecognized. ... O fingers, beautified and adorned with gold and silver, the three joints stretch the palms and they gather good things together; but now you have become strangers to this world. ... O feet, so swift and well moving ... now suddenly you are to remain unmoved. O head, hands and feet, till now I have held you fast. ... O beautiful body, hair shed by the stars, head like heaven adorned. O face anointed with sweet oil, eyes like windows, a voice like a bugle's sound, a tongue which talks so easily, a beard well trimmed ... a body adorned, light-giving, elegant and renowned, yet now after falling within the earth, your beauty beneath the earth is unseen."

DATA

Title:
The Apocalypse
of Sedrach (The
Word of Sedrach)

Original Date of
Composition:
ca.150—ca. 500ce

Original Language:
Greek

Provenance:
Uncertain

Earliest Extant
Manuscript:
15th cent. ce
(Greek)

THE TESTAMENT OF JOB

DATA

TITLE:
The Testament of
Job

ORIGINAL DATE OF
COMPOSITION:
1st cent. BCE–1st
cent. CE

ORIGINAL
LANGUAGE:
Probably Greek

PROVENANCE:
Egypt?

EARLIEST EXTANT
MANUSCRIPT:
5th cent. CE
(Coptic)

As the title suggests, the Testament of Job belongs to the testament genre, in which praise for exemplary moral behavior in general and for one virtue in particular (in this case, patience or endurance) are expressed by a dying sage to his offspring just before his death and burial. However, there is no trace of the apocalyptic concepts that are typical of testaments, while the section on moral behavior is very brief and mentions only one's duty to give alms and to avoid foreign marriages. On the other hand, the Testament of Job contains lively narrative in the style of *midrash haggadah*, the Jewish method of interpretation in which a biblical text is retold and expanded as a means of deriving new insights from it.

The Testament falls into two sections corresponding to the two distinct parts of the Book of Job. The first deals with Satan's attacks on Job, the theme of the opening prose narrative in the biblical book, which the author fills out with a mass of legendary details. Satan's hostility is provoked by Job's destruction of a heathen temple—a feat which elsewhere is attributed to Abraham—and the Bible's account of Job's wealth and generosity is greatly expanded. Although, as in the Bible, Satan has to obtain God's authority for his attacks on Job, he is depicted as a definitely hostile figure, so that in effect God is absolved of responsibility for Job's misfortunes.

In the Bible, Job passively accepts his afflictions and the author of the Testament certainly stresses his patience throughout. But the work also represents Job contending with Satan in what is described in terms of an athletic contest. In four successive scenes, Satan confronts Job

Mystical Sects and the Testament of Job

The Testament of Job is striking in its mysticism and frequent hymns, and in the importance it gives to women. These were features of the Therapeutae ("Healers"), a first-century CE Jewish sect in Egypt. The Testament, which describes Job as king of Egypt and an expert hymn-writer, very likely originates among this contemplative and ascetic group.

The emphasis on women is illustrated by a long and moving narrative about Job's first wife, Sitis. Later, after his restoration, Job distributes his prop-

erty among his sons but promises his daughters an even better inheritance: magical cords that enable them to speak in the language of angels (see extract). It has been suggested that the work was adopted by the Montanists, a heretical Christian movement of the second century CE, which gave a leading role to women prophets who spoke in tongues. The gift of angelic speech illustrates the work's mysticism, seen also in Job's faith not in the transitory present world but in the eternal celestial realm.

Job Mocked by his Wife, by Georges de La Tour (1593-1652), illustrating Job 2.9-10. The Bible does not name Job's wife, but in the Testament of Job, where she features prominently, her name is given as Sitis.

but is unable to get the better of him until he finally has to admit defeat. Job's endurance wins the day and this is the author's main message, as summarized by Job himself: "My children, you also must be patient in everything that happens to you. For patience is better than anything."

The second part of the Testament, as in the Bible, is concerned with the visit of Job's friends ("Job's comforters") Eliphas, Baldad, Sophar, and Elihu, who here are said to be kings. Most strikingly, barely anything corresponds to the biblical Job's repeated remonstrances and challenges to God. At the outset, Eliphas utters a lament over Job's sorry state, in response to which Job affirms the certainty of his vindication by God. Eliphas concludes that their attempts to help Job, by discovering what he has done to deserve his suffering, are a waste of time. However, two of his companions still try to help Job. Baldad questions Job to determine whether or not he is sane, and Sophar offers a diagnosis and medical assistance by the royal physicians, to which Job responds that "my healing and treatment are from the Lord." After this, a heavenly voice convinces the kings that they are in error in seeking to discover the reason for Job's fate. They turn on the fourth member, Elihu, who has remained obdurate, and chant a taunting hymn against him, announcing God's condemnation upon him. Finally Job is restored to an even greater prosperity than before.

From the Testament of Job, chapters 46 and 48–50

Job brought three multicolored cords whose appearance was such that no man could describe. ... And he gave each daughter a cord, saying, "Place this about your breast, so it may go well with you all the days of your life." ... Thus, when the daughter called Hemera arose, she wrapped around her own cord. ... And she took on another heart—no longer minded toward earthly things—but she spoke ecstatically in the angelic dialect, sending up a hymn to God in accord with the hymns of the angels. ... Then Kasia bound hers on. ... And her mouth took on the dialect of the archons and she praised God for the creation of the heights. ... Then the other one also, named Amaltheia's Horn, bound on her cord. And her mouth spoke ecstatically in the dialect of those on high. ... she spoke in the dialect of the cherubim, glorifying the Master of virtues by exhibiting their splendor.

THE SIBYLLINE ORACLES

The female prophets known as Sibyls were famous throughout the ancient Greco-Roman world and beyond. The word "Sibyl" may originally have referred to a particular person, but after ca. 350BCE it came to denote any one of a number of woman seers whose ecstatic utterances foretold the calamities that would befall humankind. Sibyls were usually represented as old women, and many collections of prophecies were attributed to them. Several of these compilations, which were primarily political propaganda, were of Jewish and early Christian origin and were gathered together in the present Sibylline Oracles, an extensive collection of fourteen books.

Not surprisingly, the Sibylline Oracles stand somewhat apart from the rest of the Pseudepigrapha. Like all Sybilline prophecies, they are written in Greek hexameters, quite different from the Semitic poetical forms characteristic of the Bible and Jewish tradition. They sometimes refer to biblical personalities and events (especially the Flood, which serves as an image of cosmic destruction), but these are outweighed by the more frequent references to recent history, which often allow the date and setting of the writing to be discerned.

The Oracles sometimes present the Sibyl as a Jewish figure, but allusions to her pagan origins are much more common. From a Jewish point of view it was clearly of greater value to demonstrate to Gentiles that one of their own highly esteemed prophets not only taught the

OPPOSITE This fresco by Perugino (ca. 1452–1523) in the Palazzo dei Priori in Perugia, Italy, depicts six famous Sibyls of antiquity (left to right): the Erythrean, Persian, Cumaean, Libyan, Tiburtine, and Delphic.

The Sibylline Oracles and East-West Tensions

The Sibylline Oracles provide evidence of the tension between the Eastern and Western Mediterranean around the turn of the Common Era. Eastern peoples, including the Jews, resented the imposition of European rule on their ancient religions and cultures, first by the Hellenistic empires of Alexander the Great and his successors, and latterly by the Romans. The oracles display a marked hostility toward Rome in particular. All these features can be illustrated from Book 3. At the beginning and end,

the Sibyl denounces idolatry and the moral failings of both Greeks and Romans, which is contrasted with the religious and ethical superiority of Judaism.

However, its antipathy to Rome aside (see extract, opposite), Book 3 also reveals a remarkably positive attitude toward Gentiles. It employs Greek mythological themes and literary forms and, while condemning Gentiles for idolatry and immorality, holds out the hope of their ultimate repentance and conversion to the worship of the one true God.

From the Sibylline Oracles, Book 3, lines 356–380

O luxurious golden offspring of Latium,
  Rome …
as a slave will you be wed without decorum.
Often the Mistress will cut your delicate hair
and, dispensing justice, will cast you from
  heaven to earth,
but from earth will again raise you up to
  heaven,
because mortals are involved in a wretched
  and unjust life. …
Serene peace will return to the Asian land
and Europe will then be blessed …
For all good order and righteous dealing will
  come …
and love, faithfulness, and friendship even
  from strangers.
Bad government, blame, envy, anger, folly,
poverty, will flee from men, and constraint
  will flee,
and murder, accursed strife, and grievous
  quarrels,
night robberies, and every evil in those days.

DATA

TITLE:
The Sibylline
Oracles

ORIGINAL DATE OF
COMPOSITION:
2nd cent. BCE–7th
cent. CE

ORIGINAL LANGUAGE:
Greek

PROVENANCE:
Egypt, Syria, and
the Near East

EARLIEST EXTANT
MANUSCRIPT:
14th cent. CE
(Greek)

A relief of Cleopatra VII carved during her reign at Dendera, Egypt. The queen is depicted as the goddess Isis, of whom she claimed to be an incarnation and who, like Cleopatra, was referred to as "the Mistress."

tenets of Judaism—monotheism, high ethical standards, and the Temple worship—but also uttered frequent denunciations of pagan idolatry and moral laxity (see extract, opposite).

Speculation on the end of the present world is a central theme in most of the oracles, focusing on predictions of cosmic destruction and the renewal of the world through a great universal monarch. Similar hopes were common in the Greco-Roman world, and the biblical Flood is often linked with the widespread pagan idea of a great universal conflagration.

It is often difficult to penetrate to the precise meaning of the historical allusions in the Sibyllines and the problems are well exemplified in Book 3. The main portion of the book is taken up with apocalyptic material, oracles against many different nations, and descriptions of the destruction of the world, the day of judgment, and the appearance of God's final kingdom. Here, as elsewhere in the Sibylline books, history is presented in a stylized pattern and oracles are often presented with no clear connection, because the book is essentially a collection of individual oracles of different periods.

However, Book 3 is significant because both its place of origin and date can be determined with some certainty. Its concern with Egypt clearly shows that it was compiled there, as indeed were about half the Sibylline books. Its notably conciliatory attitude toward the Gentiles (see box, p.100) can be seen to reflect the sophisticated hellenized Judaism of Egypt's capital, Alexandria, but the book also shows evidence of a more popular strand of Judaism which identified with the Egyptians in their resistance to foreign imperialism, particularly the threat posed by Rome. The book expresses a remarkable degree of loyalty to Egypt's ruling Ptolemaic dynasty, and one oracle speaks of the vengeance which will be exacted on Rome by "the Mistress," a reference to the famous Queen Cleopatra VII (ruled 51-30BCE) and the goddess Isis, with whom Cleopatra identified herself. A later oracle in Book 3 seems to reflect the widespread grief and disillusionment after Egypt's defeat by the Romans at the battle of Actium in 31BCE. Here Cleopatra is simply a "woman" and a "widow," who has brought only disaster.

Even more strikingly, Book 3 identifies one of the Egyptian monarchs with the coming messianic ruler who in Jewish belief would usher in the perfect kingdom of the final age. He is called a "king from the sun," an Egyptian royal title, and "seventh king," the seventh ruler of the Ptolemaic dynasty—probably Ptolemy IV Philometor (ruled 180–145BCE), who came into conflict with Antiochus IV Epiphanes, one of the Jews' most bitter foes (see p.28). Most of Book 3 probably dates from the later years of Ptolemy IV and forms the earliest part of the Sibylline Oracles.

From the Sibylline Oracles, Book 3, lines 1–7 and 573–598

Blessed, heavenly one, who thunders on high, who has the cherubim as your throne, I entreat you to give a little rest to me who have prophesied unfailing truth, for my heart is tired within. But why does my heart shake again? And why is my spirit lashed by a whip, compelled from within to proclaim an oracle to all? But I will utter everything again, as much as God bids me say to men. ...

There will again be a race of pious men [the Jews] who attend to the counsels and intention of the Most High, who fully honor the temple of the great God with drink offering and burnt offering and sacred hecatombs. ... at dawn they lift up holy arms toward heaven, from their beds, always sanctifying their flesh with water, and they honor only the Immortal who always rules, and then their parents. Greatly, surpassing all men, they are mindful of holy wedlock, and they do not engage in impious intercourse with male children, as do Phoenicians, Egyptians, and Romans, spacious Greece and many nations of others.

THE LETTER OF ARISTEAS

Like the Sibylline Oracles, the Letter of Aristeas stands apart from the great majority of the Pseudepigrapha because it is neither attributed to, nor about, a biblical character. The letter claims to be from Aristeas, a Jew who is closely connected with the Egyptian court, to his friend Philocrates, and gives an account of how the Bible was first translated into Greek with the support of King Ptolemy II Philadelphus of Egypt (ruled 285–247BCE). The translation that emerges is the Septuagint (from Latin *septuaginta*, "seventy") and the letter indicates how it received its name: it was translated by seventy-two Jewish scholars in seventy two days.

It is clear that this account of the origin of the Septuagint—which to this day remains the basis of the Old Testament of the Greek Orthodox church—is largely legendary and scholars generally agree that it was written over a century later than the events it purports to relate. However, parts of the Letter may be earlier and it does preserve some historically accurate reminiscences. It records the translation of only the first five books of the Bible—the Pentateuch, or Books of the Law—and historically this part of the Bible was translated first, the Greek version of the remaining books being produced some time later. According to Aristeas, the translators were Jewish scholars working in Alexandria and it is generally accepted that this was the milieu in which the Septuagint was produced.

The work's outlook on the Greek world is remarkably positive. The author, who appears to be well-acquainted with Greek literary conventions, depicts a harmonious relationship between Jews and Gentiles. Thus he writes of "God, the overseer and creator of all, whom all men worship including ourselves, … Their name for him is Zeus and Jove." Philocrates can be seen to represent intelligent Gentiles who were attracted to Judaism and whom the author wishes to inform about Jewish beliefs and institutions. When Eleazar, the high priest of the Temple who sends the scholars from Jerusalem, explains the Jewish dietary laws to the king's emissaries, he does so in rationalizing language that aims to make them comprehensible to non-Jews.

While the Letter certainly has a Gentile audience in view, it has a message for Jews as well. Whatever their mutual respect, Jews and Gentiles are not the same and the Jews must preserve, and glory in, their religious heritage. Gentile idolatry and immorality are denounced, and Eleazar emphasizes God's special choice of Israel and the fact that the practices of Judaism are designed to set Israel apart from all other nations. Throughout, the superiority of Judaism is made plain: the king, inspired by the one true God, realizes the importance of the Law and takes the lead in authorizing its translation for his subjects' benefit. There is an ecstatic account of the splendors of the Jerusalem Temple and the high priest which, while no doubt

DATA

TITLE:
The Letter of
Aristeas

ORIGINAL DATE OF
COMPOSITION:
ca. 250BCE–ca.
100CE

ORIGINAL LANGUAGE:
Greek

PROVENANCE:
Egypt

EARLIEST EXTANT
MANUSCRIPT:
11th cent. CE
(Greek)

intended to provide information for pagans, is above all a glorification of the Jewish religion.

The translation of the Law, which is recorded relatively briefly (see extract, below), is not the only concern of the Letter of Aristeas, but it is the central issue. The authority and perfect accuracy of the translation are stressed and it is not to be changed in any detail. This probably indicates the writer's need to assert the authority of the Septuagint in the face of objections by some Hebrew-speaking Jews, who felt that the translation often seemed to depart from the sense of the original. Such doubts culminated in the very literal Greek translation of the Hebrew Bible produced by Aquila in the second century CE.

A cameo of Ptolemy II Philadelphus of Egypt (right) and Queen Arsinoë, his wife and sister. The king is said to have commissioned the Greek translation of the Bible for the famous Library at Alexandria.

From the Letter of Aristeas

[King Ptolemy wrote to Eleazar, the high priest of the Temple in Jerusalem]: "We have … decided that your Law shall be translated into Greek letters from what you call the Hebrew letters, in order that they too should take their place with us in our Library with the other royal books. You will therefore act well, and in a manner worthy of our zeal, by selecting elders of exemplary lives, with experience of the Law and ability to translate it, six from each tribe, so that an agreed version may be found from the large majority." …

Eleazar offered sacrifice and selected the men and made ready an abundance of gifts for the king. … [In Alexandria, the royal librarian] Demetrius … assembled them in a … magnificent building in a quiet situation and invited the men to carry out the work of translation. … They set to completing their various tasks, reaching agreement among themselves on each by comparing versions. The result of their agreement thus was made into a fair copy by Demetrius. … The outcome was such that in seventy-two days the business of translation was completed, just as if such a result was achieved by some deliberate design. When it was completed, Demetrius assembled the company of the Jews … and read it to all, in the presence of the translators. … [The whole community] said, "Since this version has been made rightly and reverently, and in every respect accurately, it is good that this should remain exactly so, and that there should be no revision."

CHAPTER 4
PSALMS, SONGS, AND ODES
◆
THE PSALMS OF SOLOMON

The collection of eighteen poems known as the Psalms of Solomon were originally separate compositions, of varying dates and authorship. They contain no mention at all of the famous Israelite king to whom they are ascribed, but the Bible states that Solomon wrote "a thousand and five" songs (1 Kings 4.32) and two of the canonical Psalms (Pss. 72 and 127) are attributed to him. One of these, Psalm 72, has affinities with Psalm 17 of the Psalms of Solomon, which may be why the entire collection was so named when it was first assembled.

Each psalm has a title modeled on those of the Book of Psalms and the collection includes many of the literary types found in the Bible, such as hymns, psalms of thanksgiving, and

laments. Although attributed to Solomon (who ruled probably between 1000 and 900BCE), these psalms are in fact a reaction to events in Judea at a much later period. Three in particular (Pss. Sol. 2, 8, and 17) present an accurate picture of the fall of Jerusalem to the Romans under Pompey in 63BCE. Judea was ruled at this time by the Hasmonean dynasty (descendants of the Maccabees, see p.28), who were both kings of Judea and high priests of the Temple in Jerusalem. The psalms condemn the Hasmoneans as usurpers of the throne of King David, lax in their religion, and followers of Gentile customs—ironically, given that their Maccabean forebears had fought against the hellenization of Judea.

Part of a wall painting of ca. 1300CE from a south German synagogue, showing a harpist, probably King David or Solomon. He is depicted in the conical hat which medieval European Jews were forced to wear.

Pompey's intervention aimed to resolve the political instability in Judea caused by the rivalry of two Hasmonean brothers, Hyrcanus II and Aristobulus, each of whom claimed power. When Pompey approached Jerusalem, the followers of Hyrcanus opened the gates to him, but Aristobulus continued to resist, forcing Pompey to use battering rams to breach the city walls. The consequence was a great massacre, the capture and exiling of many prisoners, and the fall of the Hasmoneans. Pompey also committed the great sacrilege, from a Jewish point of view, of entering the central sanctuary of the Temple. Fifteen years later, in 48BCE, Pompey was assassinated in Egypt and his body left unburied. All these events are depicted in coded language in the Psalms of Solomon, which view the sacrilegious "dragon" Pompey as the agent of God's vengeance on the Hasmoneans for all their sins. In sharp contrast are the author's hopes for the vindication of Israel, which center on the coming Messiah (see box, p.108).

However, most of the Psalms of Solomon are not concerned with specific events but rather with personal piety. The individual psalms in the collection are moving documents, marked by profound religious reflection. The righteous know that they are far from perfect and often fall into sin, but because they are genuinely seeking to live in accord with God's purpose they can be confident that he will pardon their unintentional transgressions and that repentance and amendment of life is always open to them. Their sufferings are not a sign of God's judgment but

DATA

TITLE:
The Psalms of Solomon

ORIGINAL DATE OF COMPOSITION:
Mid–late 1st cent. BCE

ORIGINAL LANGUAGE:
Hebrew

PROVENANCE:
Jerusalem

EARLIEST EXTANT MANUSCRIPT:
10th cent. CE
(Greek)

From the Psalms of Solomon, Psalm 10

Happy is the man whom the Lord
    remembers with rebuking,
and protects from the evil way with a whip
that he may be cleansed from sin that it
    may not increase.
The one who prepares his back for the whip
    shall be purified,
for the Lord is good to those who endure
    discipline.
For he will straighten the ways of the
    righteous,
and not turn them aside by discipline;
and the mercy of the Lord is upon those who
    truly love him.
And the Lord will remember his servants
    in mercy,
for the testimony of it is in the law of the
    eternal covenant,

and the testimony of the Lord is in the ways
    of men
in his supervision.

Our Lord is just and holy in his judgments
    forever,
and Israel shall praise the Lord's name
    `in joy.
And the devout shall give thanks in the
    assembly of the people,
and God will be merciful to the poor to the
    joy of Israel.
For God is good and merciful forever,
and the synagogues of Israel will glorify the
    Lord's name.
The Lord's salvation be upon the house
    of Israel
that they may be happy forever.

are to be seen as a kindly divine discipline, to be accepted gladly as a check on their evil propensities. At all times, they can trust in God's mercy, protection, and ultimate vindication. The wicked are presented as those who have no care for God's commandments and are guilty of various immoralities. They seem to be the rich and powerful, hypocrites who manipulate the law courts and oppress and seek to mislead the righteous—who, by contrast, are poor and modest. The violent and colorful language in which the wicked are denounced shows how bitterly the authors of the Psalms of Solomon experienced their own situation.

The frequent contrast in the Psalms between the righteous and the wicked has led some scholars to propose that these refer to particular Jewish groups of the first century CE, especially the Pharisees and the Sadducees. Thus the anti-Hasmonean criticisms would reflect the general attitude of the Pharisees, who advocated strict adherence to the Jewish law, while the dynasty was supported by the Sadducees, who were based on the priestly Temple establishment. However, the idea of a division between righteous and sinners was common in Judaism, and contemporary Jewish writers such as Philo and Josephus state that most Jews did not adhere to any particular group. More recent attempts to link the Psalms of Solomon with the Qumran sect that produced the Dead Sea Scrolls also remain to be proven. Jerusalem features strongly in the Psalms of Solomon and perhaps the most that can be said is that they probably originated among "all who were looking for the redemption of Jerusalem," as Luke 2.38 puts it: pious Jews who lived in the city and lived in hope and expectation of the Messiah.

The Coming of the Messiah

Psalm 17 of the Psalms of Solomon provides the fullest picture in any Jewish work of the Messiah, the future savior of Israel, and indicates how some circles within Judaism viewed this figure in the late centuries BCE and first century CE. The Messiah is a human being and his kingdom, although it marks the end-time, will be on this earth. A descendant of King David, he is called "the Anointed," the literal meaning of "Messiah" (Hebrew *mashiach*) and the title of the Davidic monarchs in the Bible.

The author describes the coming king in language from the Bible, notably 2 Samuel 7 and Psalm 89, where God promises that David's kingdom will be re-established for all time. The Messiah will be a mighty conqueror, who will expel the Romans and their puppet rulers from Palestine, return the Jewish people to their homeland, and restore the boundaries of the ideal Davidic state. He will establish a great kingdom centered on Jerusalem, to which all the Gentiles will bring tribute and where he will rule as judge, "faithfully and righteously shepherding the Lord's flock" (Pss. Sol. 17).

Although the Messiah is a mortal, he is endowed with divine attributes, because only God himself is his superior: as Psalm 17 puts it, he is "powerful in the holy spirit and wise in the counsel of understanding, with strength and righteousness." Like the old kings of Israel, he is a source of blessing, the embodiment of wisdom and justice, and his word has the same power as the word of God.

The idealized city of Jerusalem, from the 6th-century CE church of San Vitale in Ravenna, Italy.

From the Psalms of Solomon, Psalm 17, verses 21–24 and 30–32

See, Lord, and raise up for them their king,
the son of David, to rule over your servant
   Israel
in the time known to you, O God.
Undergird him with the strength to destroy
   the unrighteous rulers,
to purge Jerusalem from Gentiles who
   trample her to destruction;
in wisdom and in righteousness to drive out
the sinners from the inheritance,
to smash the arrogance of sinners
   like a potter's jar;
To shatter all their substance with an
   iron rod;

to destroy the unlawful nations with the
   word of his mouth. ...
And he will purge Jerusalem
and make it holy as it was from the beginning,
for nations to come from the ends of the
   earth to see his glory,
to bring as gifts her children who had been
   driven out, and to see the glory of the
   Lord with which God has glorified her.
And he will be a righteous king over them,
   taught by God.
There will be no unrighteousness among
   them in his days, for all shall be holy,
And their king shall be the Lord Messiah.

LAMENTS AND CONFESSIONS

The concept of God in the non-canonical scriptures is overwhelmingly of a transcendent being, remote from the world in his heavenly dwelling place. However, the writings contain frequent prayers and hymns addressed directly to the deity, which shows that the authors felt that they could rely on a direct and deeply personal communion with their Lord. Such writings are often in poetic form and display elements from a variety of literary types found in the Hebrew Bible, especially the Book of Psalms. They are moving compositions that are often of considerable beauty and artistry.

Characteristic of the canonical Psalms are the laments, uttered either on behalf of the nation of Israel or, more frequently, by an individual. In the Hebrew Bible, laments formed part of an actual ritual observance; indeed, the original source of such laments may have been in mourning rites. National laments were usually the response to a particular disaster which had befallen Israel as a community and their object was to arouse God's concern for the sorry

state of his people and to awaken his intervention for them. Most of the Pseudepigrapha were produced against a background of disaster or subjection for the Jewish people, so it is not surprising that they should have such a tone of bitter lamentation.

A particularly fine example of a lament is uttered by the prophet Baruch in the Second Book of Baruch (see extract, p.87). It is immediately preceded by a mention of the fall of Jerusalem to the Babylonians, following which Baruch says that he and his companions "rent [their] garments, and wept and mourned, and fasted for seven days." Not the least remarkable feature of Baruch's lament is the way in which the destruction of Jerusalem affects the whole of nature: Baruch even calls on all supernatural beings to join Israel in mourning.

The most general explanation for the nation's disasters was that the people had sinned and failed to observe God's commandments, as is briefly hinted at in Baruch's lament. A strong awareness of the gravity of sin, both national but especially personal, characterizes most of the pseudepigraphical books. To restore a correct relationship with God required a sincere and humble confession of past wrongdoing, after which God would accept the sinner's repentance. The clearest instances of such a confession are the lengthy prayers attributed to Aseneth in Joseph and Aseneth (see p.63). But the need for confession and repentance, both for the individual and the nation, is perhaps most clearly expressed in the Psalms of Solomon (see pp.106–9, and extract, below).

From the Psalms of Solomon, Psalm 9, verses 6–11

To whom will you be good, O God, except
    to those who call upon the Lord?
He will cleanse from sin the soul in confessing,
so that for all these things, the shame is on us,
    and on our faces.
And whose sins will he forgive except those
    who have sinned?
You bless the righteous, and do not accuse
    them for what they sinned.
And your goodness is upon those that sin,
    when they repent.

And now, you are God and we are the people
    whom you have loved;

look and be compassionate, O God of Israel,
    for we are yours,
and do not take away your mercy from us,
    lest the peoples set upon us.
For you chose the descendants of Abraham
    above all the nations,
and you put your name upon us, Lord,
    and it will not cease for ever.
You made a covenant with our ancestors
    concerning us,
and we hope in you when we turn our souls
    toward you.
May the mercy of the Lord be upon the
    house of Israel forevermore.

OPPOSITE *By the Waters of Babylon*, by the British artist Evelyn de Morgan (1855–1919). The Jewish exiles in Babylon are shown lamenting the loss of their homeland and the destruction of Jerusalem.

THE ODES OF SOLOMON

DATA

TITLE:
The Odes of
Solomon

ORIGINAL DATE OF
COMPOSITION:
ca. 100CE

ORIGINAL LANGUAGE:
Probably Syriac

PROVENANCE:
Syria?

EARLIEST EXTANT
MANUSCRIPT:
3rd cent. CE
(Greek)

The Psalms of Solomon have a number of similarities with another collection, the Odes of Solomon, and in fact most manuscripts bring them together as a single work, under either one title or the other. The Odes make no mention whatsoever of Solomon, and it may be that they were ascribed to him only when they became linked with the earlier collection. Like the Psalms of Solomon and similar works among the Dead Sea Scrolls, the Odes belong to a genre of psalm composition that was influenced by the images and concepts of the Bible, especially those in the Book of Psalms.

However, the differences between the Psalms of Solomon and the Odes are more marked than the resemblances, and the Odes are highly distinctive writings. Above all, while the Psalms of Solomon are Jewish compositions, with no trace of Christian influence, the Odes throughout are equally clearly Christian. Christ appears explicitly and there are embellishments of the New Testament accounts of his life, such as the virgin birth, his baptism, the attacks on him, his ministry, and his descent into the underworld. In one of the Odes there is a remarkable description of the Trinity bestowing life on the universe, where God is described as having breasts and the Holy Spirit is apparently presented in feminine terms.

Recently there has been increasing support for the view that the original language of the Odes was Syriac, a Semitic language spoken in Syria. If so, the work is significant for the evidence it provides of early Syrian Christianity (see box, below). A number of concepts and expressions found in the Odes are paralleled in the letters of the Syrian writer Ignatius, bishop

Christianity in Syria

Syria was one of the first areas of Christian expansion. The New Testament relates that Paul and Barnabas undertook a mission ca. 42CE to Antioch, the Syrian capital, and states that it was in this city that the followers of Jesus were first called "Christians" (Greek *Christianoi*) (Acts 11.25–26). Little else is known about the Syrian church before the fourth century CE, which saw the beginnings of an abundant literature in Syriac that continued for many centuries and included translations of the scriptures. Hence, if the Odes are of Syrian origin, they are important because they throw light on an otherwise obscure period of Christian history.

Syriac Christianity was marked by its strong links with Judaism and the Jewish tradition of Targum (paraphrasing the Hebrew Bible into Aramaic for congregations with little knowledge of Hebrew), and much of its literature is in the form of poetry. All these features characterize the Odes and may support the hypothesis of their Syrian provenance.

The ruined 5th-century pilgrimage church at Qalat Sama'an in Syria, built around the pillar upon which St. Simon Stylites (died 459CE) had lived for 30 years. The remains of the pillar are in the foreground.

From the Odes of Solomon, Ode 19

A cup of milk was offered to me,
and I drank it in the sweetness of the Lord's
    kindness.
The Son is the cup,
and the Father is he who was milked;
and the Holy Spirit is she who milked him;
Because his breasts were full,
and it was undesirable that his milk should
    be released without purpose.
The Holy Spirit opened her bosom,

and mixed the milk of the two breasts of the
    Father.
Then she gave the mixture to the world
    without their knowing,
and those who have received it are in the
    perfection of the right hand.
The womb of the Virgin took it,
and she conceived and gave birth.
So the Virgin became a mother with great
    mercies.

A wall painting of ca. 500 CE from the tomb of a bishop called Theotecnus, his wife, and their daughter in the catacombs of San Gennaro, Naples. Their hands are raised in the "orant" gesture of prayer (see main text).

of Antioch (died 110CE), suggesting that the Odes were probably produced as early as ca. 100CE.

Ignatius' letters also reveal what appears to be the earliest systematic use of the Gospel of John, indicating that it was well known in Syrian Christian circles, and there are notable similarities between the thought and language of John and the Odes of Solomon. Like the gospel, the Odes teach that the world is governed by two spirits, the Holy Spirit and the "Evil One," but that the power of the evil spirit has been broken by the advent of Christ. The Odes' teaching of Christ as "the Word" is also close to John, and the passages in the Odes where Jesus himself speaks invite comparison with the "I am" sayings in John (6.35, 8.12, 10.7, 11.25, 14.6, 15.1).

Much in the Odes suggests that behind them lie the life and worship of a particular Christian community. At one point the odist identifies himself as a priest (see extract, opposite) and delivers what is in effect a short sermon. Frequently he appears as a divinely inspired composer of songs or odes, which he accompanies on a harp. However, he is only one of a class of "Singers" or "Odists" who chant God's praises, and it would appear that the Odes were intended as a central element in the worship of the community in which they were produced.

Often the spiritual gifts which the faithful receive are spoken of symbolically as milk or honey, or as springs or rivers of water, and the Odes mention "the ministers of that drink, who have been entrusted with his water." It is possible that these images refer to baptism and the Eucharist, but in any case the Odes seem to envisage a body of what could be described as clergy, who led the congregation in worship and delivered spiritual instruction and nourishment to its members. The Odes refer to the "orant" gesture of extending the hands in prayer, a feature of early Christian worship, especially in the eastern Church, and still employed by priests celebrating Mass. This gesture is described in the Odes as symbolizing the cross.

The predominant theme of the Odes is the picture they present of the life of the devout individual. Throughout, they express overwhelming joy and confidence in the believer's fellowship with God, which is realized through the saving experience of the coming of the Messiah. The keynote of the writer's message is love: the mutual love of Jesus for the believer and of the believer for Jesus, which makes the two virtually one. All this is a present experience—the victory over the powers of evil has already been achieved, so that, speaking in the person of Christ, the odist says: "I took courage and became strong and captured the world, and it became mine for the glory of the Most High and of God my Father."

The supreme gift which union with the Savior brings is not so much the hope of resurrection to a future life but rather immortality as a present possession, a concept which again recalls John. The odist is already admitted into Paradise. Specifically, immortality means incorruption, because the believer is united with the incorruptible risen Lord and will remain incorrupted for all time, even to "the new world."

The Odes of Solomon are an important witness to what the new faith in Jesus as the Messiah could mean for his early followers. In many respects, they strongly reflect some strands in contemporary Judaism—but these have been transformed and given a new perspective and depth by the awareness of a profound personal relationship with Jesus as the living Lord.

From the Odes of Solomon, Ode 20

I am a priest of the Lord,
and to him I serve as a priest ...
The offering of the Lord is righteousness,
and purity of heart and lips.
Offer your inward being faultlessly;
and do not let your compassion oppress
    compassion;
and do not let your soul oppress a soul. ...
But put on the grace of the Lord generously,
and come into his Paradise,
and make for yourself a crown from his tree.
Then put it on your head and be refreshed,
and recline upon his serenity.
For his glory will go before you;
and you will receive of his kindness and of
    his grace;
and you will be anointed in truth with the
    praise of his holiness.
Praise and honor to his name.
Hallelujah.

HYMNS AND SONGS

The non-canonical scriptures include a significant number of hymnic poems presenting rapturous praise of God. Such poems reflect two characteristic themes of many of the Pseudepigrapha: the concept of God's transcendence and majesty, and a belief in a highly developed hierarchy of angels.

It was natural that this exalted view of God should find expression in thanksgiving hymns, and the prime function of the angels surrounding the divine throne was the ceaseless chanting of songs of praise. Human worship was directly linked with celestial worship—some songs used in the liturgies of the community of Qumran (see p.27) claim to be the very praises and blessing uttered by the angels in heaven. The intimate union between heavenly and earthly worship is to be seen in an episode from the Apocalypse of Abraham, in which the patriarch is accompanied on his heavenly travels by the archangel Iaoel, who teaches him a song of praise to God (see extract, below) and commands him to recite it without stopping.

A number of vivid poetic compositions in the non-canonical writings display no overtly religious content. The song of Jephthah's daughter in Pseudo-Philo (see pp.68–72) is a simple human lament, in which she accepts the inevitability of her death and movingly meditates on the loss of what she could have hoped for in life. In the Book of Jubilees, Esau mocks Jacob in a dramatic example of the biblical boast or taunt, as in the song of Lamech in Genesis 4.

From the Apocalypse of Abraham, chapter 17

Eternal One, Mighty One, Holy El,
    God autocrat
self-originated, incorruptible, immaculate,
unbegotten, spotless, immortal,
self-perfected, self-devised,
without mother, without father, ungenerated,
exalted, fiery,
just, lover of men, benevolent,
    compassionate, bountiful,
jealous over me, patient one, most merciful,
Eli, my God, mighty one, holy, Sabaoth,

most glorious El, El, El, El, Iaoel. ...
Eternal, fiery, shining,
light-giving, thunder-voiced, lightning-
    visioned, many-eyed,
receiving the petitions of those who honor
    you ...
redeemer of those who dwell in the midst of
    the wicked ones. ...
Showing forth the age of the just,
you make the light shine
before the morning light upon your creation.

OPPOSITE *Angels in a Heavenly Landscape*, from the chapel in the Palazzo Medici, Florence, Italy, ca. 1460.

CHAPTER 5
WISDOM AND PHILOSOPHY
◆
THE WORDS OF AHIQAR

Originating ca. 600BCE, the Words of Ahiqar is by far the most ancient of all the pseudepigraphical books and many scholars would exclude it from the Pseudepigrapha altogether, on the grounds of its date (pre-Babylonian exile), non-Jewish origin, and content. Ahiqar himself may have been a historical figure: the book describes him as a high official at the Assyrian court, serving as counselor, scribe, and keeper of the royal seal under two rulers, Sennacherib (704–681BCE) and Esarhaddon III (681–669BCE).

At the time, Aramaic was the international diplomatic language of the Near East, and there are good grounds for believing that it was the original language of Ahiqar. In any case, the oldest surviving version is an Aramaic text discovered in 1906 in southern Egypt on the island of Elephantine in the Nile, the site of a Jewish military colony which existed there in the fifth

Ahiqar is said to have served kings Sennacherib and Esarhaddon of Assyria. In this relief from his palace at Nineveh, Sennacherib receives the submission of the Israelite city of Lachish (compare 2 Chronicles 32.9).

century BCE and had probably been established about a century earlier. Together with much other evidence, this shows that the story was increasingly adopted by Jews as their own. The Book of Tobit in the biblical Apocrypha gives a short account of the career of Ahiqar and actually makes him into a Jew and the nephew of Tobit. Another text shows that the name Ahiqar was Aramaic, so it was easy for Jews to regard him as someone who had risen to prominence in a foreign court, like Joseph, Daniel, and Mordecai in the Bible. Also,the sayings ascribed to Ahiqar have many similarities with those found in writings of the Jewish wisdom tradition.

The Elephantine document falls into two distinct parts, a narrative of Ahiqar's career and a collection of sayings. In the narrative, the ageing and childless Ahiqar adopts his nephew Nadin and trains him as his successor. In due course, the king, Esarhaddon, confirms Nadin in his uncle's position, but Nadin proves ungrateful and accuses Ahiqar of fomenting a rebellion. Esarhaddon believes the slander and orders one of his high counselors, Nabusumiskun, to seize Ahiqar and execute him. However, Ahiqar had saved Nabusumiskun from a similar fate under Esarhaddon's father, Sennacherib, and after Ahiqar has reminded Nabusumiskun of this, the counselor devises a ploy whereby Ahiqar appears to have been killed but is actually hidden away to await better times. His death is reported to the king, who believes the fiction.

At this point the Aramaic text breaks off, but there is no doubt that it originally narrated a happy conclusion, in which Ahiqar is eventually restored to favor and Nadin is executed, much as in the story of Mordecai and Haman in the Book of Esther. The author of the Book of

From the Words of Ahiqar, verses 55–71

Nabusumiskun replied to me, "Have no fear, my lord Ahiqar, father of all Assyria, on whose counsel King Sennacherib and all the Assyrian army used to rely!" At once [he] said to his companions, the two men who were accompanying him … "Listen to me: this Ahiqar was a great man. He was Esarhaddon's keeper of the seal, and all the Assyrian army used to rely on his counsel and advice. Far be it from us to kill him! There is a eunuch-slave of mine. Let him be killed between these two mountains in place of this Ahiqar. When it is reported, the king will send other men after us to see the body of this Ahiqar. Then they will see the body of this eunuch-slave of mine and that will be the end of the matter until

eventually Esarhaddon thinks of Ahiqar and wishes for his counsel, and grieves over him. Then Esarhaddon's thoughts will turn to me and he will say to his officers and courtiers, 'I would give you riches as numerous as grains of sand, if only you could find Ahiqar.' "

Now this plan seemed good to his two companions. They replied … "Do as you suggest. Let us not kill him, but you give us that eunuch in place of Ahiqar. He shall be killed between these two mountains."

At that time, word spread through the land of Assyria that Ahiqar, King Esarhaddon's scribe, had been put to death. Then officer Nabusumiskun took me to his house and hid me.

DATA

TITLE:
The Words of
Ahiqar (Ahiqar)

ORIGINAL DATE
OF COMPOSITION:
7th–6th cent. BCE

ORIGINAL LANGUAGE:
Aramaic

PROVENANCE:
Mesopotamia

EARLIEST EXTANT
MANUSCRIPT:
late 5th cent. BCE
(Aramaic)

The remains of the Roman-period temple of Baal Shamaim, the "Lord of the Heavens," one of several popular Near Eastern deities invoked in the Words of Ahiqar, in the ancient city of Palmyra in Syria.

Sayings from the Words of Ahiqar

3. Spare not your son from the rod; otherwise, can you save him from wickedness?

4. If I beat you, my son, you will not die; but if I leave you alone, you will not live.

18. A king's word is gentle, but keener and more cutting than a double-edged dagger.

35. A leopard came upon a she-goat who was cold. The leopard said to the goat, "Won't you let me cover you with my pelt?" The goat replied to the leopard, "Why should I do that, my lord? Don't take my own hide away from me! For, as they say, 'A leopard does not greet a gazelle except to suck its blood.'"

39. Do not draw your bow and shoot your arrow at the righteous man, lest the gods come to his aid and turn it back against you.

49. Whoever takes no pride in his mother's or his father's name, may Shamash not shine on him, for he is an evil man.

73. The bramble sent a message to the pomegranate as follows: "Dear Pomegranate, what good are all your thorns to him who touches your fruit?" The pomegranate replied to the bramble: "You are nothing but thorns to him who touches you!"

106. A man said one day to the wild ass, "Let me ride on you, and I will provide for you!" The wild ass replied, "Keep your care and fodder; as for me, I want nothing to do with your riding!"

Tobit clearly knew the story of Ahiqar's restoration, while later versions of Ahiqar in a number of other languages include an elaborate tale of how the king of Egypt challenges Esarhaddon to send him a wise man who can answer various hard questions and build a palace in the sky. Ahiqar is brought out of hiding, sent to Egypt and, after a successful mission, returns to upbraid Nadin, as a consequence of which the wicked nephew dies.

In the opening words of the narrative, Ahiqar is described as "a wise and skillful scribe," and it was above all as a wise teacher that Ahiqar was renowned in the Near East, the Greco-Roman world, and in Judaism and Christianity. The second part of the Aramaic text consists of a large number of sayings. It seems likely that they were originally quite separate: they do not mention Ahiqar at all, suggesting that this part was only later attributed to him. The sayings display a range of literary types, in no discernible order, and many are fragmentary. But the parallels between them and similar material both in the Bible and in older Mesopotamian and Egyptian literature clearly show that the compiler is drawing on a wide range of traditions.

The sayings bear close resemblances to those in the biblical Book of Proverbs and the proverbial sayings in the apocryphal Book of Sirach (Ecclesiasticus), notably in what Ahiqar has to say on the theme of "spare the rod and spoil the child," or the need to control one's servants. Alongside practical sayings about the danger of rash speech, the need to work hard and avoid debt, contentment with one's lot, the virtues of family life, and social harmony, there are also numerous sayings inculcating respect for the king, as well as several animal or plant fables which can be paralleled in various other sources, including the Bible (Judges 9.8–15 and 2 Kings 14.9).

Ahiqar and the Gods

The sayings of Ahiqar in the Elephantine text never mention the God of Israel, but refer instead to "the gods," at least three of which are named: El, Shamash, and Shamayn, all widely worshiped throughout the ancient Near East. El was the head of the Canaanite pantheon, Shamash was the Mesopotamian sun god, and Shamayn is almost certainly Baal-Shamaim, "Lord of the Heavens" in Syrian religions.

Unsurprisingly, in the later versions of the Ahiqar legend "the gods" become "God." However, the Bible itself provides evidence that, before the Babylonian exile, the popular religion of Israel included the worship of the sun, the "Queen of Heaven," and other deities. It is this kind of religion which is found among the Jews of Elephantine. Letters from members of the colony often invoke "the gods," and two other deities, Eshem-Bethel and Anath-Bethel, were worshiped alongside Yahweh. One letter prays to the Babylonian gods Bel, Nabu, Shamash, and Nergal. Even if the writer of this letter was not a Jew, it at least shows that his religious practices could be tolerated in a Jewish milieu at this period.

THE THIRD BOOK OF THE MACCABEES

Despite its title, the Third Book of the Maccabees (3 Maccabees) has no connection with the Maccabean movement (see p.28) and records events that are supposed to have taken place over fifty years earlier, during the reign of Ptolemy IV Philopator of Egypt (ruled 221–204 BCE). But the title can perhaps claim some justification from the fact that the work closely parallels a number of episodes and concepts found in the Second Book of the Maccabees (2 Maccabees) in the Apocrypha.

The Third Book has been described as a "pathetic history" or "historical romance," meaning that it is less interested in accurate history than in engaging the reader's emotions by the use of vivid, exaggerated, and repetitious language, exploiting all the devices of Greek rhetoric. The plot is largely fictional, but it displays a sound knowledge of Egypt in the time of Ptolemy IV: it reproduces the style of official documents and letters, and its depiction of the king as addicted to elaborate banquets and as a worshiper of his supposed ancestor, the god Dionysus, accords with other sources. The book also has close connections with the Letter of Aristeas (see pp.104–5), another product of Egyptian Judaism of the centuries around the beginning of the

A sphinx of the Ptolemaic period stands before the 2nd-century CE column known as "Pompey's Pillar" in Alexandria, a cosmopolitan city where Greek, Egyptian, and Jewish culture existed side by side.

Common Era. However, 3 Maccabees reveals that Alexandrian Judaism was far from homogeneous in its theological outlook and, unlike the Letter of Aristeas, emphasizes the hostility between Jews and Gentiles. The king in the Letter, Ptolemy II, is an ideal ruler and well disposed to the Jews, whereas Ptolemy IV is an obstinate and bloodthirsty tyrant, who only acknowledges the Jewish community's right to exist as the result of severe divine punishments.

The purpose of 3 Maccabees is to encourage the author's fellow Jews to remain constant in their faith, with the firm assurance that God will eventually reward their righteousness and overthrow their wicked opponents, as he has done in the past. This is the theme of the two key speeches in the work, by Simon, the Jerusalem high priest, and Eleazar, a priest of the Alexandrian community. The author stresses that the Jews' piety and moral rectitude make them good and loyal citizens, a fact recognized by some at least of their Gentile neighbors (see extract).

The work centers on two dramatic scenes. In the first, following his victory in 217BCE over the Seleucid king at the battle of Raphia in southern Palestine, Ptolemy IV proceeds to Jerusalem and determines to enter the Holy of Holies of the Temple. But God frustrates him, striking him down for his impiety. This closely resembles the similar attempt of Heliodorus in 2 Maccabees 3, with the difference that Ptolemy does not learn his lesson. In the second scene, Ptolemy returns home and orders all the Jews of Egypt to be rounded up and trampled to death by a herd of elephants in the hippodrome of Alexandria. However, two angels intervene and turn the beasts back on their keepers. Ptolemy finally repents and, blaming his advisers for what has happened, orders the Jews to be returned to their homes and decrees that they are no longer to be molested. To celebrate their deliverance, the Jews inaugurate a great festival which recalls the ending of the biblical Book of Esther with the establishment of the feast of Purim.

From The Third Book of the Maccabees, chapter 3

Reverencing God and conducting themselves according to his law, [the Jews] kept themselves apart in the matter of food, and for this reason they appeared hateful to some. They adorned their community life with the excellent practice of righteousness and so established a good reputation among all men. But of this excellent practice, which was common talk everywhere regarding the Jewish nation, the foreigners took no account whatever. Instead, they talked incessantly about how different they were in regard to worship and food, asserting that they did not fulfill their contracted obligations either to the king or the armed forces but were hostile and very unsympathetic to his interests. ... [But some] Greeks in the city, who were in no way wronged by them, noticed the unexpected tumult around these people. ... they were unable to help, for they lived under a tyranny, but they did give them encouragement and felt sorry for them, and they assumed that things would change for the better. ... Some of their neighbors and friends and business associates took some Jews aside secretly and pledged to support them and make every effort to assist them.

DATA

Title:
The Third Book of
the Maccabees

Original Date
of composition:
1st cent. BCE

Original Language:
Greek

Provenance:
Alexandria, Egypt

Earliest Extant
manuscript:
Late 4th cent CE
(Syriac)

THE FOURTH BOOK OF THE MACCABEES

DATA

TITLE:
The Fourth Book
of the Maccabees

ORIGINAL DATE
OF COMPOSITION:
1st cent. CE

ORIGINAL LANGUAGE:
Greek

PROVENANCE:
Antioch, Syria?

EARLIEST EXTANT
MANUSCRIPT:
4th cent. CE
(Greek)

The Fourth Book of the Maccabees (4 Maccabees) is a philosophical tract which argues that the purpose of human existence is to live according to reason, which controls and directs the passions or emotions; unchecked, these would prevent the exercise of the four cardinal virtues: prudence, temperance, justice, and courage. This teaching characterizes the two great schools of Greek philosophy, the Platonic and the Stoic. However, 4 Maccabees identifies the practice of reason with the keeping of the Jewish law.

The work regularly qualifies the term "reason" by the adjective "devout" or "religious": in other words, the duties of piety are essential to a proper understanding of reason. The practice of reason is illustrated by episodes in the careers of some of the great figures of Israel's past (Joseph, Moses, and David), and the basic outlook of 4 Maccabees is summed up in the statement: "When God fashioned man, he implanted in him his passions and inclinations, and at the same time enthroned the intellect amid the senses as the sacred guide over all. To the intellect he gave the law, and if a man lives his life by the law he shall reign over a kingdom that is temperate and just and good and brave." Following the law involves the observance of all its commandments: the Jewish food laws and the obligation to cancel debts in the sabbatical year show the supremacy of devout reason over the natural human tendencies to take pleasure in

Judaism and Martyrdom

The Fourth Book of the Maccabees reflects the great significance which the concept of martyrdom had assumed in Judaism in the wake of the persecutions of the time of Antiochus IV Epiphanes and later. The work describes the blood of the righteous Maccabean martyrs as a "ransom" and a "propitiation" for the sins of the nation: the suffering and death of martyrs make atonement for the sins of the Israelite people and bring about God's mercy and pardon. These ideas are most clearly expressed in the speech of the first Maccabean martyr, Eleazar, in his confrontation with Antiochus (see

extract). Antiochus speaks from the standpoint of Greek philosophical reason, which Eleazar interprets from the position of a pious Jew.

The reward of the martyrs for their steadfastness is immortality. The immortality of the soul was an accepted Hellenistic concept—4 Maccabees deliberately leaves out all the statements in 2 Maccabees which express the more distinctively Jewish belief in a physical resurrection. The work's view of martyrdom accounts for its great influence and popularity in the early Church, which came to regard the Maccabean victims as prototypes of its own martyrs.

eating and to value money. The larger part of 4 Maccabees is taken up with an account of the Maccabean martyrs, who resisted the policies of King Antiochus IV Epiphanes (see p.28) and were prepared to make the supreme sacrifice for their fidelity to the law. The author takes the story of the martyrs from the account in 2 Maccabees in the biblical Apocrypha (2 Macc. 6–7), which he considerably expands and embellishes—for example, by attributing lengthy speeches to the protagonists and describing their tortures in gruesome detail.

The work is addressed to Greek-speaking Jews who were well educated, deeply Hellenized, and at home within the climate of Greek philosophical speculation. At the same time, it can be seen as a propaganda text addressed to Gentiles, with the object of showing that only in Judaism could their highest aspirations be truly realized.

From the Fourth Book of the Maccabees, chapters 5

The first [of the Jews] to be brought before Antiochus was a man called Eleazar, of priestly stock, expert in the law and advanced in age, and known to many of the tyrant's entourage for his philosophy. When Antiochus saw him, he said, "Before I have the tortures begin on you, old man, I would advise you to eat of the swine's flesh and save yourself. ..."

[Eleazar replied:] "Under no circumstances whatever do we ever deem it right to transgress the law. ... Accordingly, you must not regard it as a minor sin for us to eat unclean food; minor sins are just as weighty as great sins, for in each case the law is despised. You mock at our philosophy as though our living under it were contrary to reason. On the other hand, it teaches us temperance so that we are in control of all our pleasures and desires; and it gives us a thorough training in courage so that we willingly endure all hardship; and it teaches us justice so that whatever our different attitudes may be we retain a sense of balance; and it instructs us in piety so that we most highly revere the only living God."

How Antiochus Took and Pillaged the City and Temple of Jerusalem, from a 15th-century French manuscript of Josephus' History of the Jews.

PSEUDO-PHOCYLIDES

The author of Pseudo-Phocylides adopted the name of a Greek poet of the 6th century BCE, Phocylides of Miletus, who was renowned in the ancient world for his popular maxims. It was common for Jews and early Christians to invent sayings and attribute them to Classical Greek poets, the object being to show that renowned Gentile authors had already known—and approved—the basic principles of Judaism and Christianity.

Pseudo-Phocylides is undoubtedly a Jewish composition, as shown by its dependence on the Septuagint, the Greek version of the Hebrew Scriptures, but it avoids specific references to the Bible or to distinctively Jewish practices. In its positive attitude toward the best ideals of the Gentile world, it has some similarities with the Letter of Aristeas and 4 Maccabees. The book may be designed to propagate the principle of a highly ethical monotheism that could claim universal and indeed primeval authority. Such a claim rested on the "Noachide Laws," or "Laws of Noah," seven commandments which God was believed to have delivered to Adam and again, after the Flood, to Noah. There were five prohibitions: the worship of other gods; blasphemy against the divine name; murder; incest and adultery; and stealing; in addition to these laws, humans were required to establish courts of law and to eat only permitted foods. The laws were held to be binding on all peoples, although only the Jews had proved able to live up to them.

Pseudo-Phocylides appears to refer indirectly to each of these commandments. The Greeks had a not dissimilar concept of "unwritten laws" that were binding on the human conscience, and several of the ethical rules which the author lays down in addition to the Noachide Laws seem to reproduce these as maxims for all human beings. Thus Pseudo-Phocylides bears witness to a universalistic strand in the Judaism of the late centuries BCE and early centuries CE, which largely disappeared with the increasing dominance of rabbinical Judaism after 70CE.

Jews could also read the work as a famous pagan poet's affirmation of the traditional Jewish way of life. There may be an implication that Jews need not to be tempted by Gentile culture—as not a few were—because its highest ideals have long formed part of their own faith.

In form, Pseudo-Phocylides consists of a series of verse maxims in Greek hexameters, in no clear order and from a wide variety of sources. Its original purpose was perhaps as a school textbook, since ancient tutors employed similar collections in the teaching of literacy. The sayings were widely used in this way in sixteenth-century Europe, before doubts about their authorship were raised. The maxims cover a wide range of topics, such as family life, alms-giving, and moderation, but they are often platitudinous and the author has no coherent outlook. The author's claim to literary abilities rests on two longer passages that extol the dignity of labor and condemn sexual aberrations (see extract, opposite).

DATA

TITLE:
Pseudo-Phocylides

ORIGINAL DATE
OF COMPOSITION:
1st cent. BCE—1st
cent. CE

ORIGINAL
LANGUAGE: Greek

PROVENANCE:
Probably
Alexandria, Egypt

EARLIEST EXTANT
MANUSCRIPT:
10th cent. CE
(Greek)

Noah's Sacrifice, by Michelangelo (ca. 1510), on the ceiling of the Sistine Chapel, Rome. Following this sacrifice, God established his covenant with Noah (Gen. 8.20 ff.) and, in Jewish tradition, gave him the Noachide Laws.

From Pseudo-Phocylides, lines 175–193

Do not remain unwed, lest you die nameless.

Give nature her due, you also, beget in your turn as you were begotten.

Do not prostitute your wife, defiling your children. …

Do not let a woman destroy the unborn baby in her belly,

nor after its birth throw it before the dogs and the vultures as a prey.

Do not lay your hand upon your wife when she is pregnant.

Do not cut a youth's male procreative faculty.

Do not seek sexual union with irrational animals. …

Do not transgress with unlawful sex the limits set by nature.

For even animals are not pleased by the intercourse of male with male.

And let women not imitate the sexual role of men.

Do not surrender wholly to unbridled sensuality toward your wife.

THE "LOST"
NEW TESTAMENT

OPPOSITE *Christ Appearing to St. Peter on the Appian Way*, or *Domine, Quo Vadis?*, by Annibale Carracci (1560–1609). This painting depicts a legend first found in the apocryphal Acts of Peter (see pp.178–9).

CHAPTER 1

THE MISSING YEARS OF JESUS

◆

THE GRANDPARENTS OF CHRIST

The Protevangelium of James, also known as the Book of James, claims as its author one of Jesus' disciples, but it was written at least a century after the Crucifixion. It was hugely popular and inspired the genre of writings known as "infancy gospels," which recount episodes from Jesus' early years, about which the canonical gospels say almost nothing (see pp.134–9). Often lively and entertaining, these works were much loved by ordinary Christians and were a rich source of subjects for medieval writers and artists.

The Protevangelium ("Pre-Gospel") is the origin of numerous traditions and also furnished two popular—and entirely legendary—saints, Joachim and Anna (or Anne), the parents of Mary and grandparents of Jesus. As the title suggests, the Protevangelium fills in events before the story told in the canonical gospels, beginning with the birth of Mary and ending with that of Jesus. Mary is at the heart of the work, reflecting her growing cult among the early Christians; the Protevangelium also foreshadows later teachings about the Virgin, especially the Immaculate Conception (see box, opposite). One episode, describing Mary's presentation in the Temple, is still celebrated as one of the great festivals of the Orthodox Church.

The work recounts Mary's miraculous birth in terms that echo the gospel story of the birth of Jesus, but it also draws on themes in the Hebrew Bible. An angel tells the barren and elderly

From the Protevangelium of James, chapters 4–6

DATA

TITLE:
The Protevangelium
(Book) of James

ORIGINAL DATE
OF COMPOSITION:
ca. 150CE
ORIGINAL LANGUAGE:
Latin

PROVENANCE:
Palestine?

EARLIEST EXTANT MS:
5th cent. CE (Syriac)

And behold an angel of the Lord appeared and said: "Anna, Anna, the Lord has heard your prayer. You shall conceive and bear, and your offspring shall be spoken of in the whole world." And Anna said: "As the Lord my God lives, if I bear a child, whether male or female, I will bring it as a gift to the Lord my God, and it shall serve him all the days of its life."

And her months were fulfilled, as the angel had said: in the ninth month Anna brought forth. And she said to the midwife, "What have I brought forth?" And she replied: "A female." And Anna said: "My soul is magnified this day." And she laid it down. And when the days were fulfilled, Anna purified herself from her childbed and gave suck to the child, and called her name Mary.

Day by day the child waxed strong; when she was six months old her mother stood her on the ground to try if she could stand. And she walked seven steps and came to her mother's bosom.

The Birth of the Virgin, Italian school, 15th century. Anna (St. Anne) sits up in bed while, in the foreground, the swaddled infant Mary is washed by a midwife.

Anna that she will conceive. This annunciation is couched in language drawn from the Bible, especially the story of Samuel (1 Sam. 1.11, 28). The name of Samuel's mother, Hannah, is Anna in Latin and Greek. Anna and her husband Joachim, Mary's father, are said to live in Jerusalem in Judea. The Protevangelium movingly narrates their joyful meeting at the Golden Gate of the city after Joachim has learned of his wife's conception, a scene often found in medieval art.

The tradition of Mary's Judean family ties is mentioned in the gospels—her relative Elizabeth is said to live there (Luke 1.36, 1.39–40). Given the relatively early date of the Protevangelium and the fact that Mary was well known among the early Christian community in Jerusalem (Acts 1.14), it is not inconceivable that this tradition has some authentic basis.

The Immaculate Conception

The doctrine of the Immaculate Conception, as finally defined by Pope Pius IX in 1854, states that the Virgin Mary was, from the moment of her conception, free from all stain of original sin. This belief seems to have become widespread from ca. 500CE, although it was never universally accepted and was disputed throughout the Middle Ages.

The impetus behind it was the growing veneration of Mary, which was reflected in—and in turn fuelled

by—the Protevangelium and popular writings derived from it. The book strongly emphasizes the purity of Mary, and it is the first work to affirm the belief in her perpetual virginity—it explains that the brothers of Jesus mentioned in the New Testament were in fact Joseph's sons by a former marriage. Such assertions of Mary's purity led ultimately to the claim that she had been absolutely immaculate from the beginning of her life.

OVERLEAF (PP.132 3) *Scenes from the Life of the Virgin*, mosaics in the 14th-century church of St. Savior in Chora (now Kariye Camii mosque), Istanbul, illustrating chapter 6 of the Protevangelium of James. On the left, Joachim and Anna resolve that Mary shall not walk on the ground until she has been presented in the Temple. On the right, the chief priests of Jerusalem bless Mary at a feast held by Joachim on her first birthday.

LEGENDS OF THE NATIVITY

In its original form, as the traditional name suggests, the Protevangelium of James may have dealt only with the birth and infancy of Mary. However, the existing text also has an account of the birth of Jesus, which expands and embellishes the narratives in the gospels of Matthew and Luke. Even here the emphasis is primarily on Mary and on the proof of her virginity.

According to this account, Jesus is born in a cave in the desert. Joseph goes to find a midwife, a figure who is present in some biblical birth stories, but her help is not needed and her role consists in bearing witness to the reality of the virgin birth. At this point, another character is introduced, Salome, who also seems to be depicted as a midwife. Salome (not to be confused with the figure in the story of John the Baptist) is briefly mentioned in the gospels (Mark 15.40, 16.1), but here she appears as a personality in her own right, the beginning of a development in which she was to assume an important role in some apocryphal gospels influenced by Gnostic thought (see pp.158–9). Salome doubts Mary's virginity and as she moves to examine her physically, her hand is "consumed by fire" and "falls away." Salome repents at once; an angel appears and tells her that she is forgiven and she is healed when she touches the baby Jesus. This passage, clearly an adaptation of the episode of Doubting Thomas (John 20.24–29), illustrates the increasing tendency of Christians to exalt Mary by transferring to her aspects of the life of Jesus.

In one interesting passage Joseph narrates how, on his way to find a midwife, the whole world came briefly to a complete standstill. This is to be understood as a miracle attesting the

---

The Family of Jesus

The New Testament gospels mention the brothers and sisters of Jesus, and it was easy to understand these as the natural children of Joseph and Mary. However, such a view created a problem when belief in Mary's perpetual virginity became common (see p.131) and various proposals were made to resolve it, probably the earliest of which is found in the Protevangelium. Here, Joseph is described as an ageing widower with sons by a former marriage who are adults at the time of Jesus' birth. This explanation was generally accepted until the great Latin scholar Jerome (ca. 342–420CE) argued—probably in order to advocate the perpetual virginity of Joseph as well as of Mary—that Jesus' brothers and sisters were in fact his cousins, the children of Mary's sister.

Jerome vigorously attacked the Protevangelium, which fell out of favor in the West. But its teaching on this particular question has always remained influential, especially its description of Joseph as an old man when Jesus was born.

The Nativity, a Byzantine fresco, ca. 1175, in the church of Karamlik Kilise, Cappadocia. It illustrates the apocryphal tradition that Mary gave birth in a cave attended by two midwives, including Salome.

From the Protevangelium of James, chapters 18 and 20

[Joseph] went out to look for a Hebrew midwife in the region of Bethlehem.

Now I, Joseph, was walking and yet I did not walk, and I looked up to the air and saw the air in amazement. And I looked up at the vault of heaven, and saw it standing still and the birds of the heaven motionless. And I looked at the earth, and saw a dish placed there and workmen lying round it, with their hands in the dish. But those who chewed did not chew, and those who lifted up anything lifted up nothing, and those who put something to their mouths put nothing to their mouths, but all had their faces turned upwards. And sheep were being driven and yet they did not come forward, but stood still; and the shepherd raised his hand to strike them with his staff, but his hand remained up. And I looked at the flow of the river, and saw the mouths of the kids over it and they did not drink. And then all at once everything went on its course again. ...

And the midwife went in and said to Mary: "Make yourself ready, for there is no small contention concerning you. And Salome put forward her finger to test her condition. And she cried out, saying: "Woe for my wickedness and my unbelief; for I have tempted the living God; and behold, my hand falls away from me, consumed by fire!" ... And an angel of the Lord stood [before her] and said to her: "Salome, God the Lord has heard your prayer. Stretch out your hand to the child and touch him, so will healing and joy be yours."

The Rest on the Flight into Egypt, by Joachim Patinir (ca. 1480–1524). The background depicts a medieval legend that Jesus miraculously ripened a newly sown field of wheat in order to outwit King Herod's troops. Hearing that the family had passed by when the field was sown, the soldiers abandoned their pursuit.

DATA

TITLE:
The Gospel of
Pseudo-Matthew

ORIGINAL DATE OF
COMPOSITION:
ca. 800 CE

ORIGINAL LANGUAGE:
Latin

PROVENANCE:
W. Europe

EARLIEST EXTANT
MANUSCRIPT:
14th cent. CE
(Latin)

supernatural character of the imminent birth of Jesus, which the whole universe awaits in breathless anticipation. The vision remains highly mysterious but it may have some connection with the Gnostic concept of the true nature of the celestial realm where the supreme heavenly figure, equated also with Christ and the Holy Spirit, often has the name "Silence."

A large number of "infancy gospels," collections of legends about the birth and early years of Jesus, were written in the period following the early Christian centuries. All of them borrow heavily from the Protevangelium of James and the Infancy Story of Thomas (see pp.138–9), sometimes removing the crude, offensive or theologically unsound features in both works that had led to the western Church's condemnation of the apocryphal literature from the 4th century CE. But more often, the infancy gospels expand their models with fresh material, especially on the holy family's sojourn in Egypt, an episode mentioned in neither the Protevangelium nor the Infancy Story and only briefly in the New Testament (Matt. 2.13–14, 19–21). Two compositions in particular witness to this interest in the Egyptian episode. The Arabic Gospel of the Infancy falls into three main sections. The first, dealing with the birth of Jesus, largely depends on the Protevangelium, and the third, recounting the miracles of the boy Jesus, is mainly borrowed from the Infancy Story. In between there is an extensive cycle of miracles performed in Egypt, a number of which reflect various local traditions. In all of them, Mary takes a leading part, as does the infant Jesus: he is said to know everything and is even able to foresee his crucifixion. Originally written in Syriac, the work was translated into Arabic when Christianity spread from Syria into the Arabian peninsula. The accounts it contains, not least those of the Egyptian sojourn, became known to the Arabs and many of them are echoed in the Quran.

A similar document is the Gospel of Pseudo-Matthew. It also relies heavily on the Protevangelium and the Infancy Story, to which it adds the first mention of the ox and ass at the manger, and it has its own lengthy account of miraculous events in Egypt. A comparatively late text, it represents an effort to collect together, in a more orthodox form, the legends which had become ever more popular among ordinary Christians and which official disapproval was unable to suppress. As such, Pseudo-Matthew is of great importance as the channel through which the legends of the infancy gospel tradition became widely current in the medieval West, where they enjoyed a profound influence on the art and literature of the whole period.

From the Arabic Gospel of the Infancy, chapters 23–24

Joseph and Mary came to a desert place, and when they heard that it was infested with raids by robbers, they decided to pass through this region by night. But on the way they saw two robbers lying on the road, and with them a crowd of robbers who belonged to them, also sleeping.

Now those two robbers, into whose hands they had fallen, were Titus and Dumachus. And Titus said to Dumachus, "I ask you to let these people go free, and in such a way that our companions do not observe them." But Dumachus refused and Titus said again, "Take from me forty drachmas and have them as a pledge." At the same time he reached him the girdle which he wore round him, that he might hold his tongue and not speak. When the noble lady Mary saw that this robber had shown kindness to them, she said to him,

"The Lord God will uphold you with his right hand and grant you forgiveness of sins." And the Lord Jesus spoke and said to his mother, "In thirty years, mother, the Jews will crucify me in Jerusalem, and those two robbers will be fastened to the cross with me, Titus on my right hand and Dumachus on my left, and after that day, Titus will go before me into paradise." And she said, "God preserve you from that, my son."

And they departed from there to the city of idols; and when they drew near it, they had been changed into sandhills. From there they went to that sycamore tree which today is called Matarea, and in Matarea the Lord Jesus made a spring gush forth, in which the lady Mary washed his shirt. And from the sweat of the Lord Jesus which she wrung out there, balsam appeared in that place.

DATA

TITLE:
The Arabic Gospel
of the Infancy

ORIGINAL DATE OF
COMPOSITION:
5th cent. CE?

ORIGINAL LANGUAGE:
Arabic
(from Syriac)

PROVENANCE:
Arabia

EARLIEST EXTANT
MANUSCRIPT:
Early medieval
(Arabic)

STORIES OF THE INFANT JESUS

Together with the Protevangelium of James, the Infancy Story of Thomas—also known as the Gospel of Thomas but not to be confused with the entirely different Gnostic Gospel of Thomas (see pp.166–7)—is the source of numerous later legends of Jesus' childhood. Attributed to the apostle Thomas, the Infancy Story can be seen as a kind of continuation of the Protevangelium, which ends with the birth of Jesus. It recounts events from Jesus' fifth year to the episode with the teachers in the Temple in his twelfth year, the only incident from Jesus' childhood recorded in the New Testament (Luke 2.41–49). It was natural that Christians should be curious about his life before that episode, during what have been described as his "hidden years."

The author's aim is to present the young child as an infant prodigy, a divine being already capable of all sorts of miracles. All these accounts are legendary: similar stories were commonplace in the ancient world and the author is clearly influenced by this widespread tradition. The boy Jesus is a miracle worker, acting in a setting of ordinary daily life, depicted in a succession of lively scenes. Some of his feats are little more than charming tales, as with the stories of his molding birds from clay and then bringing them to life, or of his lengthening a piece of wood to help Joseph finish a bed. As in the New Testament, Jesus is also a healer who can revive the dead. But other incidents show him as an altogether quite alarming being (see box, opposite).

Even as a child, Jesus is a great and learned teacher who possesses supernatural wisdom and knows far more than anyone can teach him. When a scholar sets out to teach him the alphabet, Jesus' obscure utterances show that he understands the inner magical secrets of the letters as the teacher does not. Here can be seen the beginnings of what were later to blossom into the speculations of the Gnostics.

Jesus Bringing Clay Sparrows to Life, from the church of Zangwill, Switzerland, 14th century. This apocryphal incident is first described in the Infancy Story of Thomas (see extract, opposite).

Malevolent Acts of Jesus

The Infancy Story of Thomas portrays the child Jesus as a boy of mysterious and dangerous power. His words can have harsh consequences when he is angered or feels insulted, as when he shrivels up one boy for a quite insignificant act and strikes another dead for merely bumping into him (see extract).

It is hard not to feel distaste at such stories, which seem so far removed from the Jesus of the canonical gospels, and one can even detect a degree of unease on the part of the author as he narrates them: while attempting to absolve Jesus from blame, he more than once records the great offense which Jesus' behavior caused, as well as the efforts of his parents to restrain him, as when Joseph asks Jesus: "Why do you do such things that these people must suffer and hate us and persecute us?" On another occasion Joseph tells Mary: "Do not let him go outside the door, for all those who provoke him die."

From the Infancy Story of Thomas, chapters 2–4

When this boy Jesus was five years old, he was playing at the ford of a brook, and he gathered together into pools the water that flowed by, and made it at once clean, and commanded it by his word alone.

He made soft clay and fashioned from it twelve sparrows. And it was the Sabbath when he did this and there were also many other children playing with him. ...

And when Joseph came to the place and saw it, he cried out to him, saying, "Why do you do on the Sabbath what ought not to be done?" But Jesus clapped his hands and cried to the sparrows, "Off with you!" And the sparrows took flight and went away chirping.

But the son of Annas the scribe was standing there with Joseph; and he took a branch of a willow and dispersed the water which Jesus had gathered together. When Jesus saw what he had done he was enraged and said to him, "You insolent, godless dunderhead, what harm did the pools and the water do to you? See, now you also shall wither like a tree and shall bear neither leaves nor root nor fruit."

And immediately that lad withered up completely. ... The parents of him that was withered took him away, bewailing his youth, and brought him to Joseph and reproached him, "What a child you have, who does such things."

After this again [Jesus] went through the village, and a lad ran and knocked against his shoulder. Jesus was exasperated and said to him, "You shall not go further on your way," and the child immediately fell down and died. But some, who saw what took place, said, "From where does this child spring, since his every word is an accomplished deed?"

And the parents of the dead child came to Joseph and blamed him and said, "Since you have such a child, you cannot dwell with us in the village; or else teach him to bless and not to curse. For he is slaying our children."

DATA

TITLE:
The Infancy Story of Thomas

ORIGINAL DATE OF COMPOSITION:
2nd cent. CE

ORIGINAL LANGUAGE:
Greek

PROVENANCE:
Palestine?

EARLIEST EXTANT MS:
ca. 500CE (Latin)

GOSPELS OF THE JEWISH CHRISTIANS

DATA

TITLE:
The Gospel of the
Hebrews

ORIGINAL DATE OF
COMPOSITION:
ca. 100–150CE

ORIGINAL LANGUAGE:
Uncertain

PROVENANCE:
Egypt?

EARLIEST EXTANT
MANUSCRIPT:
None

The important early theologians known as the Church Fathers sometimes quote from gospels used by Jewish Christians—Jews who believed in Christ as Messiah but continued to adhere to the requirements of Jewish law, including circumcision and food taboos. None of these works survives complete and their character has to be deduced from the quotations in the Church Fathers. They refer to a "Gospel of the Hebrews," a "Gospel of the Nazareans," and a "Gospel of the Ebionites," but it is unclear whether these are separate compositions or different names for the same work.

The name "Hebrews" probably indicates the Jewish Christians of Egypt, as distinct from the Gentile Christians of that country (who had their own gospel). In Acts 24.5, the apostle Paul is described as "a ringleader of the sect of the Nazareans," a Christian group within Judaism which retained many Jewish features and which, according to the theologians Epiphanius (ca. 315–403CE) and Jerome (ca. 342–420CE), still existed in Syria in their own time. The Nazareans were not regarded as heretics or out of fellowship with the Church, unlike the Ebionites, according to Epiphanius. He clearly distinguishes the Nazarean gospel from the Ebionite one, so it is perhaps most plausible to think of three separate Jewish Christian gospels, although there can be no certainty about the question. In any case, as representatives of Aramaic-speaking Jewish Christianity, they all have much in common. All of them are closely related to Matthew, the most Jewish of the canonical gospels, but they also exhibit

Mythological and Gnostic Influences

The Gospel of the Hebrews betrays the influence of mythological and Gnostic-type ideas which were perhaps especially characteristic of an Egyptian environment. The New Testament records both the pre-existence and incarnation of Jesus, concepts here transferred also to Mary, who is identified with "a mighty power" that descends from heaven. This "power," also called the archangel Michael, is in fact the Holy Spirit, and the Spirit is central to the Hebrew gospel's view of the person and nature of

Christ. At Jesus' baptism, which appears to have had a special significance for Jewish Christianity, he is proclaimed the son of the Spirit, who, as the source of prophetic inspiration, has long waited for him, and with whom he is now finally and fully united in a perfect "rest." After his temptations, Jesus is snatched away by the Holy Spirit, here explicitly described as his mother. The concept of the Spirit as female is distinctively Jewish, since, in Semitic languages, the word for "spirit" is a feminine noun.

St. James the Less with Saints Philip and Bernardine, by Carlo Crivelli (1435/40–93). St. James the Less (left), so called to distinguish him from St. James the Great, is commonly identified with Jesus' brother. He holds a fuller's club, the traditional instrument of his martyrdom, which probably took place in Jerusalem in 62CE.

syncretistic and mystical elements which are now known to be characteristic of certain circles in later Judaism and mark the beginnings of later Gnostic speculations. All these gospels are comparatively early, to be dated no later than the first half of the second century CE.

The Gospel of the Hebrews is perhaps best known from the evidence of Jerome, who refers to its frequent use by another writer, Origen (ca. 185–254CE), and claims to have translated it into Greek and Latin from the "Hebrew" (probably meaning Aramaic). Its importance lies mainly in the material it contains which seems independent of the New Testament. It displays a particular interest in James, the brother of Jesus, who according to the New Testament

Citations from the Gospel of the Hebrews

"When Christ wished to come upon the earth to humankind, the good Father summoned a mighty power in heaven, called Michael, and entrusted Christ to his care. And the power came into the world and it was called Mary, and Christ was in her womb seven months." (*Cited by Cyril of Jerusalem.*)

"When the Lord had come up out of the water, the whole fount of the Holy Spirit descended upon him and rested on him and said to him, 'My Son, in all the prophets was I waiting for you so that you should come and I might rest in you. For you are my rest; you are my first-born Son who reigns for ever.' " (*Cited by Jerome.*)

"My mother, the Holy Spirit, took me by one of my hairs and carried me away onto the great mountain Tabor." (*Cited by Origen.*)

"The Lord said, 'Bring a table and bread!' … He took the bread, blessed it, and broke it and gave it to James the Just and said to him, 'My brother, eat your bread, for the Son of Man is risen from among them that sleep.' " (*Cited by Jerome.*)

Ruins of ancient Pella in Jordan, to which the predominantly Jewish Christians of Jerusalem are reported to have fled before the destruction of the city in 70CE.

╬╬╬╬╬╬╬╬╬╬╬╬╬

DATA

TITLE:
The Gospel of the
Nazareans

ORIGINAL DATE OF
COMPOSITION:
ca. 100–150CE

ORIGINAL LANGUAGE:
Uncertain

PROVENANCE:
Syria?

EARLIEST EXTANT
MANUSCRIPT:
None

╬╬╬╬╬╬╬╬╬╬╬╬╬

was the head of the Jerusalem church and the leading advocate of those who, unlike Paul, wanted Christians to abide by the Jewish law, eventually presenting a compromise (Acts 15.13–21). Paul records an appearance of the risen Christ to James (1 Cor. 15.7), but only after Christ has appeared to others. However, in the Gospel of the Hebrews, James is the first and most important witness to the Resurrection and is also said to have been present at the Last Supper. In addition, James takes the place of the two men on the walk to Emmaus in Luke 24.

The Gospel of the Nazareans has no heretical features and consists largely of expansions and embellishments of the canonical Matthew (see box, opposite). Together with the Gospel of the Hebrews, it stands somewhat apart from the Gospel of the Ebionites, which clearly reveals the distinctive outlook and beliefs of a particular sect. The name "Ebionite" is derived from a Hebrew word meaning "poor," and the Ebionites, who were based in the Transjordanian region, viewed themselves as the successors to the "poor" in the biblical sense of those who adhered devoutly to the law and were persecuted by the "wicked" (Pss. 9.17–18, 10.9, 11.5, and many other examples). All that is known of the Ebionites comes from Epiphanius, who cites passages from their gospel to illustrate their "heretical" beliefs.

These beliefs included the denial of the virgin birth of Jesus. According to Epiphanius, the Ebionite gospel was a "forged and mutilated" form of Matthew that omitted Matthew's nativity stories. For the Ebionites, Jesus became the Son of God not at his birth but only at his baptism, when the Holy Spirit entered into him to unite his manhood with a celestial being. All this is in line with the main thrust of Jewish Messianism. Like the Jewish sect at Qumran that produced the Dead Sea Scrolls, the Ebionites were hostile to the ritual practices of the Jerusalem Temple, and the Ebionite gospel shows Jesus as abolishing the Jewish sacrificial system. The Ebionites were also vegetarians, and their gospel removes Matthew's reference to locusts as part of John the Baptist's diet (Matt. 3.4), and makes Jesus implicitly deny that he will eat the Passover lamb.

DATA

TITLE:
The Gospel of the Ebionites

ORIGINAL DATE OF COMPOSITION:
ca. 100–150CE

ORIGINAL LANGUAGE:
Greek

PROVENANCE:
Transjordan?

EARLIEST EXTANT MANUSCRIPT:
None

Citations by Epiphanius from the Gospel of the Ebionites

"When the people were baptized, Jesus also came and was baptized by John. And as he came up from the water, the heavens opened and he saw the Holy Spirit in the form of a dove descend and enter into him. And a voice sounded from heaven that said, 'You are my beloved Son, in you I am well pleased.' And again, 'I have this day begotten you.' And immediately a great light shone round about."

"[The Ebionites] say that Christ was not begotten of God the Father, but created as one of the archangels ... and that he came and declared, as their gospel ... reports, 'I am come to do away with sacrifices, and if you cease not from sacrificing, the wrath of God will not cease from you.' "

"[The Ebionites] ... let the disciples say [to Jesus], 'Where will we prepare the Passover for you?' And him to answer, 'Do I desire at this Passover to eat flesh with you?' "

The Gospel of the Nazareans

Epiphanius says that the Nazareans used a Hebrew or Aramaic version of Matthew. The ways in which the Nazarean gospel develops the canonical text can be seen in the story of the rich young man (Matt. 19.16–22), where the Nazarean gospel has two rich men and introduces social and ethical motifs, and in the detail that the man with a withered hand (Matt. 12.10–13) was a stonemason. The Nazarean gospel says that at the time of the Crucifixion it was not the veil of the Temple (Matt. 27.51) that split but rather its huge lintel, a tradition also found in Josephus. The gospel also has an interesting interpretation of the obscure Greek word *epiousion* ("supersubstantial") in the Lord's Prayer. Jerome records that in the Nazarean gospel "instead of 'supersubstantial bread' I found *mahar*, meaning 'of tomorrow,' so that the sense is 'Give us this day our bread of tomorrow,' that is, of the future." This interpretation has proved attractive to many commentators and is sometimes given as an alternative in modern Bibles.

CHAPTER 2
GOSPELS OF THE PASSION
◆
THE GOSPEL OF PETER

Alongside the infancy gospels there is a category of "Passion gospels" which show similar features and legendary developments, but deal with the conclusion of Jesus' earthly life. The earliest of these works is the Gospel of Peter, to which several of the Church Fathers (see p.140) refer. It was lost for many centuries until a fragment missing the beginning and end was discovered in Egypt in the late nineteenth century.

The first known witness to the work is Serapion, bishop of Antioch (died ca. 211CE), who knew of a copy of it in the church of Rhossus in Asia Minor, where some of the congregation had asked for it to be read in public worship. At the latest, therefore, the gospel dates from 150–200CE, but it should probably be dated considerably earlier. Serapion says that the original authors were "Docetists," who were not so much a distinct sect but rather represented a widespread tendency which played down the reality of Christ's humanity.

Docetism saw his manhood, sufferings, and death as apparent rather than real, anticipating aspects of later Gnostic speculations.

There are certainly features of the Gospel of Peter which lend credence to Serapion's view. Christ's word from the cross in the canonical gospels, "My God, my God, why have you forsaken me?" (Mark 15.34, Matt. 27.46), appears as "My power, my power, you have forsaken me!" This is followed by the words "And having said this, he was taken up." This may illustrate the view that the person of Christ was constituted by a union of a heavenly "power" with the man Jesus, and only when this power left him could the human body die. Again, on the cross, Jesus is said to have remained silent, "as if he felt no pain," perhaps indicating that his sufferings were only apparent. A remarkable passage depicts the

The Crucifixion with Scenes of Christ's Passion, Italian, Tuscan school, ca. 1175.

cross as walking and speaking after the Resurrection, which certainly recalls later Gnostic statements about the nature of the cross (see extract, below). But it is probably going too far to label such features in the Gospel of Peter as "Gnostic": rather they should be seen as concepts which later thinkers could seize upon and develop in their own way.

Although the gospel is presented as the direct testimony of Peter, it shows little accurate knowledge of Palestine in Jesus' time. It diverges notably from the canonical gospels, even Matthew, to which it is most closely related. The Crucifixion is blamed entirely on the Jews: Pilate is entirely whitewashed and actually witnesses to Jesus as God's son. Herod, not Pilate, condemns Jesus to death, after which Pilate hands him over to the "people," and it is they, not the Roman soldiers, who mock and scourge him, crucify him, and cast lots for his clothing. According to the gospel, Jesus' legs are left unbroken "so that he might die in agony" and not because he is already dead (John 19.33). There is no mention of the desertion of the disciples, who here remain faithful, fasting and mourning in memory of their Lord. Uniquely, this work reports that the Resurrection took place openly in the middle of the night in the presence of the Roman soldiers and the Jewish leaders. The Resurrection and Ascension are a single event, and, at least in the text as it stands, there are no appearances of the risen Jesus to the apostles.

Most scholars view the Gospel of Peter as essentially a reworking and expansion of the canonical accounts of the Passion. However, its numerous divergences from the New Testament mean that it should perhaps be assessed in its own right as evidence of a strand of early Christianity with a somewhat different outlook from that which eventually became Church orthodoxy.

From the Gospel of Peter, verses 31–42

Pilate [ordered] Petronius the centurion and some soldiers to watch the tomb. And with them there came elders and scribes to the tomb. And all who were there, together with the centurion and the soldiers, rolled a great stone and laid it against the entrance to the tomb and put on it seven seals, pitched a tent, and kept watch. ...

Now in the night in which the Lord's day dawned, when the soldiers ... were keeping guard, a loud voice rang out in heaven, and they saw the heavens open and two men came down from there in great brightness. The stone which had been laid against the entrance to the tomb began to roll of its own accord ... and the tomb was opened, and both the young men entered. When the soldiers saw this, they woke the centurion and the elders, for they also were there to assist at the watch. They saw again three men came out from the tomb, two of them sustaining the other, and a cross following them, and the heads of the two reaching to heaven, but that of him whom they led by the hand over-passing the heavens. And they heard a voice out of the heavens crying, "Have you preached to them that sleep?" and from the cross there was heard the answer, "Yes."

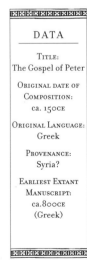

DATA

TITLE:
The Gospel of Peter

ORIGINAL DATE OF
COMPOSITION:
ca. 150CE

ORIGINAL LANGUAGE:
Greek

PROVENANCE:
Syria?

EARLIEST EXTANT
MANUSCRIPT:
ca.800CE
(Greek)

THE GOSPEL OF NICODEMUS

The Gospel of Nicodemus, also known as the Acts of Pilate, claims to be a translation of an account of Christ's Passion written in Hebrew by Nicodemus, who appears only in the Gospel of John as visiting Jesus secretly and later assisting at his burial. Pilate figures only in the opening chapters and disappears from the rest of the document.

The work's main aim is to provide indisputable proof of the Resurrection and, especially, the ascension of Jesus. This accounts for the prominence in the narrative of Nicodemus and Joseph of Arimathea—the only two of Jesus' followers referred to—because they were both leading members of the Jewish community and thus trustworthy witnesses. The version of Jesus' trial before Pilate places the responsibility for his fate on the Jewish chief priests and scribes. However, the author is careful to stress that many ordinary Jews revered Jesus and were prepared to speak on his behalf. A central accusation against Jesus—also found in the canonical gospels—is that he was a sorcerer, whose miracles were the work of evil spirits. This charge is refuted by witnesses who have been healed by a simple word from Jesus, without any magical incantations. A second slander is that Jesus was the child of illicit intercourse. The issue is not the Virgin Birth: the gospel seems to take it for granted that Jesus was the natural son of Joseph and Mary, leading some scholars to propose an Ebionite background for the work (see p.142–3). The problem

---

From the Gospel of Nicodemus, chapter 2

The elders of the Jews said to Jesus, "What should we see? Firstly, that you were born of fornication; secondly, that your birth meant the death of the children in Bethlehem; thirdly, that your father Joseph and your mother Mary fled into Egypt because they counted for nothing among the people." Then declared some of the Jews that stood by, devout men, "We deny that he came of fornication, for we know that Joseph was betrothed to Mary, and he was not born of fornication." Pilate then said to the Jews who said that he came of fornication, "Your statement is not true; for there was a betrothal, as your own fellow countrymen say." Annas and Caiaphas said to Pilate ... "These are proselytes and disciples of his." And Pilate called to him Annas and Caiaphas and said to them, "What are proselytes?" They answered, "They were born children of Greeks, and now have become Jews." Then said those who said that he was not born of fornication, [twelve men,] "We are not proselytes, but are children of Jews and speak the truth; for we were present at the betrothal of Joseph and Mary."

OPPOSITE *The Lamentation*, by Roger van der Weyden (1399/1400–1464). Nicodemus and Joseph of Arimathea support the body of Christ, alongside the Virgin (left), Mary Magdalene, and John.

The Anastasis (Resurrection), a late 14th-century Russian icon of the Novgorod School. Taking Adam—who is surrounded by other biblical figures—by the hand, Christ leads the dead out of hell.

is Mary's pregnancy before her marriage to Joseph, but this is justified when it is proved that the couple were betrothed—by Jewish custom, a betrothal permitted a couple to have intercourse before their formal wedding.

Pilate and the Romans appear throughout in a favorable light. Pilate attributes Jesus' casting out of demons not to an evil spirit but to Asclepius, or Aesculapius, the benevolent Greco-Roman god of healing, and he cites the history of Israel to condemn the Jews. Pilate's famous question, "What is truth?" (John 18.38), which in John goes unanswered, is here expanded into a dialogue. Jesus replies, "Truth is from heaven" and Pilate then asks, "Is there not truth upon earth?" and receives the stinging retort, "You see how those who speak the truth are judged by those who have authority on earth." The messenger sent to summon Jesus to Pilate—there is no trace of a forcible arrest—is instructed to bring him "with gentleness" and spreads his kerchief on the ground for Jesus to walk upon. When Jesus enters the governor's palace, the images of the emperor on the Roman standards miraculously bow down before him. Pilate's wife is described as a God-fearer who favors the customs of the Jews.

The gospel attaches a legend about Joseph of Arimathea. He is imprisoned by the Jews for having given the body of Jesus an honorable burial, but when they come to execute him his cell is empty. Joseph is discovered safe and sound in his hometown. He returns in triumph to Nicodemus in Jerusalem and gives an account of his escape to the high priests. The Jews remain divided in their attitude to Jesus, but there is a final psalm of penitence and praise.

Attached to the Gospel of Nicodemus is an account of Christ's descent to the underworld. Originally a separate work, it probably predates the gospel, because speculation about Jesus' descent became popular among Christians from an early period (see box, opposite). The two works were perhaps linked because of the prominence in both of Nicodemus and Joseph of Arimathea. Christ descends to Hades, which—as in Greek myth—is primarily a person rather than

---

The Influence of Christ's Descent into Hell

The account of Christ's descent into hell in the Gospel of Nicodemus is the earliest written example of a theme with its roots in two brief New Testament passages. The First Letter of Peter states that Jesus made a proclamation to "the spirits in prison" (1 Pet. 3.19), while Matthew tells of a mass resurrection after Jesus himself has risen (Matt. 27.53). The legend, which was also influenced by Psalm 24 (see main text), exerted a profound influence on medieval Christianity. For theologians, it explained how the great biblical figures who lived before Jesus and prophesied his coming were finally able to share in the salvation which he alone brought. Its dramatic scenes also captured the popular imagination and inspired writers and artists. In the West, the descent is known as the Harrowing of Hell or Descent into Limbo; in the East, it forms part of the depiction of the Resurrection (see opposite and pp.150–51).

---

a place. He is a stern jailer but not evil, and his realm is simply the destination of all the dead and not a region of eternal torments for the damned, like the later Christian concept of hell. Behind this presentation of the underworld lies the Hebrew Sheol, the home of the departed, which the Bible describes as a gloomy city beneath the earth, surrounded by bars and gates. Against Hades stands Satan, who seeks to prevent Jesus from releasing the inhabitants of the underworld, but is himself finally consigned to Hades, who is thus seen to act under the authority of Christ.

The descent narrative begins with a scene in which Joseph of Arimathea mentions that many were raised from the dead along with Jesus, referring specifically to the two sons of the aged Simeon, "who took Jesus in his arms" (Luke 2.28). The Jewish leaders find them and demand to know how they had risen from the grave and the brothers write an account that takes up the remainder of the work. The two were in the underworld with "all who have died from the beginning of the world" when a bright light illuminated the darkness. The biblical prophets and patriarchs, together with John the Baptist and Adam, joyfully recognize this as heralding the advent of the Savior, but Satan appears and tells Hades that Jesus is only another dead man who is due to join all the other dead. However, a loud voice utters the words of Psalm 24.7 (23.7 in the Septuagint): "Lift up your gates, O rulers ... and the King of glory shall come in." The gates and bars of the underworld are crushed, Jesus enters (see pp.150–51), the dead are freed, and Satan is handed over to Hades for a grisly fate. Finally, Christ brings all the departed, with Adam at their head, into paradise, where they meet Enoch and Elijah, who had already ascended to heaven, and the penitent thief who was crucified with Jesus and had gone directly to paradise. At the end of the work the two sons of Simeon relate what had happened to them after their own resurrection before finally departing from the earth.

DATA

TITLE:
The Gospel of Nicodemus

ORIGINAL DATE OF COMPOSITION:
2nd–4th cent. CE

ORIGINAL LANGUAGE:
Greek

PROVENANCE:
Uncertain

EARLIEST EXTANT MANUSCRIPT:
5th cent. CE
(Greek)

From the Gospel of Nicodemus, chapters 5–7: The Descent into Hell

Again the voice sounded, "Lift up the gates." When Hades heard the voice the second time, he answered as if he did not know it and said, *"Who is this King of glory?¹"* The angels of the Lord said, *"The Lord strong and mighty, the Lord mighty in battle.²"* And immediately at this answer the gates of brass were broken in pieces and the bars of iron were crushed and all the dead who were bound were loosed from their chains, and we with them. And the King of glory entered in like a man, and all the dark places of Hades were illumined. ...

Then the King of glory seized the chief ruler Satan by the head and handed him over to the angels, saying, "Bind with iron fetters his hands and his feet and his neck and his mouth." Then he gave him to Hades and said, "Take him and hold him fast until my second coming." And Hades took Satan and said to him, ... "Turn and see that not one dead man is left in me, but that all which you gained through the tree of knowledge you have lost through the tree of the cross. ... You wished to kill the King of glory, but have killed yourself. ... you shall learn by experience what evils I shall inflict upon you. O arch-devil, the beginning of death, the root of sin, the summit of all evil, what evil did you find in Jesus that you went about to destroy him?"

¹Ps.24.10   ²Ps.24.8

The Descent into Limbo, by the Master of the Osservanza, Italian, ca. 1440–44. Satan lies crushed beneath the gates of the underworld as Christ, bearing the banner of the Resurrection, prepares to lead out Adam and other holy figures.

THE REPORT AND DEATH OF PILATE

DATA

TITLE:
The Anaphora
(Report) of Pilate

ORIGINAL DATE OF
COMPOSITION:
2nd cent. CE?

ORIGINAL LANGUAGE:
Greek

PROVENANCE:
Uncertain

EARLIEST EXTANT
MANUSCRIPT:
Early medieval
(Latin)

Early Christians showed considerable interest in Pontius Pilate and there are many apocryphal writings about him. In all of them, there is an increasing tendency—already apparent in the canonical gospels—to exonerate him for the death of Christ. The most important of these texts is his supposed report to the emperor about the fate of Jesus.

Roman governors were expected to submit reports to Rome about important events in their regions, but for the real Pilate one executed Jew among many would not have merited such imperial attention. For Christians, of course, the Crucifixion was an event of supreme and universal significance and some such report was probably invented at a very early period. The extant work has the Greek title Anaphora ("Report") and is addressed to the emperor Claudius (reigned 41–54CE) rather than the historically correct Tiberius (reigned 14–37CE). The Report largely reproduces the narrative of the Descent into Hell (see pp.148–51). Attached to it is another text known as the Paradosis ("Handing Over") of Pilate, one of a number of works which speculate on his fate. Pilate disappeared from history in 36CE, when he returned to Rome from Judea to answer serious charges brought against him by the Samaritans. This fact may be loosely recalled in the Paradosis, in which the emperor summons Pilate to Rome and interrogates him before the Senate about the death of Jesus. In spite of his attempt to shift the blame onto the Jews, Pilate is condemned to death and executed—but not before he has expressed repentance for his deeds (see box, below).

Pilate: Saint and Villain

A striking feature of the Report of Pilate is the description of how Pilate meets his death. He appears as virtually a Christian, who prays to Jesus for forgiveness for himself and his wife Procla. A voice from heaven assures him that he will be among the blessed, and when he is beheaded his head is taken up by an angel. This highly favorable picture of Pilate is representative of the general tradition of Eastern Christendom: in the Coptic Church, Pilate and his wife Procla are honored as saints and martyrs.

A very different view of Pilate prevails in the Western tradition. In three Latin accounts of his death, as well as in the famous medieval collection The Golden Legend by Jacobus de Voragine, he is regarded as merely a criminal in the grip of evil. In one version of the story the emperor compels him to commit suicide, after which his corpse is flung into the Tiber, where it is surrounded by demons. Only after various adventures does his body find a resting place in the Alps, where a mountain by Lake Lucerne bears his name, Mount Pilatus.

From the Paradosis of Pilate, chapters 8–10

Caesar questioned Pilate, and commanded an officer called Albius to behead him, saying, "As this man raised his hand against the righteous man called Christ, so shall he fall in the same way, and find no deliverance." And when Pilate came to the place of execution, he prayed silently, "Lord, do not destroy me with the wicked Hebrews, for it was through the lawless nation of the Jews that I raised my hand against you, because they plotted a revolt against me. You know that I acted in ignorance. Therefore do not condemn me because of this sin, but pardon me, Lord, and your servant Procla, who stands with me in this hour of my death, whom you made to prophesy that you must be nailed to the cross. Do not condemn her also because of my sin, but pardon us and number us among your righteous ones." And behold, when Pilate had finished his prayer, there sounded a voice from heaven, "All generations and families of the Gentiles shall call you blessed, because in your governorship all was fulfilled which the prophets foretold about me."

DATA

TITLE:
The Paradosis
(Handing Over)
of Pilate

ORIGINAL DATE OF
COMPOSITION:
2nd cent. CE?

ORIGINAL LANGUAGE:
Greek

PROVENANCE:
Uncertain

EARLIEST EXTANT
MANUSCRIPT:
Early medieval
(Latin)

Pilate Washing His Hands (left) and *The Mocking of Christ* (right), from an Armenian manuscript of the gospels illuminated by Youhannes de Berkri in 1392.

THE GOSPEL OF BARTHOLOMEW

The Gospel of Bartholomew is the most important and complete of the numerous apocryphal writings ascribed to Bartholomew. The New Testament merely lists him as one of the twelve apostles and records nothing further about him. This opened the way for later authors to use his name as a vehicle for their own ideas.

The gospel may be classed as a "Passion gospel," although it is set entirely in the period after Jesus' resurrection. In the manuscripts, the work is called The Questions of Bartholomew and this describes its character. In the first chapter, he asks Jesus where he went when he disappeared from the cross and he is given an account of the descent into hell, ending with a curious discussion about the number of people who die every day and how many of their souls reach paradise. In the second chapter, it is Mary who is questioned about the circumstances of the Incarnation and her reply centers on an account of the Annunciation. Mary is described in highly exalted language and, although she several times asserts male superiority and her unworthiness to speak compared with the apostles, her pre-eminence and the supreme honor owing to her are made plain.

The following chapter has the apostles asking Jesus to show them the bottomless pit of the underworld and being duly terrified by the sight. In chapter four, Bartholomew asks to be shown the devil, named as Beliar and Satan, who reveals to the apostle the secrets of cosmic geography and the angels. The devil also gives an entertaining account of how he and his minions entrap and punish sinners. Finally, Bartholomew asks Jesus about the deadly sins and he and the other apostles are endowed with the Holy Spirit in order to instruct human beings how to avoid them.

St. Bartholomew, an Italian painted panel of ca. 1360–65. He holds a flaying knife, the traditional instrument of his martyrdom.

It has been claimed that the book reflects Gnostic concepts, but in reality there is little in the work to justify this claim. Like the Gospel of Bartholomew, many of the Gnostic gospels take the form of a series of questions to the risen Jesus by his followers, but all such works may be independent expansions of the New Testament, which states that the disciples interrogated Jesus after his resurrection. Much more convincing is the theory that the Gospel of Bartholomew shows the influence of Docetism, an early heresy which claimed that Jesus was a heavenly "power" with only the appearance of human form. In the gospel, Jesus vanishes from the cross to descend to Hades, and this may refer to the idea of the "power." The work also says that Jesus received sacrifices in paradise even when he was on earth, which may reflect the Docetic notion that Christ was constituted by the union of a man and a heavenly being.

However, there is also much in the work which seems to place it within the regular life and worship of the early Church. For example, it echoes liturgical language, not least in the great veneration of Mary, and features in the narrative of the Annunciation may well point to the sacraments of baptism and the eucharist (see extract, below).

From the Gospel of Bartholomew, chapters 2 and 4

[Mary] began, "When I lived in the temple of God and received my food from the hand of an angel, one day there appeared to me one in the form of an angel; but his face was indescribable. ... And I looked toward heaven; and there came a cloud of dew on my face and sprinkled me from head to foot, and the angel wiped me with his robe. Then he said to me, 'Hail, you who are highly favored, the chosen vessel.' And then he struck the right side of his garment and there came forth an exceedingly large loaf, and he placed it upon the altar of the temple, and first ate of it himself and then gave to me also. And again he struck his garment, on the left side, and I looked and saw a cup full of wine. And he placed it upon the altar of the temple, and drank from it first himself and gave it also to me. And I looked and saw that the bread did not diminish and the cup was full as before. Then he said, 'Three years more, and I will send my word and you shall conceive my son, and through him the whole world shall be saved. But you will bring salvation to the world.' " ...

Peter said to Mary, "You who are favored, ask the Lord to reveal to us all that is in the heavens." And Mary answered Peter, "O rock hewn above, did not the Lord build his church upon you? You therefore should be the first to go and ask him. ... You are the image of Adam. Was he not formed first and then Eve? Look at the sun. It shines like Adam. Look at the moon. It is full of clay, because Eve transgressed the commandment. For God placed Adam in the east and Eve in the west, and he commanded the two lights to shine, so that the sun with its fiery chariot should shine on Adam in the east and the moon in the west should shine on Eve its milk-white light. But she defiled the Lord's commandment, and therefore the moon became soiled, and its light does not gleam."

DATA

TITLE:
The Gospel of Bartholomew

ORIGINAL DATE OF COMPOSITION:
3rd cent. CE

ORIGINAL LANGUAGE:
Greek

PROVENANCE:
Possibly Egypt

EARLIEST EXTANT MANUSCRIPT:
Early medieval (Greek)

CHAPTER 3
GNOSTIC MYSTERIES

◆

THE GNOSTIC HERESY

"Gnosticism" is a modern name given by scholars to a religious movement which—whatever its ultimate origins—emerged as a Christian heresy during the first three centuries CE and was particularly important and widespread in the second century CE. It was a highly individual system of belief, and embraced a bewildering variety of ideas and speculations which cannot easily be harmonized into a coherent system.

Irenaeus, bishop of Lyons (ca. 180CE), provides the earliest detailed account of a number of Gnostic groups and says of just one of them: "You can hardly find two or three people who agree on anything." Nevertheless, it is possible to some extent to construct a general picture of an underlying Gnostic belief system. The word Gnosticism derives from the Greek word *gnosis*, meaning "knowledge." All religions seek to convey the true knowledge of the divine, the world,

The Rediscovery of the Gnostics

As a result of the efforts of the early Church, Gnostic beliefs and practices largely disappeared from the Christian community after the fourth century CE and for a long period the Gnostics were known only from descriptions and quotations from Gnostic books in the writings of the Church Fathers. This meant that Gnosticism was only viewed through the eyes of its opponents.

It was only in the nineteenth century that discoveries made available some original texts from the Gnostics themselves. However, the most dramatic breakthrough came in 1945 with the discovery of a large collection of Gnostic writings at Nag Hammadi in Upper Egypt. They are all in Coptic, the Egyptian language, and date from the fourth century CE, but it is generally accepted that they are translations of earlier Greek originals. This discovery has brought about a new understanding and appreciation of the whole significance of the Gnostic movement. The Nag Hammadi texts show how complex Gnosticism was, since they represent a wide variety of literary forms and theological speculations. They also suggest that one of the reasons for the wide appeal of Gnosticism was that it incorporated an extensive range of influences drawn not only from Christian tradition, but also from the broader Near Eastern religious background, particularly Judaism. Some of the texts show no trace of Christian beliefs and may even indicate the existence of a pre-Christian Gnosticism.

and human nature. "Knowledge" is a vital concept in the New Testament, and the theologian Clement of Alexandria (ca. 150–215CE) uses the term "gnostic" in a general sense to describe a Christian who has acquired an especially deep knowledge of truth. The Gnostics had a distinctive understanding of religious knowledge, but the Church Fathers considered their beliefs to be false and heretical and saw them as a serious threat to the emerging Christian orthodoxy.

The Gnostics were concerned above all with how human beings might find salvation. They taught that there is an absolute division between the material world and the transcendent God, and they rejected the Hebrew Bible, with its teaching that the material universe was made by the one creator deity. In the most influential Gnostic groups, the "divine" is not a monotheistic unity but is made up of an evolving succession of beings called "aeons," or divine emanations, which together form the Pleroma, or "divine fullness." (By contrast, Paul identifies the Pleroma with Christ.) One of these aeons, often viewed as the Jewish God, goes astray and this separation produces the cosmos, which—totally unlike the divine realm—is a region of confusion and error, in which humanity is enmeshed.

An understanding of the true underlying nature of all existence is one part of what the Gnostics meant by "knowledge." Another is self-knowledge. Human beings in their true

DATA

TITLE:
The Gospel of the Egyptians

ORIGINAL DATE OF COMPOSITION:
ca. 100–150CE

ORIGINAL LANGUAGE:
Greek

PROVENANCE:
Probably Egypt

EARLIEST EXTANT MANUSCRIPT:
None

OPPOSITE A view across the Nile at Nag Hammadi in Egypt, where an ancient Gnostic library was found in 1945.

The Gospel of the Egyptians

One relatively early text with clear Gnostic characteristics is the Gospel of the Egyptians (ca. 100–150CE). The main source for this work—not to be confused with a book of the same title from Nag Hammadi—is Clement of Alexandria, whose brief citations suggest that it took the typically Gnostic form of a series of questions put to Jesus by his followers, notably Salome. She was a witness of the Crucifixion and Resurrection (Mark 15.40–41, 16.1) and was an important figure in Gnostic circles.

The gospel seems to have been used in place of the canonical gospels by various groups in Egypt, in particular an ascetic sect called the Encratites, which took a negative view of sex and marriage—most Gnostics regarded sexuality as a sign of enslavement to the world of matter. Clement's extracts seem to imply that when people recognize their divine nature, the distinction between the sexes which belongs to the material world is abolished (see extract, opposite).

nature—the spirit or the inner person—are divine, at one with the supreme divinity, but they are weighed down by a material body and do not recognize their divine nature. For Gnostics, salvation is the realization of the truth about oneself, which frees the individual from enslavement by the created world and restores a lost union, not to say identity, with the divine.

For the Gnostics, Christ comes to earth to reveal to human beings the truth about themselves: his teaching, rather than his miracles, death, and resurrection, is the means of salvation. The Gnostic Christ appears in spiritual form as a heavenly Redeemer, and Gnostic writings do not concern themselves with what could be described as "the historical Jesus." Those Gnostic texts that have some relation to the canonical gospels and New Testament aim to interpret the deeper, hidden meaning of the sayings of Jesus and other New Testament texts. Some Gnostic writings claimed that the special knowledge was a secret teaching which Jesus had given to his disciples in the period between his resurrection and ascension, and which continued to be handed down, in both written and oral form, among "those who know"—a privileged esoteric group who enjoyed a revelation denied to ordinary believers.

Such a brief summary can only be a very inadequate account of this complicated subject, but it is perhaps sufficient to show why Gnosticism was so firmly combated by those promoting what was to become Christianity. Owing to the discovery of the Gnostic library at Nag Hammadi (see box on p.157), Gnosticism can now be viewed much more positively than it often was in the past, when it appeared as a strange and outlandish heresy. It was a belief system in its own right which offered a resolution of the human predicament and a promise of dignity and freedom from the toils of existence. Gnostic writings often express the joy and hope which Gnostics experienced when they felt they had awakened, as from a bad dream, from the illusions of the material world.

Clement of Alexandria on the Gospel of the Egyptians

When Salome asked when that which she had inquired about would be known, the Lord said, "When you have trampled on the garment of shame and when the two become one and the male with the female is neither male nor female." Now ... we have not this word in the four gospels that have been handed down to us, but in the Gospel of the Egyptians. ...

When Salome asked, "How long will death have power?" the Lord answered, "So long as you women bear children"—not as if life was something bad and creation evil, but as teaching the sequence of nature: for in all cases birth is followed by decay. ...

Those who are opposed to God's creation because of continence, which has a fair-sounding name, also quote the words addressed to Salome which I mentioned earlier. ... Why do they not also adduce what follows the words spoken to Salome? ... For when she said, "I have then done well in not bearing children," as if it were improper to engage in procreation, then the Lord answered and said, "Eat every plant, but that which has bitterness eat not."

The Victory of Light over Darkness, a 4th-century mosaic from Aquileia, Italy, symbolizing the victory of Church orthodoxy (the cock, which heralds the light) over heresy at the Council of Nicea (Iznik, Turkey) in 325CE.

THE GOSPEL OF TRUTH

One of the most attractive of the Gnostic manuscripts from Nag Hammadi (see p.157) is known, from its opening words, as the Gospel of Truth. It is important as one of the fullest surviving accounts of the essential character of Gnosticism, and it is also of considerable literary quality, far superior in this respect to most other Gnostic writing. In deeply moving and often rhapsodical language, it conveys the utter joy and release which Gnostic believers found in the truth revealed to them.

According to Bishop Irenaeus, a book called the Gospel of Truth had recently been produced, as a sort of fifth gospel, by a group called the Valentinians (see box on p.162), and scholars are generally agreed that the Nag Hammadi text is a Valentinian composition. The Gospel of Truth contains no connected narrative of the life and deeds of Jesus (although it refers to a number of individual episodes) and does not quote any of his sayings, nor does it have the form common to other Gnostic gospels of secret teaching given by Jesus to a chosen group of disciples. It is much more like a sermon or lecture, punctuated by direct exhortation to the hearers and clos-

Valentinian Gnosticism (see p.162) was characterized by esoteric initiation rituals similar to those of mystery religions. A rite of one such group, the Eleusinians, is depicted in this 1st century CE Roman mosaic.

ing with a heartfelt personal testimony from the author himself. Its opening words summarize its whole theme: it is a message of "discovery" of one's true self, which comes from the knowledge of the supreme God, the Father, revealed through Jesus, the Father's intimate Word, who brings redemption for lost humanity and the consequent promise of joy and hope.

The book can be viewed as a meditation on the Christian Gospel, to bring out its deeper meaning in the light of the author's own distinctive theology. It assumes a knowledge of much of the New Testament, especially the four gospels, and refers to Christ's meeting with the Temple teachers, his confrontations with the Pharisees, to the little children as the recipients of revelation, to the Crucifixion (see extract below), to the parable of the lost sheep, and to the freeing of the sheep from a pit on the Sabbath (see extract on p.163). For the author, those who oppose Jesus represent those unable to respond to the truth, in contrast to the little children, who represent the true Gnostic believers. The Crucifixion is Jesus' unveiling of the living book, in which the names of the chosen are written, and the death of the immortal Savior is only apparent. The reference to the parable of the lost sheep includes a numerological interpretation that is known from Irenaeus to have been current among the Valentinians. The release of the sheep on the Sabbath becomes the release and enlightenment of the individual Gnostic.

The Gospel of Truth lacks any orderly, systematic arrangement. Rather it consists of a number of themes to which the author returns throughout the work. He propounds the teaching, common to all Gnostic systems, of the absolute division between the fundamentally evil created world and the transcendent realm of the essentially unknowable Father. The material world is

From the Gospel of Truth, pages 19–20

In the midst of a school he appeared and proclaimed the Word, even as a Master. There came to him those who were wise in their own hearts, putting him to the proof. But he convinced them that they were empty. They hated him, for they were not truly wise.

Following in their turn, came the little children to whom belongs the *gnosis* of the Father. When they had been confirmed in their faith, they learned to contemplate the aspects of the face of the Father. They knew and were known. They were glorified and they glorified. The living Book of the Living, which was written in the Thought and in the Mind of the Father, manifested itself in their hearts. ... the merciful, the faithful Jesus patiently accepted the endurance of suffering until he had received the Book, since he knew that his death meant life for many. ... For this reason Jesus appeared and took that Book for himself. He was nailed to a cross of wood and attached the decree of the Father upon the cross. O great, sublime Teaching! He humbled himself even to death, although he was clothed with eternal life. After he had stripped off these perishable rags, he clothed himself in incorruptibility, which no one can take away from him.

Valentinianism

Valentinus, the most influential Gnostic figure of his day, was active in Rome ca. 140–160CE. His teaching attracted numerous followers, and made him the chief heretic in the eyes of the Church. Valentinus systematized the body of Gnostic speculations into a basic coherent theology, although this was much developed and modified by his disciples. His concept of the spiritual world was an evolutionary one, consisting of a succession of male and female pairs of aeons which constituted the Pleroma or "divine fullness" (see p.157).

Like many thinkers, Valentinus was concerned with the problem of evil. For him evil was embodied in the material world, which had been brought about by the defection of one of the aeons, the female Sophia. Together with a being known as the Demiurge—often identified with the God of the Hebrew Bible—Sophia had caused the creation of this world.

Valentinus and his followers also provided Gnosticism with an organizational structure, in many ways an alternative Church. Salvific knowledge, or *gnosis*, was conveyed through a process of initiation involving both doctrinal instruction and esoteric rituals similar to those of Greco-Roman mystery religions. These varied among different Valentinian groups, but there are references to a second baptism for a chosen few and to an obscure ceremony which took place in the "bridal chamber."

---

the creation of Error, one of the "aeons" that make up the Pleroma (see p.157) and this seems to be a version of the central Valentinian myth of the fall of Sophia and the role of the Demiurge, the creator deity. The setting for human existence is not so much a world which has fallen away from God through sin, but a world characterized by ignorance of the Father, where men and women walk in the gloom of anguish and nightmares.

This tragic state can be remedied only by a revelation of *gnosis*, the true knowledge, which for the author sums up all that is meant by the Christian Gospel, in its original sense of the "good news." Such revelation is the work of Jesus, who is central to the whole book. There is little trace of the elaborate account of the emanations of other divine beings that is characteristic of full-blown Valentinianism: although terms such as aeon and Pleroma occur, they are not developed and often seem almost incidental, and all the emphasis falls on the figure and function of Christ. Several titles are applied to him but the most common is Logos or Word: Jesus is the Teacher-Redeemer who brings to light the Word of the Father. The author is concerned to make clear that Jesus is able to reveal to humanity the truth, which consists in knowing the Father, because of his perfect union, almost to the point of identity, with the supreme God. A lengthy reflection on the relationship between the Father and Son, which probably reflects such New Testament passages as Philippians 2.9–10, centers on the Son as the "Name" of the Father, with a repeated refrain "The Name of the Father is the Son." It may in fact be said that the identity of the two is all that matters for the writer in his presentation of the person of Jesus.

DATA

TITLE:
The Gospel of Truth

ORIGINAL DATE OF COMPOSITION:
2nd cent. CE?

ORIGINAL LANGUAGE:
Greek

PROVENANCE:
Uncertain

EARLIEST EXTANT MANUSCRIPT:
4th cent. CE
(Coptic)

Jesus and the Lost Sheep, from a Roman sarcophagus of the 4th century CE. Depictions of Jesus as the Good Shepherd were popular among the early Christians.

Even more important is the gospel's account of what the work of the Redeemer means for individuals. There is a dramatic description of the pitiable condition of humanity before the advent of Christ, and of the wonderful experience of freedom and new life that comes to those who accept his message. *Gnosis* is primarily self-knowledge. Gnostics, to whom the writer is speaking, find the knowledge of the Father through knowing the truth about themselves: that their origin is from God and that they are themselves divine, children of the Father. Revelation is found within the believer even more than in the person of Christ. The believer realizes that his or her ultimate destiny is to recover the primal state of being by ascending to the Pleroma and to the place of "Rest," a term denoting the being of the Father. The whole picture is one of the complete harmony and union of the Father, the Son, the divine sphere, and the Gnostic: "All beings which have emanated from the Father are Pleromas and all beings which have emanated from him have their roots in him, who caused them all to grow in himself."

From the Gospel of Truth, pages 31–32

He is the shepherd who left the ninety-nine sheep that did not go astray. He went in search for the one that was lost. He rejoiced when he found it. ... He labored even on the Sabbath for the sheep whom he found fallen into a pit. He saved the life of this sheep, because he drew it out of the pit, that you, children of the knowledge of the heart, may know in your hearts what is the Sabbath on which the work of redemption must not remain inactive, that you may say of that day from on high, which has no night, and of the light which does not pass away, being perfect —say then in your hearts that you are this perfect day and that this light which does not grow dim dwells in you.

THE GOSPEL OF PHILIP

Another important text from Nag Hammadi that originates in the Valentinian sect (see p.162) is the Gospel of Philip. The title occurs only in the colophon at the end, which may well be a later addition, and in the work itself the apostle Philip is mentioned only once. However, Philip was an important figure in Christian tradition and this single reference may well have been sufficient for the attribution to him of the whole work.

The gospel is essentially a theological treatise which exhibits many general Gnostic ideas, especially about the redemption of the soul from the world of matter and the attainment of self-knowledge when the believer realizes that he or she is one with the Father, Christ, and the Holy Spirit. In form, the work consists of an anthology of disconnected sayings, often very short, displaying a range of literary genres and theological themes and most likely taken from several sources. However, it is possible that the sayings derive from a single work that was a sort of manual of instruction for Gnostic initiates—if so, the sayings could be viewed as something like lecture titles, which the initiate could memorize or copy down.

Many passages center on Jesus as the bringer of salvation, through his revelation of truth and knowledge and through his restoration of perfect harmony—not least by abolishing the difference between the sexes. As in other Gnostic writings, Jesus' female followers are prominent, especially the three Marys (his mother, his sister, and Mary Magdalene, who is referred to as Jesus' "companion"). There is a remarkable saying about Mary Magdalene in which she is made to correspond to the Beloved Disciple of John's gospel (see extract, opposite). There are frequent references to the imagery of the bride and the bridegroom, behind which there appears to lie the distinctive Valentinian concept of the Redeemer as the bridegroom of the aeon Sophia ("Wisdom"), and his angels as the bridegrooms of Sophia's offspring. The gospel reveals that the Valentinian community practiced five sacraments, listed as baptism, chrism ("anointing"), eucharist, redemption, and "bridal chamber." The most important sacrament was the mystic rite of the bridal chamber, which had no parallel in the mainstream Church and was probably characteristic of several Gnostic groups. Exactly what occurred in the "bridal chamber" is unclear, but it would seem to have involved a kind of reenactment of the marriage of the Redeemer and Sophia, the divine bridegroom and bride, through whom the original unity of male and female was restored. One passage lists the sacraments in ascending order of importance, culminating in the bridal chamber, and this suggests that together they made up a single complex initiation ceremony into the sect.

DATA

TITLE:
The Gospel of Philip

ORIGINAL DATE OF COMPOSITION:
2nd–3rd cent. CE

ORIGINAL LANGUAGE:
Greek

PROVENANCE:
Syria?

EARLIEST EXTANT MANUSCRIPT:
4th cent. CE (Coptic)

OPPOSITE *St. Philip and the Dragon*, by Filippino Lippi (1457–1504). In this apocryphal legend, the apostle Philip vanquished a dragon from a temple of Mars and converted the pagan idol's devotees.

Sayings from the Gospel of Philip

55b. The Savior loved Mary Magdalene more than all the disciples and kissed [her] on her mouth often. The other disciples … said to him, "Why do you love her more than all of us?" The Savior answered and said to them, "Why do I not love you like her?"

78. If the woman had not separated from the man, she would not have died with the man. The separation from him became the origin of death. Because of this, Christ came, to remove the separation which existed from the beginning and again unite the two. …

79. But the woman is united to her husband in the bridal chamber. But those who have united in the bridal chamber can no longer be separated. That is why Eve separated from Adam, because she had not united with him in the bridal chamber.

THE COPTIC GOSPEL OF THOMAS

The Coptic Gospel of Thomas consists of 114 sayings attributed to Jesus—many of them found in the gospels, but some otherwise unrecorded—and recounts nothing of his ministry, passion, or resurrection. As such it stands somewhat apart from the other Nag Hammadi texts, although it has links with some of them, such as the Gospel of Philip (see pp.164–5) and the Pistis Sophia (see pp.170–71).

Parts of the gospel—not to be confused with the Infancy Gospel of Thomas (see p.138)—were found in the cache of papyrus documents discovered around the turn of the twentieth century at Oxyrhyncus in Egypt. These fragments suggest that it was originally written in Greek. The Coptic text, which appears to reflect a marked development of the original, claims to contain "the secret words" spoken by Jesus and written down by the apostle Thomas. This reference to a hidden revelation indicates a Gnostic outlook, while Thomas was an important figure in Christian tradition, especially in Gnostic circles, and a considerable body of writings is ascribed to him. He was of particular significance in the Syrian church (see p.200), and it is probable that Syria, where Christianity had early taken root, was the home of the original work, which may be dated to the middle of the second century CE.

However, there are grounds for thinking that some at least of the sayings may go as far back as the first century CE and this raises the question—which is the subject of much scholarly debate—of the relationship of the earliest form of the Gospel of Thomas to the canonical gospels. The Gospel of Thomas invites comparison with the hypothetical document "Q" (from German *Quelle*, "source") which many scholars claim was used, together with Mark's gospel, by the authors of Matthew and Luke. According to the numerous scholarly reconstructions of "Q," it too was a collection of Jesus' sayings. This may indicate that several such collections existed and constituted an early Christian literary genre.

Around half of the sayings in the Gospel of Thomas have close parallels in the synoptic gospels (Matthew, Mark, and Luke). Many of these are virtually identical with their canonical counterparts, while others display significant divergences. It is therefore possible that the sayings in the Gospel of Thomas were selected directly from the canonical gospels and were either reproduced more or less exactly or amended to fit the author's distinctive theological outlook.

On the other hand, many scholars would claim that the Gospel of Thomas is independent of the New Testament and not only contains genuine sayings of Jesus not found elsewhere but also preserves some of his words in a simpler and more authentic form than that found in the canonical gospels. For instance, Thomas includes several of Jesus' parables, but they almost always lack any of the interpretative elements found in the canonical gospels.

The Incredulity of Thomas, an 11th-century Spanish relief by the Master of Silos illustrating John 20.24–29.

Sayings from the Coptic Gospel of Thomas

These are the secret words which the living Jesus spoke, and which Didymus Judas Thomas wrote down. 1. And he said: He who shall find the interpretation of these words shall not taste death.

2. Jesus said: He who seeks, let him not cease seeking until he finds; and when he finds he will be troubled, and when he is troubled he will be amazed, and he will reign over the All.

10. Jesus said: I have cast a fire upon the world, and see, I watch over it until it is ablaze.

31. Jesus said: No prophet is accepted in his own village, no physician heals those who know him.

47. Jesus said: It is not possible for a man to ride two horses or stretch two bows; and it is not possible for a servant to serve two masters, unless he honors the one and insults the other.

The Assumption of the Virgin and Saints, by Bicci di Lorenzo (1373–1452). According to an early legend, Mary was miraculously taken up to heaven after her death. Thomas was not present and doubted the event, so to convince him she sent down her belt into his hands (center).

Thus there are no allegorical features and no references to the future or to the end-time.

In Thomas's version of the Parable of the Wicked Tenants (see extract, opposite), the owner of a vineyard sends a servant to collect fruit from his tenants, but they just assault the servant. The same happens with a second servant, so the owner sends his son, but the tenants kill him. The parable concludes at this point, with the characteristic words "He who has ears, let him hear." But the synoptic version of the parable (Mark 12.1–11 and parallels in Matthew and Luke) has a whole succession of servants (representing the prophets of Israel), all of whom are beaten or killed before the owner sends his son, who also dies (Mark. 12.5–8). In addition, the parable adds that the tenants will be replaced, and there is a quotation from the Hebrew Bible (Mark 12.10–11). It has been suggested that the simpler form in the Gospel of Thomas represents Jesus' original teaching, in which the vineyard stands for the ancestral land of Israel in Jesus' own time. The two servants symbolize its population, who are oppressed by foreign occupation, and the son is Jesus, Israel's Messiah. The synoptic version, it is claimed, has expanded this into a picture of the disobedience of Israel down the ages, with the succession of killed or beaten servants representing the biblical prophets and the expulsion of the tenants symbolizing God's rejection of Israel in favor of the Gentiles. The son is Jesus as a universal savior rather than a national one. Similarly, the Parable of the Net in Matthew 13 is an allegory of the Last Judgment, but this theme does not occur in the Gospel of Thomas, where the emphasis is on the fisherman as the model of the man who acts according to wisdom (see extract, below).

However, caution is necessary before such examples in Thomas are accepted as the "authentic" teaching of Jesus. Much in the Gospel of Thomas represents the common currency of Gnostic thought and the work should probably be considered—certainly in its extant Coptic form—as a broadly Gnostic composition. Thus the theme of the kingdom of heaven is as prominent in Thomas as it is in the canonical gospels, but in Thomas it is a wholly present and spiritual reality, rather than the New Testament's kingdom of the future. In Thomas, entering the kingdom is the equivalent of the disciple's discovery of his or her own divine nature. Thomas's version of the Parable of the Net emphasizes one large fish which is preserved, and similarly its account of the Parable of the Lost Sheep describes the straying animal as the biggest of the flock (see extracts below). The fish and the sheep both probably refer to the true Gnostic, who alone is the recipient of salvation. In Thomas, the words "He who has ears to hear, let him hear," which also occur in the canonical gospels, are certainly a call to human beings to recognize both the truth about Jesus and also their true nature as belonging to the divine world in unity with the supreme Father.

Sayings from the Coptic Gospel of Thomas

8. Man is like a wise fisherman who cast his net into the sea; he drew it up from the sea full of small fish; among them he found a large good fish, the wise fisherman; he threw all the small fish into the sea, he chose the large fish without difficulty. He who has ears to hear, let him hear!

65. A good man had a vineyard; he leased it to tenants, that they might work in it and he receive the fruits from them. He sent his servant, that the tenants might give him the fruits of the vineyard. They seized his servant, beat him, and all but killed him. The servant went away and told his master. His master said, "Perhaps they did not know him." He sent another servant; the tenants beat the other also. Then the master sent his son. He said, "Perhaps they will have respect for my son." Those tenants, since they knew that he was the heir of the vineyard, they seized him and killed him. He who has ears, let him hear.

107. The kingdom is like a shepherd who had a hundred sheep; one of them, the biggest, went astray; he left the ninety-nine and sought after the one until he found it. After he had labored, he said to the sheep, "I love you more than the ninety-nine."

DIALOGUES WITH CHRIST

One group of Gnostic writings in the Nag Hammadi library constitutes a distinct literary genre: it consists of dialogues between Jesus and his disciples after the Resurrection and may be classed as typically Gnostic gospels. Examples are the Sophia Jesu Christi and the Dialogue of the Savior, to which may be added two Coptic documents discovered earlier, the Pistis Sophia and the two Books of Jeu.

The characteristic themes and concepts of Gnosticism recur throughout all of these texts. They convey esoteric teaching that can be received and understood only by a select group of initiates, who in turn must keep the revelation secret from all but the elect. This feature is particularly prominent in the Books of Jeu. The word "Jeu" denotes the "True God" who came forth from the bosom of the Father and from whom there issued twenty-eight emanations, or aeons. Their names and number, described in careful detail, form the hidden instruction to be learned by the initiate. In one strongly worded passage, Jesus dictates how stringently such knowledge is to be kept secret (see extract, opposite). The opening words of the work can be seen as a succinct statement of what the Gnostics understood as the "gospel" or "good news": "This is the book of the knowledge of the invisible God through the medium of the hidden mysteries which

show the way to the chosen race, leading into rest to the life of the Father." The text goes on to describe how those of the "chosen race" are initiated through three baptisms bestowed by Jesus: by water, fire, and the Holy Spirit.

In the Pistis Sophia ("Faithful Sophia") Jesus gives an account of his journey through the heavens, during which he finds the disconsolate aeon Sophia, the Mother (see pp.162 and 164), who has fallen into the realm of matter. Jesus restores her to her primal state to be his consort. His female followers, especially Mary Magdalene and his mother Mary, play an important part in the dialogues.

A 17th-century Russian icon of the enthroned figure of Sophia (the Holy Wisdom), personified in the form of a fiery winged angel.

The Sophia Jesu Christi is a reworking of a Gnostic treatise without any clear Christian elements that is also among the Nag Hammadi texts. The title may simply mean "the Wisdom of Jesus Christ," that is, a book of his teaching, or the word "Sophia" may denote the aeon Sophia, who is mentioned in the work. The beginning narrates Jesus' meeting with his disciples in Galilee after his resurrection. The twelve male disciples are accompanied by seven female followers, one of whom, Mary Magdalene, later questions Jesus. The Redeemer appears to them, in typical Gnostic imagery, as a heavenly and spiritual being, suffused by light. The disciples are unable to understand Jesus' real nature, the salvation that he brings, or the mysteries of the supernatural realm. He instructs them in response to a series of questions and the work concludes with a brief summary of the teaching he has given.

The Dialogue of the Savior, a work probably of the second century CE, exists in a very damaged state, but seems to be a sayings collection, which has been expanded by a series of questions and answers between the disciples and Jesus that expounds typical Gnostic teaching about the creation of the world and the mysteries of the cosmos.

DATA

TITLES:
The Books of Jeu
The Pistis Sophia

ORIGINAL DATE OF
COMPOSITION:
3rd cent. CE

ORIGINAL LANGUAGE:
Greek

PROVENANCE:
Egypt

EARLIEST EXTANT
MANUSCRIPTS:
3rd cent. CE
(Jeu); 4th cent. CE
(Pistis Sophia)
(both Coptic)

From the Books of Jeu, chapter 43

Jesus said, "These mysteries which I shall give you, preserve, and give them to no man except he be worthy of them. Give them not to father nor to mother, or to brother or to sister or to kinsman, neither for food nor for drink, nor for woman-kind, neither for gold nor for silver, nor for anything at all of this world. Preserve them, and give them to no one whatsoever for the sake of the good of this whole world."

From the Sophia Jesu Christi

The Son of Man agreed with Sophia, his consort, and revealed himself in a great light as androgynous. His male nature is called "the Savior, the Begetter of all Things," but his female "Sophia, mother of all," whom some call Pistis. ...

[Jesus said to his disciples], "Behold, I have taught you the name of the Perfect One, the whole will of the holy angels and of the Mother, that the manly host may here be made perfect, that they may appear in all aeons from the Unlimited up to those which have arisen in the unsearchable riches of the great invisible Spirit; that they all may receive of his goodness and of the riches of his place of rest above which there is no dominion. But I am come from the First, who was sent that I might reveal to you that which was from the beginning, because of the arrogance of the leader and his angels who say of themselves that they are gods. But I am come to lead them out of their blindness, that I may make known to everyone the God who is over the All. But you, trample down their graves, break their yoke asunder, and awaken that which is mine!"

CHAPTER 4
LEGENDS OF THE APOSTLES
◆
APOCRYPHAL ACTS

Within the New Testament apocryphal literature, the largest category comprises the acts of various apostles. There is a considerable number of comparatively late and minor acts, but the most important group is made up of five great acts—of Peter, John, Paul, Andrew, and Thomas—dating from the second and third centuries CE. They are written for the edification and entertainment of ordinary Christians and as such they throw valuable light on the life and concerns of the Church of the early centuries.

The basic model of all the apocryphal acts is the Acts of the Apostles in the New Testament, but they also develop their own distinctive characteristics, as can easily be seen by comparing the account of Paul in the canonical Acts with that in the apocryphal Acts of Paul. Certain features are common to all these apocryphal compositions. They take the form of a narrative of the travels of the apostle in question (see map, right), which relates how he journeyed throughout the Levant and beyond, spreading the word of Christ from Rome to India.

This basic structure is filled out with a succession of actions or deeds performed by the apostle—predominantly healing miracles—which would have a special appeal for the audience to which they are addressed. These accounts stress the marvelous and supernatural powers of the apostle, who appears very much like the "divine man," or "miracle-worker," found in Greek thought and writings. The works reveal the influence of the Hellenistic literary genre known as "aretalogy" (from *arete*, "virtue," which can also mean "manifestation of divine power," or "miracle"), which recounts the wonderful doings of a godlike man, such as Alexander the Great and other famous heroes. But aretalogy was also commonly employed to convey the essential beliefs of a religious or philosophical movement, and each of the apocryphal acts represents a particular theological tradition which often diverges from the outlook of the mainstream Church.

The apostles are also teachers and the speeches attributed to them constitute another distinct genre. Also present in the apocryphal acts are folktales, legends, and edifying fables, many of which had long captured the popular imagination in the ancient Near East. Noteworthy too are the sexual elements, represented on the one hand by love stories and love motifs (in which women feature prominently) and on the other hand by passages praising virginity and asceticism. In this respect the apocryphal acts display many parallels with features of

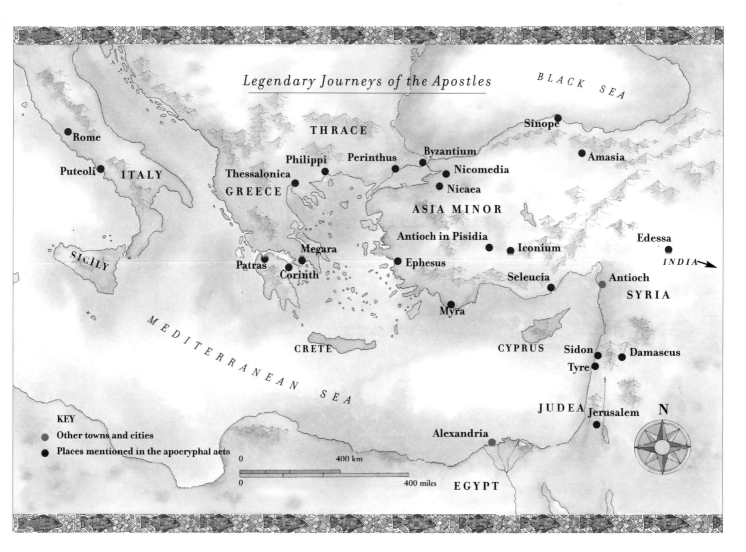

Legendary Journeys of the Apostles

BLACK SEA

THRACE

Sinope

Rome

Amasia

Puteoli ITALY

Philippi Perinthus Byzantium

Thessalonica Nicomedia

GREECE Nicaea

ASIA MINOR

Edessa

Antioch in Pisidia

Megara Iconium

SICILY Patras Ephesus INDIA

Corinth Seleucia Antioch

Myra SYRIA

MEDITERRANEAN SEA

CRETE CYPRUS Sidon Damascus

Tyre

JUDEA Jerusalem N

KEY

● Other towns and cities

● Places mentioned in the apocryphal acts

0   400 km

0   400 miles   EGYPT

Alexandria

This map shows the cities and lands mentioned in the apocryphal acts of Peter, John, Paul, Andrew,
and Thomas. The narratives of journeys which are interspersed with great deeds, conform to a
common Hellenistic literary genre of the period.

Hellenistic novels, and to a certain extent they may be viewed as adaptations of this genre for
the use of Christian congregations. However, although the apocryphal acts all share similar
characteristics, they differ considerably from one another and each author employs the common stock of motifs in his own way.

Whatever their literary models, the apocryphal acts bear witness to an increasing interest in the apostles as great saintly figures in the early Christian era, and to a desire among
ordinary Christians to know more about their lives—especially those about whom comparatively little is related in the New Testament.

THE ACTS OF PETER

The Acts of Peter represents one of the earliest developments of the episode in the Acts of the Apostles, where the apostle Peter rebukes a figure called Simon Magus ("Simon the Magician") for wishing to buy the apostles' power to convey the gift of the Holy Spirit by a simple laying on of hands (Acts 8.18–24). In Christian tradition, Simon Magus came to be viewed as the arch-heretic, the father of Gnosticism and the foe of Peter. It is this last aspect which forms the central theme of the Acts of Peter.

The narrative recounts a contest between two miracle-workers: Simon Peter, representing true religion, and Simon Magus, "the angel of the devil." Apart from a brief account of the voyage from Palestine, all the events take place in Rome, which is likely to have been where the book originated. The text is preserved in a single Latin manuscript, known as the Vercelli Acts, but the original was certainly a Greek writing, probably from the late second century CE.

Simon Magus Attempts to Buy the Power to Confer the Holy Spirit, by Liberale da Verona (ca. 1445–ca. 1525). Simon's act is the origin of "simony," the sin of offering money for a spiritual benefit or religious office.

There are a number of similarities between the Acts of Peter and the Acts of John (see pp.180–83). Both texts detail how the earthly Jesus appeared to his disciples in a variety of forms and in both there occurs teaching about the mystery of the cross, which, as the Acts of Peter explains, means that, "for you who hope in Christ, the cross must not be this thing that is visible, for this passion, like the passion of Christ, is something other than this which is visible." The two texts set out a list of designations for Jesus and each has a tendency virtually to identify Christ with the whole Godhead—so, in his final prayer, Peter can say to Jesus, "you are my Father, you are my Mother, you [are] my Brother, you are Friend, you are Servant, you are House-keeper, you are the All, and the All is in you; you are Being, and there is nothing that is, except you." In the two works, there is a strongly ascetic note—the eucharist is celebrated without wine, and chastity is demanded as a condition of salvation, exemplified especially by the prominence in the narratives of devout women. It has been suggested that the author of the Acts of Peter knew and used the Acts of John, but their common themes are employed in somewhat different ways, nor can there be any certainty about the chronological order of composition of the two texts. It is therefore probably best to view them as independent writings but both reflecting the popular piety of Christian circles in the early centuries CE.

The central motif of the contest between Peter and Simon is supplemented by two other sections. The opening part records how Paul establishes the Church in Rome, from where he is summoned away by Jesus to carry the Gospel to Spain. Simon then arrives in Rome and proves

From the Acts of Peter, chapters 9 and 12

Peter, seeing a great dog tied ... with a massive chain, went up to him and let him loose. And when the dog was let loose he acquired a human voice and said to Peter, "What do you bid me do, you servant of the ineffable living God?" And Peter said ... "Go in and tell Simon in the presence of his company, 'Peter says to you, Come out in public; for on your account I have come to Rome, you wicked man and troubler of simple souls.'" And immediately the dog ... rushed into the middle of Simon's companions and ... called out with a loud voice, "I tell you Simon, Peter the servant of Christ is standing at the door, and says to you, 'Come out in public.'" ... But Simon said to the dog, "Tell Peter that I am not in the house." And the dog answered him in the presence of Marcellus, "You most wicked and shameless man, you enemy of all that live and believe in Christ Jesus, here is a dumb animal sent to you and taking a human voice to convict you and prove you a cheat and a deceiver." ... Having said these words, the dog ... came to Peter ... and reported his dealings. ... So the dog said, "Messenger and apostle of the true God, Peter, you shall have a great contest with Simon, the enemy of Christ and with his servants; and you shall convert many to the faith that were deceived by him."... And when the dog had said this, he fell down at the apostle Peter's feet and gave up his spirit.

The Story of Simon and Eubula

Before the final encounter between Peter and Simon Magus in the Forum, a self-contained section has been inserted in the work which tells of an earlier confrontation in Judea. The story shows Simon not only as a magician but also as a lover of money, in accordance with the account in the Acts of the Apostles. Peter relates that Simon was staying with a wealthy woman called Eubula and repaid her hospitality by stealing all her valuables, including a golden satyr which she worshiped. The theft was revealed to Peter in a dream, along with details of how Simon was proposing to sell the stolen property. The apostle arranged for Simon's agents to be apprehended when they attempted to conclude the transaction and under torture they implicated Simon, forcing him to flee the country. Eubula was converted to Christianity and embraced an ascetic life, giving up her property for the relief of the poor.

his miraculous power by flying through the air above the city gate. He rapidly succeeds in persuading most of the members of the Church to accept him as their God and Savior in place of the Christ preached by Paul. In this emergency, God reminds Peter, who is living in Jerusalem, of how he had once driven Simon from Judea (Acts 8) and must now go to Rome to do the same.

Peter finds Simon living in the house of a senator, Marcellus, who has been seduced by the sorceror's charms. Peter endeavors to compel Simon to confront him, by means of various miracles typical of folklore: a talking dog (see extract, p.175), a smoked fish made to swim again, and a seven-month-old child who speaks with a man's voice. Peter's feats convince the crowd and bring about the recovery of the Roman church. Marcellus takes the lead in returning to the true faith and he expels Simon from his home. Peter then proceeds with the restoration of the Church by holding a service of prayer in Marcellus's house (during which the room is suffused

DATA

TITLE:
The Acts of Peter

ORIGINAL DATE OF
COMPOSITION:
Late 2nd cent. CE

ORIGINAL LANGUAGE:
Greek

PROVENANCE:
Probably Rome

EARLIEST EXTANT
MANUSCRIPT:
ca. 600CE
(Latin)

From the Acts of Peter, chapters 31 and 32

[Simon said], "Men of Rome, at present you think that Peter has mastered me ... but you are deceived. For tomorrow I shall leave you ... and fly up to God, whose power I am ... If then you have fallen, behold I am He that Stands." ... And by the following day a large crowd had assembled ... to see him fly ... And lo and behold, he was carried up into the air, and everyone saw him all over Rome, passing over its temples and its hills ... And Peter ... cried out ... "Make haste, Lord, with your grace; and let him fall down from this height, and be crippled, but not die."... And he fell down ... and broke his leg in three places. ... But Simon in his misfortune found some ... who carried him on a stretcher by night from Rome to Aricia; and after staying there he was taken to a man named Castor ... and there he underwent an operation; and thus Simon, the angel of the devil, ended his life.

St. Peter in Rome, a fresco by Filippino Lippi (1457–1504) in the church of Santa Maria del Carmine, Rome. Peter and Paul argue with Simon Magus before the emperor Nero (right), a scene derived from the adaptation of the Acts of Peter in the 13th-century *Golden Legend*. For the scene on the left, see pp.178–9.

with supernatural light) and by performing some miraculous cures. Then Peter has a vision in which Jesus promises him a great trial of faith with Simon on the coming Sabbath. This is duly arranged to take place in the Forum, where, Marcellus reports, the crowd are saying, "Tomorrow at dawn two Jews will contend in this place concerning the worship of God."

The scene in the Forum begins with a challenge from Simon, who turns to the crowd and utters the kind of anti-Christian statements that could be made by pagans: "You men of Rome, is God born? Is he crucified? He who owns a Lord is no God!" There follows a series of episodes in which Peter and Simon vie with one another to restore various dead people to life. Simon's miraculous powers are not in question, only their inadequacy—thus he can make a dead young man open his eyes and nod his head, but only Peter can cause him to stand up and be fully restored to life. Peter appears as a model of Christian charity toward Simon, saving him from being lynched by the mob for his failure to restore the dead man.

The confrontation reaches a dramatic climax when Simon promises that he will prove his superiority once and for all by flying through the air, as he had done on his first appearance in Rome. Peter prays that Simon may fall from the sky but suffer only a broken leg, and this duly occurs. However, he later dies from his injuries (see extract, opposite).

THE MARTYRDOM OF PETER

The conclusion to the Acts of Peter is an account of the apostle's martyrdom, which circulated as an independent piece from an early date. The defeat of Simon (see p.177) led to a revival in the church of Rome, marked especially by the adoption of sexual abstinence, enabling men and women to "worship God in sobriety and purity."

Interestingly, Peter is shown as not unduly rigorous. A wealthy woman nicknamed Chryse ("the golden") gave Peter a large donation. His companions objected, pointing out that she was a notorious fornicator, but Peter replied, "I do not know what this woman is as regards her

The Crucifixion of St. Peter, a late fresco by Michelangelo (1475–1564) in the Cappella Paolina in the Vatican.

usual way of life; but I did not take it [the money] without reason; for she was bringing it as a debtor to Christ, and is giving it to Christ's servants; for he himself has provided for them."

The issue of celibacy brings about Peter's downfall. Some concubines of the prefect Agrippa and the wife of Albinus, a prominent citizen, convert to Christianity. Albinus blames Peter, and seeks his arrest. After being warned by Albinus's wife, Peter heeds his companions' pleas to leave. As he exits the city gate he encounters Jesus in a famous meeting known as "Quo Vadis," for which this work is the earliest source (see illustration, p.128). The apostle asks, "Lord, where are you going?" (in Latin, *"Domine, quo vadis?"*), a question which reproduces the words of John's gospel (John 13.36). The author of the Acts of Peter does not quote Jesus' reply in the gospel, but clearly understood it as an indirect prophecy of Peter's martyrdom: "Where I am going, you cannot follow me now; but you will follow afterward."

The meeting with Christ causes Peter to turn back to Rome, where he is promptly arrested and sentenced to be crucified. At the place of execution, he makes two speeches, his final message to his followers. Peter asks to be crucified head downward—this became a widely accepted tradition, frequently depicted in art (see opposite and on p.177)—and he goes on to explain what this request signifies in terms of the religious symbolism of the cross (see extract, below).

From the Acts of Peter, chapters 35 and 38

As [Peter] went out of the gate he saw the Lord entering Rome; and when he saw him he said, "Lord, where are you going?" And the Lord said to him, "I am coming to Rome to be crucified." And Peter said to him, "Lord, are you being crucified again?" He said to him, "Yes, Peter, I am being crucified again." ... Then [Peter] returned to Rome rejoicing and giving praise to the Lord, because he said, "I am being crucified"; since this was to happen to Peter. ...

When they had hanged him up in the way which he had requested, [Peter] began to speak again, "Men whose duty it is to hear, ... you must know the mystery of all nature, and the beginning of all things ... For the first man, whose likeness I have in my appearance, in falling head downward showed a manner of birth that was not so before ... He

therefore, being drawn down, ... established the whole of this cosmic system, being hung up as an image of the calling, in which he showed what is on the right hand as on the left, and those on the left as on the right, and changed all the signs of their nature, so as to consider fair those things that were not fair, and take those that were really evil to be good. ... You then, my beloved, ... must leave your former error ... You should come up to the cross of Christ, who is the Word stretched out, the one and only, of whom the Spirit says, 'For what else is Christ but the Word, the sound of God?' So that the Word is this upright tree on which I am crucified; but the sound is the cross-piece, the nature of man; and the nail that holds the cross-piece to the upright in the middle is the conversion and repentance of man."

THE ACTS OF JOHN

The Acts of John is formed from two travel accounts relating to the apostle John, son of Zebedee—however, very little concerning his travels is actually recorded. These details may have been omitted by the author, who lays great emphasis on John's miracles and preaching. The setting is mainly Ephesus in Asia Minor, which reflects the existing tradition that the apostle had been active in the region and had died in the city.

The work may be seen as reflecting the views of one particular Christian group which felt an affinity with the apostle John and persevered with its own understanding of his life and teaching, as well as its own distinctive religious practices. Thus in the Acts of John, the eucharist is a breaking of bread, without any mention of wine, celebrating the glorification of Christ. The book was probably written in eastern Syria in the early part of the third century CE.

The first half of the Acts finds John in the city of Miletus, whence he journeys to Ephesus and performs various miracles, of which the most dramatic is his destruction of the temple of Artemis and the subsequent conversion of the Ephesians (see extract, below). Within the account of John's first stay at Ephesus, there is a distinct section which contains the apostle's preaching of the Gospel and defines the theological outlook of the work as a whole. It has

From the Acts of John, chapters 38–42

DATA

TITLE:
The Acts of John

ORIGINAL DATE OF
COMPOSITION:
3rd cent. CE

ORIGINAL LANGUAGE:
Greek or Syriac

PROVENANCE:
Probably eastern
Syria

EARLIEST EXTANT
MANUSCRIPT:
5th cent. CE
(Armenian)

Two days later there was the dedication-festival of the idol-temple. So while everyone was wearing white, John alone put on black clothing and went up to the temple; and they seized him and tried to kill him … And he went up on a high platform, and said to them … "How many miracles and cures of diseases have you seen performed through me? And yet you are blinded in your hearts, and cannot recover your sight. … See, here I stand. You all say that you have Artemis as your goddess; pray to her, then, that I, and I alone, may die; or if you cannot do this, then I alone will call upon my own God." … So saying, he uttered this prayer: "O God, who is God above all that are called gods … who does convict every form of worship, by converting men to you; at whose name every idol takes flight, and every demon, every power and every unclean nature; now let the demon that is here take flight at your name … and show your mercy in this place, for they have been led astray." And while John was saying this, of a sudden the altar of Artemis split into many pieces, and all the offerings … fell to the floor and its glory was shattered, and so were more than seven images; and half the temple fell down, so that the priest was killed at one stroke … Then the assembled Ephesians cried out, "There is but one God, the God of John! … We are converted, now that we have seen your marvelous works! Have mercy upon us … and save us from our great error!"

three parts—a discussion of the earthly appearance of Jesus, a hymn uttered by Christ, and his revelation of the mystery of the cross. It is generally agreed that this section is older than the narrative and that it was incorporated into the latter in an already fixed form.

It is clear that this material has a Gnostic character. The hymn speaks of the union of the disciple with the Redeemer and the need to keep the revelation of his true nature secret. This knowledge initiates the believer into a cosmic event which is realized through the Cross of Light—this is the true cross of which the actual one of wood was only a symbol (the passion of Christ also is to be understood symbolically). Jesus is described as being encountered by his followers in many different guises—his human form has no real importance.

All these features can be seen as representative of an incipient stage of the process which was to lead to a fully developed Gnosticism. As a whole, the Acts of John is not of a specifically Gnostic character but it is possible to understand much of it in the light of Gnostic concepts,

Curetes Way, one of the main streets of ancient Ephesus, with the 2nd-century CE temple of Hadrian.

The Raising of Drusiana by St. John the Evangelist, by Girolamo Mazzola Bedoli (ca. 1500–1569). This episode occurs at the end of the Acts of John (see box, opposite). The apostle John is traditionally identified as the author of the Gospel of John and of the Book of Revelation.

From the Acts of John, chapters 60 and 61

On the first day we arrived at a lonely inn; and while we were trying to find a bed for John we saw a curious thing. There was one bed there lying ... not made up; so we spread the cloaks which we were wearing over it, and begged him to lie down on it ... But when he lay down he was troubled by the numerous bugs; and as they became more and more troublesome to him, and it was already midnight, he said to them in the hearing of us all, "I tell you, you bugs, to behave yourselves, one and all; you must leave your home for tonight and be quiet in one place and keep your distance from the servants of God." And while we laughed and went on talking, John went to sleep ... Now as the day was breaking I got up first, and Verus and Andronicus with me; and we saw by the door of the room a mass of bugs collected ... John went on sleeping [and] when he woke up we explained to him what we had seen. And he sat up in the bed and looked at them and said to the bugs, "Since you have behaved yourselves and avoided my punishment go back to your own place" ... The bugs came running from the door toward the bed and climbed up its legs and disappeared into the joints. Then John said again, "This creature listened to a man's voice and kept to itself and was quiet and obedient; but we who hear the voice of God disobey his commandments and are irresponsible; how long will this go on?"

Callimachus and Drusiana

An episode toward the end of the Acts of John became well known in the Middle Ages after being made into a Latin drama by the 10th-century German nun Hroswitha. At Ephesus, a certain Callimachus seeks to seduce a woman called Drusiana. She is the wife of John's companion Andronicus, but has vowed to live a life of chastity. Troubled by Callimachus's attentions, Drusiana dies of depression and is buried. Callimachus, aided by a man called Fortunatus, breaks into her tomb to commit a necrophilic act, but an angel strikes them dead.

When John and his followers visit the tomb the next day, they find the bodies of the two intruders.

John first restores Callimachus to life: he confesses his sins and converts to Christianity. The apostle then restores Drusiana, who is shown as a model of Christian charity in that she forgives Fortunatus and asks that he too may be revived. Callimachus objects, but John rebukes him, pointing to the example of Jesus, who forgave his enemies. Drusiana is given the privilege of reviving Fortunatus, but he remains unrepentant and John denounces him as a representative of those who do not accept the true Christian faith and refuse the spiritual nourishment of the sacraments. Fortunatus suffers a horrible death and John declares: "Devil, you have your son."

and the author may have deliberately intended to point his readers toward such an interpretation. But modern scholarship has shown that the sharp opposition between Gnosticism and the theology of the mainstream Church was not yet apparent at the period in which the Acts of John was produced. What came to be recognized as Gnostic concepts and the beliefs of "early Catholicism" still had much in common during the early Christian centuries, and the boundaries between them were fluid.

The hymn of Christ is accompanied by a dance. Sacred dancing features in many religions, not least Judaism, and a third-century CE Jewish commentary on the Song of Songs says that "In time to come the Holy One will lead the dance among the righteous." It seems likely that this dance was a rite among the community for whom the work was written.

The second section of the work brings John back to Ephesus. The author includes an entertaining story about how John dealt with an infestation of bedbugs to drive home a religious message (see extract, opposite). The Acts of John ends with an account of the apostle's death, an element found in all the other apocryphal acts. Elsewhere, however, the hero is martyred, but Church tradition was unanimous that John had died peacefully in Ephesus.

John celebrates a final eucharist, which is depicted as a rite celebrating not the death of Jesus but his divine glory. Christ is pictured in a long string of epithets: "the Seed, the Word, Grace, Faith, the Salt, the inexpressible Pearl, the Treasure, the Plough, the Net, the Greatness, the Diadem." Immediately before his death, John utters a long prayer in which the ideals of asceticism and chastity characteristic of the work as a whole receive their clearest expression.

THE ACTS OF PAUL

A travel narrative—the basic structure of all the apocryphal acts—is very clearly visible in the Acts of Paul. The work is made up of eleven separate scenes set in various cities of the Near East in the course of the apostle's journeyings which take him from Damascus to Rome, where he meets his end.

The text seems to be intended as a supplement to the account of Paul in the canonical Acts of the Apostles. The episodes in each scene follow the same pattern—a journey, preaching by Paul which leads to his persecution, followed by his performing of miracles and, finally, his departure. The book is mentioned by the Christian author Tertullian, writing ca. 200CE, so it was composed some time before that date. He attributes it to a heretical presbyter of Asia Minor and the fact that it mainly concentrates on sites in that region strongly indicates Asia Minor as its provenance. The dating is also supported by the dependence of the Acts of Paul on the Acts of Peter, which the former's author appears to have known and used. The work is not primarily a theological treatise but rather a series of stories, both to entertain and confirm the faith of ordinary Christians who were often persecuted by their fellow citizens.

There are certain theological ideas and tendencies—not always wholly consistent with one another—that the work shares not only with the Acts of Peter but with the apocryphal acts in general. Paul's first sermon is described as "the word of God concerning continence and the Resurrection" and these are the two great theological themes throughout (see box, below). But the teaching is markedly orthodox, with no traces of what could be described as Gnosticism. The

---

Chastity and Saint Thecla

Almost every episode in the Acts of Paul turns on the motif of sexual abstinence as the reason for the persecution of Paul and his followers. An ascetic outlook is prominent—worldly possessions are transient and believers must set their hope on resurrection to the life to come, which is for them both a present and a future reality. Again, the eucharist is celebrated only with bread and water, not wine.

The work's summons to sexual self-restraint means that it gives a prominent role to those women who display the virtue of chastity. This is especially the case in the opening episode (the Acts of Paul and Thecla), which subsequently became widely known as a separate work. This composition reflects a local cult of Saint Thecla in Asia Minor, which rapidly spread throughout both the Eastern and Western Church, where she was honored as the most famous of the class of virgin martyrs—although the Acts of Paul recounts that in fact Thecla died peacefully in her bed.

author shows considerable knowledge of the Hebrew Bible and strongly affirms the reality of Christ's humanity, as in the statement in a letter attributed to Paul, "our Lord Jesus Christ was born of Mary of the seed of David, when the Holy Spirit was sent from heaven by the Father into her, that he might come into this world and redeem all flesh through his own flesh, and that he might raise up from the dead us who are fleshly, even as he has shown himself as our example."

The work begins with a section known as the Acts of Paul and Thecla. A celebrated saint

From the Acts of Paul and Thecla, chapters 5 and 6

Blessed are the pure in heart, for they shall see God.

Blessed are they who have kept the flesh pure, for they shall become a temple of God.

Blessed are the continent, for to them will God speak.

Blessed are they who have renounced this world, for they shall be well pleasing to God.

Blessed are they who have wives as if they had them not, for they shall be heirs to God.

Blessed are they who have fear of God, for they shall become angels of God.

Blessed are they who tremble at the words of God, for they shall be comforted.

Blessed are they who have received the wisdom of Jesus Christ, for they shall be called sons of the Most High.

Blessed are they who have kept their baptism secure, for they shall rest with the Father and the Son.

Blessed are they who have laid hold upon the understanding of Jesus Christ, for they shall be in light.

Blessed are they who through love of God have departed from the form of this world, for they shall judge angels and at the right hand of the Father they shall be blessed.

Blessed are the merciful, for they shall obtain mercy, and shall not see the bitter day of judgment.

Blessed are the bodies of the virgins, for they shall be well pleasing to God, and shall not lose the reward of their purity.

St. Paul Enthroned, With Angels, a 12th-century Catalan painting, perhaps representing the ascension of Paul to the heavens (see p.214).

and martyr (see box, p.184), Thecla is the central figure and Paul plays only a subsidiary part. The narrative falls into two main sections set in the city of Iconium in Asia Minor, followed by a concluding epilogue set in Antioch in Pisidia—the New Testament records that Paul visited both cities. Each section has a similar content and structure and each reaches a climax when Thecla is condemned to death, a fate from which she is saved by divine intervention.

The beginning of the narrative centers on Paul's arrival in Iconium. There he is accosted by a certain Onesiphorus, who recognizes the apostle from a description given by Paul's disciple Titus: "a man of small stature, with a bald head and crooked legs, in a good state of body, with eyebrows meeting and nose somewhat hooked, full of friendliness." This description, in particular the reference to the apostle's baldness, was to determine the traditional depiction

of Paul in Christian art (for example, see illustrations on pp.177, 185, 194, and 216). Paul then preaches a sermon modeled on the Beatitudes (see extract, p.185)—two of which are quoted verbatim from Matthew—but they are much expanded and transformed into a paean in praise of virginity, and a promise that those who receive the wisdom of Christ and remain faithful to their baptism will achieve the status of angels.

There is more than a hint of the erotic about Thecla. She appears obsessed with Paul —the first mention of her finds her sitting by a window for three days and nights where she can listen to Paul's preaching, and later she is said to seek for him "as a lamb in the wilderness looks about for the shepherd." The text refers more than once to her beauty and it is stated that she went naked to the stake.

In the first section of the narrative, set in Iconium, Thecla is converted to celibacy by Paul's teaching of continence. This has the

St. Thecla Delivers Este from the Plague, by Giambattista Tiepolo (1696–1770). Painted in 1759 for Este cathedral, Italy, it commemorates a tradition that the saint interceded to save the city from an epidemic in 1638.

usual result found in most of the apocryphal acts: her rebuffed fiancé rouses the populace and the authorities against Paul, who is arrested. But the governor, rather like Pilate in the case of Jesus, is impressed by the apostle's words and merely has him flogged and expelled from the city. However, it transpires that Thecla has bribed the jailer and visited Paul in prison, where she is discovered "bound with him in affection." All the blame for what has occurred is now transferred to her, and the governor accedes to demands that she be burnt to death. But when the pyre is lit, God causes "a noise beneath the earth and a cloud above, full of rain and hail," so that the fire is quenched and Thecla is saved. She now joins Paul, who has taken refuge with Onesiphorus and his family outside the city, where she vows to follow him wherever he goes. Paul at first has his doubts, telling her that "the season is unfavorable and you are comely," nor does he consider her yet ready to be baptized, as she requests. However, he eventually takes her with him to Antioch in Pisidia, where the second section of the story is set.

Here all the attention is on Thecla. A leading citizen, Alexander, falls in love with her and tries to bribe Paul to support his suit but the apostle replies, "I do not know the woman of whom you speak, nor is she mine." When Thecla rebuffs Alexander, he persuades the governor to condemn her to fight against beasts in the arena at the public games. When she is faced with the animals, Thecla baptizes herself. The beasts lose all their power to harm Thecla and she is released (see extract, below), gaining a host of Christian converts.

Thecla still yearns for Paul and discovers that he has gone to the town of Myra. She joins him there and tells him of all her adventures. The apostle commissions her to return to Iconium as a missionary. From Iconium she later moves to Seleucia "and after enlightening many with the word of God she slept with a noble sleep."

From the Acts of Paul and Thecla, chapters 33–38

Thecla was taken ... and [was] stripped, and ... flung into the stadium. ... They sent in many beasts, while she stood and stretched out her hands and prayed. And when she had finished her prayer, she turned and saw a great pit full of water, and said, "Now is the time for me to wash." And she threw herself in, saying, "In the name of Jesus Christ I baptize myself on the last day!"... So, then, she threw herself into the water ... but the seals, seeing the light of a lightning-flash, floated dead on the surface. And there was about her a cloud of fire, so that neither could the beasts touch her nor could she be seen naked. ... So Alexander said to the governor, "I have some very fearsome bulls—let us tie her to them."... And they bound her by the feet between the bulls, and set red-hot irons beneath their bellies that being the more enraged they might kill her. The bulls indeed leaped forward, but the flame that blazed around her burned through the ropes, and she was as if she were not bound. ... And immediately the governor issued a decree, saying, "I release to you Thecla, the pious handmaid of God."

DATA

Title:
The Acts of Paul

Original Date of Composition:
ca. 185–ca. 195CE

Original Language:
Greek

Provenance:
Asia Minor

Earliest Extant Manuscript:
ca. 300CE
(Greek)

PAUL AND THE LION

Following the episode of Paul and Thecla, the narrative of the Acts of Paul returns to the apostle's activity in Myra, followed by accounts of his visits to Sidon, Tyre, and Ephesus. This section of the text is at times fragmentary—for example, it records virtually nothing of his stay in Tyre—but the main narrative themes are reasonably clear.

At Myra, Paul cures a number of citizens, beginning with a man called Hermocrates. He and his wife are then baptized, but their elder son, Hermippus, is angry because he wanted to inherit his father's property. With a band of men he attacks Paul, who confronts them with words influenced by the gospel accounts of Christ in the garden of Gethsemane: "I am not a robber, nor am I a murderer. The God of all things, the Father of Christ, will turn your sword into its sheath, and will transform your strength into weakness." Hermippus is struck blind and immediately repents. Paul and his parents, who have been baptized, pray for him and his sight is restored.

At Sidon, the chief event would seem to be Paul's destruction of the temple of Apollo, for which he and his companions are arrested. But they escape by sea to Tyre, from where Paul proceeds to Ephesus. He preaches a sermon against idols to the city governor, who is impressed but—as in the similar episode in Acts 19—is forced by the objections of the idol-makers to condemn Paul to face the beasts in the arena. As in the earlier narrative about Thecla, a violent hailstorm intervenes. It kills most of the beasts in the arena and many of the onlookers, but Paul escapes, together with a lion he had once baptized (see box).

Animals in the Apocryphal Acts

Talking animals are characteristic of folklore and literary fables and are common in the apocryphal acts, as they are in other ancient writings on the saints. Particularly notable is the motif of the lion who submits to the power of holy men and women. In the Acts of Paul, Thecla in the arena is protected by a lioness. Later, Paul himself faces the same ordeal in an account inspired by his statement in 1 Corinthians: "I fought with wild animals at Ephesus" (1 Cor. 15.32). In the arena, he recognizes a fierce lion as an animal that he had once baptized in Palestine. The background to this is provided by a charming story preserved only in a Coptic fragment of the Acts of Paul (see extract, opposite).

Aspects of this episode point to the author's awareness of a close kinship between human beings and other creatures, to the extent that even animals require baptism as the gateway to salvation. Just as Christian baptism involves, for humans, the embracing of a life of continence, so it does for the lion in the story, who after its baptism met a lioness "and did not yield himself to her but ran off."

Ancient Lycian rock-cut tombs dating from the 6th or 7th century BCE at Myra in Asia Minor, where, according to the Acts of Paul, the apostle performed various healing miracles.

From the Acts of Paul (the Coptic Papyrus)

I [Paul] went out, accompanied by the widow Lemma and her daughter Ammia. I was walking in the night, meaning to go to Jericho in Phoenicia. ... There came a great and terrible lion out of the valley ... But we were praying, so that through the prayer Lemma and Ammia did not come upon the beast. But when I had finished praying, the beast had cast himself at my feet. I was filled with the Spirit and looked upon him, and said to him, "Lion, what do you want?" But he said, "I wish to be baptized." I glorified God, who had given speech to the beast and salvation to his servants. Now there was a great river in that place; I went down into it and he followed me. ... I myself was in fear and wonderment, in that I was on the point of leading the lion like an ox and baptizing him in the water. But I stood on the bank ... and cried out, saying, "You who dwell in the heights ... who with Daniel shut the mouths of the lions, who sent to me our Lord Jesus Christ, grant that we escape the beast, and accomplish the plan which you have appointed." When I had prayed thus, I took the lion by his mane and in the name of Jesus Christ immersed him three times. But when he came up out of the water he shook out his mane and said to me, "Grace be with you!" And I said to him, "And likewise with you."

PAUL AT PHILIPPI

Following his escape from the arena at Ephesus (see p.188), Paul takes a ship to Philippi in Macedonia in the north of Greece. The account of the apostle at Philippi has, for the most part, a different character from the rest of the Acts of Paul and consists of an interchange of letters between him and members of the church at Corinth. This correspondence is often referred to as the "Third Letter to the Corinthians" (3 Corinthians) and probably represents an originally independent work.

First, there is a narrative section which tells how two teachers, Simon and Cleobius, had arrived at Corinth, expounding a doctrinal system different from that which the Christians there had received from Paul. They taught "that there was no resurrection of the flesh but only of the spirit, and that the body of man is not the creation of God; and the world they said that God did not create it, and that God does not know the world; and that Jesus Christ was not crucified, but was only a semblance, and that he was not born of Mary, or of the seed of David."

St. Paul Preaching, by Giovanni Ricco (1817–73). This painting depicts Paul's speech before "the chief priests and the council" of the Jews in Jerusalem in defense of his preaching (Acts 22.3ff.).

As a consequence, the leaders of the Corinthian community send a letter to Philippi, asking Paul to test the validity of the views of Simon and Cleobius, who claim that: "We must not appeal to the prophets, and that God is not almighty, and that there is no resurrection of the flesh, and that the creation of man is not God's work, and that the Lord is not come in the flesh, nor was he born of Mary, and that the world is not of God, but of the angels."

Clearly, the false teaching was essentially an early and popular form of Gnosticism, which was emerging in the first two centuries CE. There is no evidence of fully developed Gnostic concepts, such as the doctrine of the aeons or the divine nature of human beings (see pp.157–8). There is also a connection with the Corinthian letters in the New Testament, where Paul is deeply engaged against false teachers, possibly with Gnostic tendencies, who have infiltrated the community.

In reply, Paul sends back a letter as his correspondents had requested. His answer is in two parts. First, he sets out what he had "received from the apostles who were before me, who at all times were together with the Lord Jesus Christ"—in fact, he simply restates the ortho-dox faith without argument. In the second part, he turns to the doctrine of the Resurrection, which, for the author of the Acts of Paul, was one of the key themes of the apostle's preaching. Here he brings forward proofs for the truth of a bodily resurrection, reproducing some of the discussion in 1 Corinthians 15 but also citing passages from the Hebrew Bible, one of which also occurs in the canonical gospels.

The remainder of what is related about events in Philippi is in a very incomplete condi-tion, but it seems to involve the persecution, execution, and revival of a young woman called Frontina, a disciple of Paul. After the apostle revives her—an event which apparently leads to the conversion of her family—he finally sets out for Corinth.

From the Third Letter to the Corinthians, chapter 3

As for those who tell you that there is no res-urrection of the flesh, for them there is no resurrection, who do not believe in him who is thus risen. For indeed, you men of Corinth, they do not know about the sowing of wheat or the other seeds, that they are cast naked into the ground and when they have perished below are raised again by the will of God in a body and clothed. And not only is the body which was cast into the earth raised up, but also abundantly blessed. And if we must not derive the similitude from the seeds alone, but from nobler bodies, you know that Jonah the son of Amathios, when he would not preach in Nineveh, was swal-lowed by a whale, and after three days and three nights God heard Jonah's prayer out of deepest hell, and no part of him was cor-rupted, not even a hair or an eyelid. How much more, O you of little faith, will he raise up you who have believed in Christ Jesus, as he himself rose up?

PAUL IN CORINTH

What is narrated about Paul's stay in Corinth is remarkably brief, in view of the city's importance for the apostle in the New Testament. There is no mention of any miracles performed there and he is only recorded as preaching regularly for forty days.

It is surprising that he does not deal with the threat of the false missionaries, to which he had been alerted at Philippi—rather his theme is said to be "the word of perseverance, relating in what place anything had befallen him and what great deeds had been granted to him," and this is the clue as to the significance of the time in Corinth for the author of the Acts of Paul.

It is from Corinth that Paul sets out for Rome and the martyrdom that awaits him there. He prepares with faithful perseverance, saying, "Behold, I go away to the furnace of fire and I am not strong unless the Lord grants me power. ... The grace of the Lord will go with me, that

From the Acts of Paul ("Corinth to Italy")

When they were on the open sea ... Paul fell asleep. ... And the Lord came to him, walking upon the sea, and he nudged Paul and said, "Stand up and see!" And he awakening said, "You are my Lord Jesus Christ, the king. But why so gloomy and downcast, Lord? ... For I am not a little distressed that you are so." And the Lord said, "Paul, I am about to be crucified afresh." And Paul said, "God forbid, Lord, that I should see this!" But the Lord said to Paul, "Paul, get up, go to Rome and admonish the brethren, that they abide in the calling to the Father." ...

Paul laid aside his mood of sadness and taught the word of truth and said, "Fellow soldiers of Christ, listen! How often did God deliver Israel out of the hand of the lawless! And so long as they kept the things of God he did not forsake them. ... He sent them in addition prophets to proclaim our Lord Jesus Christ; and these in succession received share and portion of the Spirit of Christ. ... And now, brethren, a great temptation lies before us. If we endure, we shall have access to the Lord, and shall receive as the refuge and shield of his good pleasure Jesus Christ, who gave himself for us. ... For in these last times God for our sakes has sent down a spirit of power into the flesh, that is, into Mary the Galilean, according to the prophetic word; who ... gave birth to Jesus the Christ, our King, of Bethlehem in Judea, ... who went to Jerusalem and taught all Judea. ... And he did great and wonderful works, so that he chose from the tribes twelve men whom he had with him in understanding and faith, as he raised the dead, healed diseases, cleansed lepers, healed the blind, made cripples whole, raised up paralytics, cleansed those possessed by demons."

OPPOSITE Remains of ancient Corinth. In the background stands the temple of Apollo, built ca. 540 BCE.

I may fulfill the dispensation with steadfastness." Paul goes not as a prisoner, as in the canonical Acts of the Apostles, but as a free man who voluntarily accepts God's purpose for him.

The account of the journey to Italy is also brief and bears little relation to the narrative of Paul's voyage in the New Testament—again, the author's concern is to bring out its real meaning in terms of the plan that God had foreordained for Paul. The only episode during the journey itself is a vision, when Paul sees Christ walking on the sea (see extract, opposite). Afterward, Jesus walks ahead of the ship, showing the way—the voyage is thus under divine direction.

On his arrival, Paul is welcomed by members of the Church and then preaches a sermon, the conclusion of which has been lost. As it stands, it is an exhortation to perseverance and endurance, in the certainty that God will never desert those who trust in him. God's faithfulness is exemplified firstly in his dealings with the old Israel and secondly by his sending of the Savior into the world, to redeem it by his teaching and miracles. Thus the address once more sets out the true meaning of Paul's ultimate destiny, and of all suffering and martyrdom.

THE MARTYRDOM OF PAUL

Like the corresponding sections of other apocryphal acts, the account of the martyrdom of Paul was transmitted as a separate piece and was probably employed in liturgies on the apostle's feast day. The theme of the confrontation between Paul and Nero contrasts the soldiers of Christ, the universal king, and the subjects of the Roman state.

Paul has hired a barn outside Rome as a preaching house and among the many who come to hear him are some members of the imperial household. Patroclus, Nero's cupbearer, finds the barn crowded and instead listens to the apostle's message from a neighboring window. He falls to his death, but Paul restores him to life—a recapitulation of the episode of Paul and Eutychus in the Acts of the Apostles (Acts 20.9ff.). Patroclus returns to Nero, who had earlier been told of his cupbearer's death, and the emperor asks him who has brought him back to life (see extract,

St. Paul Led to Martyrdom, by Luca di Tomme (1333–89). The traditional site of Paul's death, Tre Fontane (Three Fountains) in Rome, is so called from a legend that his head bounced three times, a spring appearing at each spot.

below). Finding that Patroclus and other courtiers have joined Christ's army, the emperor decrees "that all who were found to be Christians and soldiers of Christ should be put to death."

Nero recognizes Paul as the ringleader of the Christians and has the apostle interrogated. But Paul's replies simply enrage the emperor, who orders all the Christian prisoners to be burned except Paul, who is a Roman citizen. He is "to be beheaded according to the law of the Romans." Paul promises to appear after his execution in proof of the resurrection of the body.

At this point the narrative introduces the prefect Longus and the centurion Cestus, who are impressed by Paul's teaching. Paul promises that if they visit his grave the next morning they will be given the seal of baptism by two of his long serving companions, Luke and Titus. After praying, Paul is decapitated with a sword but instead of blood, "milk spurted upon the soldier's clothing." Later, Paul appears to the emperor and threatens him with imminent doom. Terrified, Nero orders the Christians to be released. In the closing scene, Longus and Cestus come to Paul's tomb, where they see Titus and Luke praying with the risen apostle, and are baptized. This probably points to the Church's increasing veneration of the tombs of martyrs.

From the Acts of Paul (the Martyrdom of Paul)

When [Nero] saw Patroclus ... he cried out, "Patroclus, are you alive?" And he said, "I am alive, Caesar." But he said, "Who is he who made you to live?" And the youth ... said, "Christ Jesus, the king of the ages." But Caesar ... said, "So he is to be king of the ages, and destroy all the kingdoms?" ... [And] he struck him on the face and said, "Patroclus, do you also serve in that king's army?" And he said, "Yes, lord Caesar, for indeed he raised me up when I was dead." And ... Nero's chief men said, "We also are in the army of that king of the ages." But he shut them up in prison ... and commanded that the soldiers of the great king be sought out. ...

[Nero said to Paul], "Man of the great king, but now my prisoner, why did it seem good to you to come secretly into the empire of the Romans and enlist soldiers from my province?" But Paul, filled with the Holy Spirit, said before them all, "Caesar, not only from your province do we enlist soldiers, but from the whole world. For this charge has been laid upon us, that no man be excluded who wishes to serve my king. ... Caesar, it is not for a short time that I live for my king. And if you behead me, this will I do: I will arise and appear to you in proof that I am not dead, but alive to my Lord Christ Jesus, who is coming to judge the world."

But Longus and Cestus said to Paul, "Whence have you this king, that you believe in him without change of heart, even unto death?" Paul communicated the word to them [and they said] "We entreat you, help us and we will let you go." But he answered and said, "I am no deserter from Christ, but a lawful soldier of the living God. Had I known that I was to die, I would have done it. But since I live to God and love myself, I go to the Lord that I may come again with him in the glory of his Father."

THE ACTS OF ANDREW

In its original form the Acts of Andrew was almost certainly the longest of all the apocryphal acts. Unfortunately it is also the worst preserved, and any attempt at a reconstruction has to take the form of a mosaic of a variety of witnesses. It is also one of the earliest of the acts, to be dated probably ca. 150CE.

Between the third and ninth centuries CE the Acts of Andrew was disseminated throughout both Eastern and Western Christendom, and it was used particularly by heretical groups, such as the Manicheans (see p.222) and the Priscillianists (see p.229). As a result it was rejected by the mainstream Church, but it was a long time before the work was consigned to oblivion.

What is known of its scope is derived from the summary of it in the Book of the Miracles of the Blessed Apostle Andrew, by Gregory of Tours (ca. 540–594CE). From this, it can be seen that the composition followed a typical pattern: a travel narrative and an account of a martyrdom. From Palestine, Andrew travels westward to cities in northern Asia Minor and Greece, finally ending in Achaia (southern Greece). He is particularly active in Philippi and in Patras, where he is executed and buried. Gregory concentrates almost exclusively on the apostle's miracles and removes his speeches. In fact, these are the most significant part of the Acts of Andrew because they express the author's particular theology, which does not wholly accord with the orthodox Catholic outlook of Gregory—hence his suppression of these passages.

The Acts of Andrew belongs to the same popular religious milieu as the Acts of Peter, with which it has some close connections and similar gnosticizing elements (see box, below). On

Gnosticism and the Acts of Andrew

The Acts of Andrew represents a mode of thought which is not to be defined as developed Gnosticism but rather as displaying the "gnosticizing tendencies" that frequently emerge in the Christianity of the period. There is the dualism between the spiritual and the material world and the concept of salvation as being the discovery by individuals of the divine nature within themselves. Such awareness is achieved through the revelation brought by the Redeemer, who is not the incarnate Jesus, but a wholly divine being who is hard to distinguish from God himself. The visible world is the sphere of illusion and transitoriness, from which humans free themselves by realizing their real inner being, leading to a renunciation of the things of the flesh: sex, a rich diet, wealth, and public honors. The apostle Andrew is the medium through whom this is made known—he is described as the "midwife" of salvation and he is at once the revealer and the example which humanity should follow.

the other hand, the work also shows evidence of the influence of Hellenistic philosophy. Compared with other apocryphal acts, the author is something of a philosopher and an intellectual, at home in the general philosophical and religious climate of the second century CE.

Apart from the information supplied by Gregory of Tours, the only event at Philippi is recounted in an incomplete Coptic papyrus (see extract, below). It tells of a young soldier who is possessed by a demon. Andrew performs an exorcism and, after the young man is restored to his right mind, the soldier enlists in the spiritual service of Christ.

The account of the martyrdom of Andrew, and the events leading up to it, displays the ingredients common to such texts: miraculous healings, conversions, persecution and finally

From the Utrecht Coptic Papyrus

[Andrew said to the demon], "Why then should you not tremble ...? I tremble wholly in all my limbs and I glorify the receiver who is coming for the souls of the saints. O champions of virtue, not in vain have you contended: see, the judge of the contest prepares for you the crown unfading. ... O virgins, not in vain have you guarded the purity, and not in vain have you persevered in prayers, while your lamps burned in the midst of the night, until the call reached you, 'Arise, go out to meet the bridegroom.'"

When the demon had departed ... the young man ... put off his uniform of soldiery ... saying, "O man of God, I have spent ... pieces of gold to acquire this ephemeral garment ... but now I will give all that I possess that I may obtain for myself the uniform of your God." His comrades ... said to him, "... if you deny the emperor's uniform, you will be punished." The young man replied, "Truly I am wretched because of my former sins. Would that my punishment were only because of this, that I denied the uniform of the emperor, and that I be not punished because I have despised the baptismal garment of the immortal King of the ages."

Scenes from the Life of St. Andrew, a Russian icon of the apostle, who was widely revered in the Middle Ages and was adopted as the patron of Greece, Russia, Scotland, and several other countries.

crucifixion. As well as the apostle, the protagonists at Patras are the proconsul Aegeates, his brother Stratocles, the proconsul's wife Maximilla, and her maidservant Iphidama. Stratocles has come to the city "to turn to philosophy": he has abandoned worldly ambition for a quest to discover the truth. Andrew expels a spirit possessing a servant of Stratocles and fully restores the slave to health—as a consequence, Stratocles is eager to learn the apostle's teaching. Andrew first exhorts him to realize his true nature, telling him, "Bring forth, my child, what you have. ... I know him who is silent, I know him who yearns, already your new man speaks to me" and then continues to show that this self-realization, the new man, will lead him to see that his searchings can only be resolved by his conversion to the Christian faith. And in a speech, which may well have been originally addressed to him, Andrew gives a full description of what the awareness of the individual's innermost nature really means and effects. Stratocles is won over and henceforward becomes the apostle's devoted follower.

However, the main emphasis falls on Maximilla. Andrew convinces her to leave her husband and embrace a life of continence. All attempts by Aegeates to win her back are rebuffed and Andrew is duly thrown into prison, with the sarcastic remark, "You corrupter, for your good deeds to Maximilla these thanks are returned by me." She maintains contact with the imprisoned apostle, who strengthens her in her resolve, so that finally Aegeates is driven to order his execution. The narrative of the martyrdom focuses particularly on two features: Andrew's speech to the cross, similar to that in the Acts of Peter, and his final message of the vanity of all earthly things compared with the rewards of the heavenly life.

From the Acts of Andrew

DATA

TITLE:
The Acts of Andrew

ORIGINAL DATE OF COMPOSITION:
ca. 150 CE

ORIGINAL LANGUAGE:
Greek

PROVENANCE:
Unknown

EARLIEST EXTANT MANUSCRIPT:
4th cent. CE (Coptic)

"If, O human being, you understand all these things ... namely that you are immaterial, holy, light, akin to the unbegotten, intellectual, heavenly, translucent, pure, superior to the flesh, superior to the world, superior to powers, superior to authorities, over whom you really are, ... then take knowledge in what you are superior. ...

"Hail, O cross ... I am come to you whom I recognize as my own; I am come to you, who long for me. I know the mystery for which you have indeed been set up. For you are set up in the cosmos to establish the unstable. And one part of you stretches up to heaven so that you may point out ... Logos, the head of all things. Another part of you is stretched out to right and left that you may put to flight the fearful and inimical power and draw the cosmos into unity. And another part of you is set on the earth, rooted in the depths, that you may bring what is on earth and under the earth into contact with what is in heaven. ... Well done, O cross, that you have bound the circumference of the world!"

OPPOSITE *St. Andrew and St. Francis*, by El Greco (1540–1614). Andrew is shown with an X-shaped cross, in accordance with a relatively late tradition—the Acts of Andrew indicate that his cross was a standard one.

THOMAS IN INDIA

Of the five principal apocryphal acts, the Acts of Thomas is the only work that is preserved entire. The earliest complete version is in Greek but scholars generally agree that this is a translation of an original Syriac text. As such, the work is significant for the evidence it provides about early Christianity in Syria, centered on the city of Edessa.

The thought of the Acts of Thomas shows close connections with two great theologians of Syrian Christianity, Tatian (ca. 120–173CE) and Bardaisan (154–222CE), both of whom were later considered heretical. The work comprises thirteen scenes, followed by the account of the apostle's martyrdom. The setting is almost entirely various cities in India, the association with that country probably accounted for by the close ties between Edessa and north India around the beginning of the third century CE, the most likely date for the work's composition.

Thomas was an important figure for the early Church. He is called Judas Thomas and also Didymus, "the Twin," and regarded as the twin brother of Jesus. The motif of the "twin" is a central feature of the Acts of Thomas—it is hardly an exaggeration to say that the apostle appears virtually as Jesus' identical twin, and their roles are often interchangeable.

The author of the Acts of Thomas is concerned less with doctrinal issues than with recounting a series of wonder stories, including talking animals and reviving the dead.

From the Acts of Thomas, chapters 6 and 7

The maiden is the daughter of light,
Upon her stands and rests the majestic
    effulgence of kings,
Delightful is the sight of her,
Radiant with shining beauty. ...
Her two hands make signs and secret
    patterns, proclaiming the dance of
    blessed aeons,
Her fingers open the gates of the city. ...
Her groomsmen keep her compassed about,
    whose number is seven, ...
And her bridesmaids are seven,
Who dance before her. ...
Having their gaze and look toward the
    bridegroom,

That by the sight of him they may be
    enlightened;
And forever shall they be with him in that
    eternal joy, ...
And they shall glorify the Father of all,
Whose proud light they received
And were enlightened by the vision of their
    Lord,
Whose ambrosial food they received,
Which has no deficiency at all,
And they drank too of his wine
Which gives them neither thirst nor desire;
And they glorified and praised, with the
    living Spirit,
The Father of Truth and Mother of Wisdom.

Scenes from the Life of St. Thomas, from a 13th-century window in Bourges cathedral, France. The legendary episodes depicted include the tale of Thomas at the wedding feast (see p.203).

Nevertheless, the works display a theological outlook common to all the apocryphal acts, representing popular beliefs and practices among Christians. Central is the preaching of asceticism, particularly sexual abstinence. A sharp contrast is drawn between the present world and the heavenly existence which Christ reveals, and the calling of the believers is to renounce the pleasures of the material world and, by a life of holiness, to realize their true spiritual nature. Jesus is above all the Revealer and the Redeemer, although the events of his earthly life are certainly referred to in an orthodox fashion. The work makes greater use of the canonical biblical writings than any other apocryphal text, but it concentrates largely on the teachings and parables of Jesus.

Although the work is intended for a popular audience, the author is a sophisticated thinker, who welds together a wide range of traditions and concepts into his own richly symbolical pattern. The book begins with the apostles in Jerusalem dividing the world among

The 1st-century CE Buddhist monastery at Takht-i-Bahi, Pakistan. Legends of apostolic activity in India may stem from early accounts of India as a land "teeming with monks," as the *Golden Legend* puts it. This was true—but the thriving monasteries of the region were Buddhist ones.

From the Acts of Thomas, chapters 31–32

DATA

TITLE:
The Acts of Thomas

ORIGINAL DATE OF
COMPOSITION:
ca. 200–250CE

ORIGINAL LANGUAGE:
Syriac

PROVENANCE:
East Syria

EARLIEST EXTANT
MANUSCRIPT:
ca. 11th cent.
(Greek)

[The serpent said to Thomas:] "I am a reptile of reptile nature, the baleful son of a baleful father. ... I am son of him who sits upon the throne and has power over the creation which is under heaven ... I am a kinsman of him who is outside the ocean, whose tail is set in his own mouth; I am he who entered through the fence into Paradise and said to Eve all the things my father charged me to say to her; I am he who kindled and inflamed Cain to slay his own brother, and because of me thorns and thistles sprang up on the earth; I am he who hurled the angels down from above, and bound them in lusts for women, that earth-born children might come from them and I fulfill my will in them; I am he who hardened Pharaoh's heart ... I am he who led the multitude astray in the wilderness, when they made the calf; I am he who inflamed Herod and kindled Caiaphas to the false accusation of the lie before Pilate ... I am he who kindled Judas and bribed him to betray Christ to death. ... I am a kinsman of him who is to come from the east, to whom also is given power to do what he will on the earth."

them for their missionary work. Thomas is assigned to India but refuses to go. At this point, there arrives an Indian merchant called Abban, sent by King Gundaphorus to buy a slave-carpenter. In a reversal of the selling of Jesus by Judas Iscariot, Jesus takes the initiative and effects the sale of Judas Thomas, who is now described as a carpenter like himself.

Abban and Thomas set out by ship and arrive first at Andrapolis, probably in Egypt. While there, Thomas sings a hymn during a wedding which at first sight seems to be a paean to erotic love, but in fact is an allegory supplanting bodily union for that between Christ and the believer (see extract, p.200). The sequel confirms this when Jesus appears, in the guise of Thomas, to the newly married pair, and tells them to renounce sexual intercourse in favor of "that incorruptible and true marriage, in which you shall be groomsmen entering into that bridal chamber which is full of immortality and light." The couple duly separate.

After arriving in India, Thomas is introduced to King Gundaphorus, who commissions him to build a palace. The apostle uses the money for the relief of the poor, later explaining that he has indeed built a palace but it is in heaven and the king will see it only after his death. Gundaphorus is furious and condemns Thomas to be flayed alive. But then the king's brother dies and angels take his soul to heaven, where he discovers the palace. The angels allow him to return to earth and report to his brother, and the two of them are converted to Christianity. This narrative illustrates one of the main themes of the work—the absolute contrast between the present world, which is corrupt and transitory, and the immortal, heavenly realm, which is humanity's true home. The author sets out another of his main concerns, that men and women can only free themselves from the slavery of their present existence by realizing their true spiritual nature and renouncing the claims of the material world, following the example of Jesus.

The Children of Satan

The narrative of Thomas in the kingdom of Gundaphorus includes prominent accounts of the apostle's expulsion and destruction of demons, and these have great significance in the author's theological outlook. The demons form part of the sad lot which humanity endures in the present world—they appear in many forms and are the children of Satan, the material world's ruler, who continually afflicts human beings, "coming in by stealth and casting men into doubt." In a retrospective narrative drawn from the Bible which demonstrates the author's knowledge and use of the canonical scriptures, a great serpent recounts the various demonic shapes it has assumed throughout history (see extract, opposite). It ends its speech with a prophecy of the coming of a cryptic figure "from the east," probably a reference to the well-known legend of the return of the emperor Nero, who will stand at the end of time as the champion of Satan in a final confrontation with his nemesis, God's Messiah.

MYGDONIA AND CHARISIUS

The first section of the Acts of Thomas, set in the kingdom of Gundaphorus, consists of individual miracle stories, with no clear connection between them. In the second section, the scene moves to another Indian city, ruled by a king called Misdaeus, and the character of the writing changes markedly.

Accounts of the apostle's miracles largely disappear: perhaps the only clear example is Misdaeus' attempt to torture Thomas by attaching hot metal plates to his feet. But "immediately water gushed abundantly from the ground, so that the plates were swallowed up," and the king is in danger of drowning and is only saved when the apostle prays for the flood to disappear. Instead, all the emphasis falls on the sermons and prayers of Thomas, expounding the nature and demands of the faith, and the conversions which his words effect. The whole sequence is much more coherent, with the particular episodes closely linked together, and the emotions and personalities of the participants are more fully developed.

The center of the whole represents a motif common to all the apocryphal acts—women who are persuaded to live apart from their husbands and then to adopt the Christian religion. The principal figure is a wealthy woman Mygdonia, accompanied by her nurse Marcia, but there is also an account of the conversion of the king's wife, Tertia. Won over, too, by Thomas is Siphor, one of the royal captains and the king's son, Vazan. Here can be seen another common element—a concern to show the success of Christianity's appeal with the upper classes.

From the Acts of Thomas, chapters 128 and 130

Charisius came up [to the apostle] and said to him in entreaty, "I pray you, O man: I have never sinned at all, neither against you or anyone else, nor against the gods. Why have you stirred up so great an evil against me? ... For what reason do you drive me out of my mind, and cast yourself into destruction? For if you do not persuade her, I will both kill you and take my own life. And if, as you say, there is life and death beyond, and also condemnation and victory and a tribunal, I too will go in there to be judged with you. And if the God whom you preach is just, and awards the punishments justly, I ... shall obtain justice.

... Therefore listen to me and come home with me, and persuade Mygdonia to become with me as formerly, before she saw you!" ... Thomas said to Mygdonia, "My daughter, obey what brother Charisius says!" And Mygdonia said, "If you could not name the deed in word, how do you compel me to endure the act? ... But now you say this because you are afraid. But who does something, and having been praised ... then changes it? Who builds a tower and then demolishes it from the foundations? Who digs a well of water in a thirsty place and fills it in again? Who finds a treasure and does not make use of it?"

Mygdonia is married to Charisius, a kinsman of the king, who is depicted in a remarkably sympathetic light. His deep love for his wife is brought out by the moving and pathetic pleas with which he attempts to persuade her to return to him: though he occasionally utters threats against her, he does not carry them out. He shows considerable respect for Thomas and, in a striking passage, points to his honorable and upright life, which has not deserved the confusion which the apostle's teaching has brought upon him (see extract, opposite), and asks Thomas to beg Mygdonia to live with him as before. Thomas does so, but his intervention only serves to confirm Mygdonia in her resolution. Finally, Charisius takes his case to the king but, even then, he begs Misdaeus not to carry out his intention of executing Thomas, saying, "Have patience a little while, O king. First terrify the man with words and persuade him, that he may persuade Mygdonia to become to me as formerly." However, after repeated warnings from the king, Thomas is finally imprisoned—the prelude to martyrdom.

The chapel on St. Thomas's Mount near Madras, India. It stands on the hill where Thomas is traditionally said to have been martyred. It is said that his body was later moved to Edessa and thence to Italy.

SACRED RITES AND PRAYERS

One of the most interesting features of the Acts of Thomas is the information it provides about the liturgical practices and beliefs of the early Syrian church. The conversions of Gundaphorus and his brother and of the various individuals in the kingdom of Misdaeus all climax in an initiation ritual through which the new believers are admitted into the communion of the Church.

The fullest account of this rite is given in the case of Mygdonia and referred to more briefly elsewhere. It was made up of three stages: first, there was an anointing with holy oil, then baptism in water in the name of the Trinity, followed by the celebration of the eucharist. The anointing took the form of the pouring of oil on the head of the initiate, reflecting what was done in the case of kings in the Hebrew Scriptures, and on one occasion it is related that

Thomas ordered Mygdonia so to anoint the women candidates, while he himself anointed the male candidate Vazan: that this distinction was the regular practice of the Syrian church is confirmed by the third-century CE Church order known as the Teaching of the Apostles, which comes from the same area as the Acts of Thomas, and directs that deaconesses are to anoint the women, "since it is not fitting that a woman should be seen by men," probably indicating that oil was applied not only to the head but also the naked body, as the Acts of Thomas also indicates on at least one occasion. Anointing and water baptism go together in all the Syrian initiatory rituals but it would seem that special significance was ascribed to the former.

The meaning of the anointing and the eucharist is expounded in the apostle's prayers which accompany them. They take the regular liturgical form of the *epiklesis*, the

St. Thomas Blessing, a 15th-century Macedonian icon.

invocation of the Holy Spirit over the material elements (see extract, below). Anointing signifies the Spirit, which transforms the believers into new men and women. The Spirit is depicted as female, for it must be remembered that the word for "spirit" is feminine in Syriac, as in other Semitic languages. Thus the Spirit is addressed as the "compassionate mother," and as such is the mother of the Savior, with whom she is closely linked as "the power established in Christ" and the one who reveals the hidden mysteries of his teaching. But also she is the mother of the sacramentally new-born believer, who becomes the twin of the Redeemer. She is also identified with the biblical figure of the Divine Wisdom, another female personage, and when she is described as "mother of the seven houses," there is a clear echo of the seven pillars of the house built by Wisdom according to Proverbs 9.

The Spirit is also the power invoked for the celebration of the eucharist, which has a number of distinctive features in the Acts of Thomas. The elements are solely bread and water, as found in other apocryphal writings, which points to the strongly ascetic outlook of the circles in which such texts originated. In particular, it is the bread, and its blessing, breaking and distribution, that is the central element—the cup of water being little more than an accompanying feature. So the clearest account of the ritual in the work has Thomas bringing a stool, over which he spreads a linen cloth and sets on it "the bread of blessing," utters a consecratory prayer and then marks the bread with the sign of the cross, breaks and distributes it, saying, "Let this be to you for the forgiveness of sins and eternal transgressions": there is no mention of either water or wine.

This reflects the custom of the early church in Syria, where the breaking of bread was the heart of the liturgy. Sacraments are thus as vital an element in the work of Thomas as his teaching and miracles and it is not surprising that King Misdaeus should describe the apostle as one who "bewitches men with oil and water and bread."

From the Acts of Thomas, chapter 27

The apostle took the oil and pouring it on their heads anointed and chrismed them, and began to say:
"Come, holy name of Christ that is above
    every name;
Come, power of the Most High and perfect
    compassion;
Come, you highest gift;
Come, compassionate mother;
Come, fellowship of the male;

Come, you female one who reveals the
    hidden mysteries;
Come, mother of the seven houses, that your
    rest may be in the eighth house;
Come, elder of the five members,
    understanding, thought, prudence,
    consideration, reasoning ...
Come, Holy Spirit, and purify [them]
And give them the added seal in the name of
    the Father and Son and Holy Spirit."

THE SONG OF THE PEARL

The most famous part of the Acts of Thomas is the Song of the Pearl, a long poem in the story of Mygdonia, where it is spoken by the apostle. Most scholars agree that this particularly beautiful example of Syriac poetry was originally an independent work.

The language of the hymn is symbolic and allusive and its interpretation has been much debated. Nevertheless, the plot is clear. A young prince is divested of his royal garments and sent by his parents to go down to Egypt to "bring the one pearl which is in the midst of the sea, in the abode of the loud-breathing serpent." Eventually, the prince casts a spell on the serpent, seizes the pearl, and sets out for home. On his return, he is invested once more with his royal robe and recognized, with his brother, as the heir to the kingdom.

The Song of the Pearl subtly interweaves a number of motifs and themes. It is based on two of Jesus' parables, that of the Prodigal Son who leaves home but eventually returns, and that of the merchant who sells all his possessions to gain one precious pearl, which represents the kingdom of heaven. The main concern is actually not the pearl but the prince's robe. The restoration of the robe is the climax of the poem: it represents the recovery of the image of God and the union of the believer (the prince) with Jesus (the prince's brother), with whom he will inherit the kingdom of heaven. The prince also represents Thomas as the perfect example of what every human being may achieve, and the apostle's union with Jesus accords with the concept of Jesus and Judas Thomas as twins (see p.200).

The Prince and Human Destiny

In one respect the prince represents Adam, who is often viewed in apocryphal texts as originally a heavenly and kingly being (see pp.22–3). As a result of the Fall, Adam lost the image of God, symbolized by the prince's removal of his royal robe. Adam is also the representative of humankind as a whole, and so the Song of the Pearl is above all about the true nature of human destiny. Humans are enslaved in the world of matter, symbolized by Egypt, where they live in ignorance and oblivion, from which they must awaken to realize their true heavenly existence, represented by the acquisition of the pearl. This awakening is brought about by the revelation of the Christian gospel, symbolized by a letter to the prince from his parents, which urges him to complete his task and return, drawing him home "with its love." Humanity was expelled from Eden but people can return to Paradise by embracing a life of holiness and purity. In doing so they reverse the victory of Satan—the serpent in the Song of the Pearl—over Adam. A summons to the holy life is the main doctrine of the entire Acts of Thomas.

The Parable of the Prodigal Son, by the Master of the Female Half Lengths (active ca. 1490–1540). The Acts of Thomas interprets this episode somewhat differently from the canonical gospels.

From the Song of the Pearl, lines 82–102

My splendid robe adorned
Gleaming in glorious colors,
With gold and beryls,
Chalcedonies and opals …
And the likeness of the king of kings
Was embroidered all over it …
And again I saw that all over it
The motions of knowledge were stirring.
And I saw too
That it was preparing as for speech.
I heard the sound of its songs
Which it whispered at its descent:
"I belong to the most valiant servant,
For whom they reared me before my father,
And I perceived also in myself

That my stature grew according to his
   labors."
And with its royal movements
It poured itself entirely toward me …
And my love also spurred me
To run to meet it and receive it …
I clothed myself with it and mounted up
To the gate of greeting and homage.
I bowed my head and worshipped
The splendor of the father who had sent it
   to me,
Whose commands I had accomplished,
As he also had done what he promised. …
For he rejoiced over me and received me,
And I was with him in his kingdom.

THE MARTYRDOM OF THOMAS

The episodes which precede the account of the apostle's martyrdom are carefully developed to foreshadow and lead up to that final event. On the one hand, in a series of speeches Thomas anticipates his death, bears witness to his faithful ministry in the past and prepares himself and his followers for what is to come. On the other hand, the author shows that Thomas has established an enduring Christian community.

The final scene before the martyrdom describes a ceremony when the remaining prominent converts he has made are admitted into the Church's fellowship, culminating in the eucharist in which they all share and, after they have uttered the concluding Amen, this is repeated by a heavenly word of assurance, "Amen, fear not but only believe."

The narrative of the martyrdom follows immediately on this valedictory scene. It seems likely that the account was often transmitted as a separate text. It is not clearly explained why King Misdaeus, who hitherto has done no more than imprison Thomas, should now decide to execute him. However, it would seem that sorcery was the capital charge, as the king says to the apostle: "But now I will so deal with you that your sorceries may perish with you." Reflecting what is said in the canonical gospels about the attitude of the Jerusalem hierarchy toward Jesus, Misdaeus is afraid of the apostle's popularity with the people and decides to kill him secretly: he hands him over to four soldiers, "commanding them to take him to the mountain and dispatch him with spears." Thomas meets his fate with a speech that expresses his awareness of his human condition: "Behold, how four have laid hold of me, since from the four elements I came into being! And one leads me, since I belong to one, to whom I depart. But now I learn that my Lord, since he was of one, to whom I depart and who is forever invisibly with me, was struck by one; but I, since I am of four, am struck by four."

The Efficacy of Relics

Two features in the account of the martyrdom reveal the ecclesiastical interests of the author. Thomas was accompanied by some of his followers on the mountain, where he ordains Siphor, the royal captain, as a presbyter, and Vazan, the king's son, as a deacon, thus establishing a church, which continued in existence, since "the Lord helped them and increased the faith through them." An epilogue to the story relates how, after a long time had elapsed, a son of Misdaeus was afflicted by a demon and the king decided to open the apostle's tomb to take one of the bones to fasten on his son so that he might be healed. But he found the tomb empty of any bones, because "one of the believers had stolen them away and carried them to the regions of the West." This may well be a reference to the tradition of the translation of Thomas' relics back to Edessa in 394CE. Misdaeus has to be satisfied with some dust from where the body had rested and this proves efficacious—the book ends with the king's conversion, "becoming submissive to Siphor," thus completing the acts of Judas Thomas "which he performed in the land of the Indians, fulfilling the command of him who sent him."

From the Acts of Thomas, chapters 159–162

Judas [Thomas] went away to be imprisoned. And not only so, but Tertia and Mygdonia and Marcia too went away to be imprisoned. ... When [the apostle] had completed his word to them, he went into the dark house and said, "My Savior, ... let these doors become as they were, and let them be sealed with their seals!" And leaving the women he went away to be shut up. ... When he returned, [he] found the guards fighting and saying, "What sin have we committed against that sorcerer, that by magic art he opened the doors of the prison, and wishes all the prisoners to escape? But let us go and inform the king." ... And as soon as day broke, they arose and went off to king Misdaeus, and said, "Lord, release that sorcerer or command him to be kept in custody somewhere else. For twice has your good fortune kept the prisoners together. Though we shut the doors at the proper time, yet when we wake we find them open. And moreover, your wife and your son, together with those others, do not stay away from the man." When he heard this, the king went to inspect the seals which he had set upon the doors; and he found the seals as they were before. And he said to the jailers, "Why do you lie? For indeed these seals are still intact. And how say you, that Tertia and Mygdonia went into the prison?" And the guards said, "We told you the truth."

OPPOSITE *The Apostle Thomas*, by Georges de la Tour (1593–1652). The apostle holds a spear, traditionally said to be the instrument of his martyrdom (see main text, opposite).

CHAPTER 5

VISIONS OF THE END OF TIME

◆

THE APOCALYPSE OF PETER

The existence of numerous Christian apocalypses bears witness to the great significance of apocalyptic concepts in the early Church. Such works represent a development of themes in the New Testament, which they often quote, and they share many features with the Jewish apocalyptic tradition (see p.236), of which they are the heirs.

The rabbinical Judaism that developed under Roman rule after 70CE largely suppressed the apocalyptic writings—partly for political reasons, since many described the overthrow of imperial tyrannies—but the texts were preserved and venerated by Christians, who christianized them in various degrees. Jewish apocalypses purport to be by great figures of Israel's past, and Christian works similarly claim famous characters in the history of the Church as their authors. As the term apocalypse ("revelation") implies, the essential element in all Christian apocalyptic texts is a secret revelation given by Jesus to one of his followers. These teachings generally take the form of a description of the end of the world, which in Christian works usually centers on the second coming of Christ. An important feature of Jewish apocalyptic is a review of national or world history presented as prediction, but this is rarely found in Christian works.

The most notable, and generally the earliest, Christian apocalypses are those attributed to Peter, Paul, and Thomas. There are two completely different works called the Apocalypse of Peter, one of which is a Coptic work in the Nag Hammadi library (see pp.216–17). The other

DATA

TITLE:
The Apocalypse
of Peter

ORIGINAL DATE OF
COMPOSITION:
100–150CE

ORIGINAL LANGUAGE:
Greek

PROVENANCE:
Egypt

EARLIEST EXTANT
MANUSCRIPT:
3rd–4th cent. CE
(Greek)

From the Apocalypse of Peter, chapter 8

Near this flame there is a great and very deep pit ... And the women are swallowed up, up to their necks and are punished with great pain. These are they who have procured abortions and have ruined the work of God which he has created. Opposite them is another place where the children sit, ... and they cry to God. And lightnings go forth from those children which pierce the eyes of those who, by fornication, have brought about their destruction. ... And they sigh and cry to God because of their parents, "These are they who neglected and cursed and transgressed your commandment. They killed us and cursed the angel who created us, and hung us up. And they withheld from us the light which you have appointed for all." ... And the children shall be given to the angel Temlakos. And those who killed them will be tortured for ever, for God wills it to be so.

probably dates from the first half of the second century CE and comes from Egypt, where Peter was a significant figure, because the church of Alexandria was traditionally founded by his disciple, Mark. The work was widely known and respected and it is often cited by the Church Fathers—Clement of Alexandria (ca. 150–ca. 215CE) even accounts it as inspired Scripture.

The first part of the book has the same setting as the first chapter of the canonical Acts of the Apostles. Here, though, the disciples ask Jesus not about the restoration of the kingdom to Israel, but about "the signs of your second coming and of the end of the world," a phrase drawn from the Gospel of Matthew. Jesus describes the coming day of judgment, when the world will be destroyed by fire. The second part takes the well-known form of a tour of the cosmos, where Peter is shown the place of punishment for the wicked, whose sins and torments, which are inflicted by archangels, are described in exhaustive detail. The punishments are for sexual offenses or the failure to lead an ascetic life, and there is an especially interesting passage condemning abortion (see extract, opposite), although according to Clement of Alexandria this passage refers to the common ancient practice of exposing unwanted children to death. Finally, there is a retelling of the Transfiguration (Mark 9.2–8; Matt.17.1–8; Luke 9.28–36), in the course of which Peter is shown paradise, where the righteous dwell in bliss with the angels.

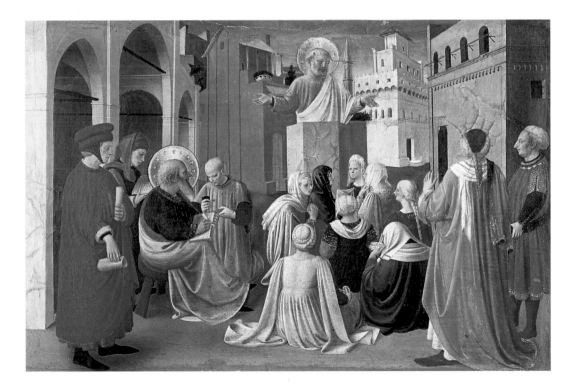

St Peter Preaching, by Fra Angelico (ca. 1387–1455). The seated figure with a halo and holding a book is generally agreed to be the evangelist Mark, who according to Christian tradition was Peter's disciple.

THE APOCALYPSE OF PAUL

The starting point of the Apocalypse of Paul is the apostle's account in the New Testament of how he was "caught up to the third heaven" and "heard things that are not to be told, that no mortal is permitted to repeat" (2 Cor. 12.3–4). It was typical of apocalyptic writers to seize on mysterious scriptural verses such as this and to attempt to satisfy the curiosity which they inevitably aroused about the celestial world.

The work recounts that Paul recorded his heavenly experiences in a scroll which he concealed under his house in Tarsus, his hometown. At the command of Jesus, an angel led to its "discovery" during the reign of the emperor Theodosius (ruled 379–395CE), very likely the period during which the text was actually composed. Although rejected by the ecclesiastical authorities, the Apocalypse became widely popular and was translated into several languages, and its influence on Christian concepts of heaven and hell endured beyond the Middle Ages. It is relatively late in its present form, but its use of various older traditions is reflected in its repetitive style—most notably its two almost identical visions of paradise.

Paul's account of his heavenly journey begins with the whole of creation complaining to God that "mankind alone sins." The apostle is shown the righteous and the wicked souls (see extract, opposite) and there is a long description of the torments inflicted on sinners that closely resembles the Apocalypse of Peter (see pp.212–13)—almost certainly one of the author's sources. Paul is depicted as a powerful figure, equal to the angels and the great heroes of Israel. On his second visit to paradise, which forms the book's climax, he is welcomed and honored by the Virgin Mary and the biblical patriarchs and prophets.

Heresy and Orthodoxy

The Apocalypse of Paul reflects the state of the Church in the fourth and fifth centuries CE, when Church leaders often propagated doctrines that were eventually judged as heretical, while monks and ordinary Christians continued to uphold orthodox beliefs. In Paul's account of the cosmos, the most severely judged class of sinners are the heretics, who, as the author says bluntly, "have not confessed that Christ came in the flesh and that the Virgin Mary bore him," or "say that Christ has not risen from the dead and that this flesh does not rise," or "that the bread of the eucharist and the cup of blessing are not the body and blood of Christ." Members of the Church hierarchy—a bishop, a presbyter, a deacon, and a lector—are tormented for failing in their duties. By contrast, the simple monastic life of the desert is presented as the ideal, and it is likely that the author was a monk.

The Rapture of St. Paul to the Third Heaven, by Nicolas Poussin (1593–1665). This depiction of Paul's ascension to heaven is influenced by the tradition of the Apocalypse of Paul.

From the Apocalypse of Paul, chapter 18

The Lord said to the soul of the sinner: "I say to you, soul, confess the deeds which you committed against these souls which you see, when they were in the world." And it answered and said: "Lord, it is not a full year since I killed this soul and shed its blood on the ground, and with that other I committed fornication; but that is not all, for I also injured it greatly by taking away its property." … And I heard the voice of one who said: "Let that soul be handed over into the hands of Tartarus, and it must be led down to the underworld … and be cast into torments and be left there until the great day of judgment." And again I heard thousands of thousands of angels who were singing a hymn to the Lord.

DATA

TITLE:
The Apocalypse
of Paul

ORIGINAL DATE OF
COMPOSITION:
Late 4th cent. CE

ORIGINAL LANGUAGE:
Greek

PROVENANCE:
Unknown

EARLIEST EXTANT
MANUSCRIPT:
Early medieval
(Latin)

THE GNOSTIC APOCALYPSES

DATA

TITLE:
The Coptic
Apocalypse of Peter

ORIGINAL DATE OF
COMPOSITION:
ca. 200CE

ORIGINAL LANGUAGE:
Greek

PROVENANCE:
Uncertain

EARLIEST EXTANT
MANUSCRIPT:
4th cent. CE (Coptic)

The Coptic Apocalypse of Peter from Nag Hammadi represents the beliefs of a particular Gnostic Christian group. In it, Jesus gives Peter a secret revelation to pass on to this sect, which views itself as an elect society of those who are alone able to receive Jesus' teaching and realize their true immortal natures. The revelation is presented as a prediction of events in the author's own day, very likely the turn of the third century CE.

The members of the sect are "aliens" in the existing world order and are persecuted by other Christians with false doctrines, who are described as being in the grip of demonic powers. Sometimes rival Gnostic groups seem to be in view, such as those who call themselves "after the name of a man with a naked woman of many forms and many sufferings." This probably denotes the followers of Simon Magus (see pp.174–7), the traditional founder of Gnosticism, whose companion Helena was believed to be constantly reborn in various female shapes. The work also

A 4th-century CE Roman relief of the apostles Peter (left) and Paul. Evidently unfinished, it perhaps depicts their legendary meeting in Rome, where both were traditionally said to have been martyred.

The Coptic Apocalypse of Paul

Also in the Nag Hammadi collection there is a Coptic Apocalypse of Paul, which, like the work of the same title (see pp.214–15) is an interpretation of 2 Corinthians 12.2–4. One of its concerns is to promote the status of Paul, since the purpose of his heavenly ascent is to meet the twelve apostles, who welcome him as their equal. He also witnesses the torments of the damned.

The text is only preserved in a fragmentary form but enough survives to prove its Gnostic outlook. This appears in particular in its understanding of the "Ancient One" of Daniel 7. The "old man in white raiment" whom Paul encounters in the seventh heaven is the lower creator deity of Gnostic thought, who tries to prevent Paul from ascending further, saying: "How will you be able to escape me? Look here and see these rulers and authorities!"—that is, the rulers of the created world. But a figure called the Spirit, identified with Christ, tells Paul to give a sign that is the proof of Paul's immortal nature and his freedom from the material world. When Paul does so, the way to the higher heavens is opened for him.

contrasts the true "brotherhood" with a false "sisterhood," perhaps referring to the prominence of female prophets in some Christian circles, notably the Montanists (see box on p.98).

However, the work reserves its main polemic for the emerging Great, or Catholic ("universal"), Church. Its leaders, the bishops and deacons, are denounced as falsely claiming authority from God. For the writer, the Lord is a wholly heavenly and spiritual being and Jesus says: "I myself am the Spirit, perceptible only spiritually, filled with radiant light." A clear line is drawn between the Son of Man in heaven and the human Jesus on earth, who is dismissed as the "imitator." The earthly Jesus is composed of a divine nature and a human nature that are distinct from one another. Only this Jesus can suffer and die and, when Peter is shown a vision of the Crucifixion, he sees the Redeemer leave his bodily counterpart on the cross and mock those who are deluded into believing they have killed the Savior (see extract, below). The author's principal opponents are therefore those "who adhere to the name of a dead man"—the historical Jesus.

From the Coptic Apocalypse of Peter

The Savior said to me: "He whom you see beside the tree glad and laughing, this is the living Jesus. But he into whose hands and feet they drive the nails is his fleshly likeness, the "ransom," which alone they are able to put to shame. That came into being after his likeness. But look on him and on me!"

But when I had looked, I said: "Lord, no one sees you, let us flee from here!" But he said to me: "I have told you that they are blind. ..." But I saw one about to approach us, like to him and to the one who laughed beside the tree—but it was woven in Holy Spirit, and this was the Savior.

DATA

TITLE:
The Coptic Apocalypse of Paul

ORIGINAL DATE OF COMPOSITION:
2nd–4th cent. CE

ORIGINAL LANGUAGE:
Greek

PROVENANCE:
Uncertain

EARLIEST EXTANT MANUSCRIPT:
4th cent. CE (Coptic)

THE APOCALYPSE OF THOMAS

The Apocalypse of Thomas was lost until the beginning of the twentieth century, although its existence was known from its condemnation in the "Gelasian Decree," a text probably of the sixth century CE. It is extant in a shorter and a longer version, both in Latin. It is generally agreed that the shorter text is the more authentic and that it was originally written in Greek.

The shorter version is distinguished from other apocalypses by its description of the events marking the end of the world. These are uniquely said to take place over seven days, consciously recalling the seven days of creation in the Book of Genesis and thus producing a symmetry between the beginning and end of the universe. The Apocalypse was also clearly inspired by the Book of Revelation, of which it contains numerous reminiscences, such as the prominence of the number seven. There is no particular order to the events of the seven days, rather each vividly relates a variety of cosmic catastrophes. These are followed by a final eighth day, when "a gentle and pleasant voice in heaven from the east" is heard and the elect are saved, rejoicing "that the destruction of the world has come."

The work's repeated references to light have suggested to some scholars a connection with Gnostic circles, where the motif of light was also a central concept. However, the author of the Apocalypse may simply have been inspired by his scriptural models: the appearance of light is the first creative act in Genesis (Gen. 1.3), while the climax of Revelation is the appearance of

From the Apocalypse of Thomas (shorter version)

DATA

TITLE:
The Apocalypse
of Thomas

ORIGINAL DATE OF
COMPOSITION:
Pre-400CE (shorter
vers.); 5th cent. CE
(longer vers.)

ORIGINAL LANGUAGE:
Greek

PROVENANCE:
Uncertain

EARLIEST EXTANT MS:
5th cent. (shorter);
8th cent. (longer)
(both Latin)

At the fourth hour of the sixth day there will be a great voice in heaven. ... Then the spirits and souls of the saints will come forth from paradise and come into all the earth, and each go to its own body where it is laid up; and each of them will say: "Here my body is laid up."

And when the great voice of those spirits is heard there will be an earthquake everywhere in the earth and by the force of that earthquake the mountains will be shattered above and the rocks beneath. Then each spirit will return to its own vessel and the bodies of the saints who sleep will rise. Then their bodies will be changed into the image and likeness and honor of the holy angels and into the power of the image of my holy Father. Then they will put on the garment of eternal life: the garment from the cloud of light which has never been seen in this world. ... Then they will be carried off in a cloud of light into the air, and rejoicing go with me into the heavens and remain in the light and honor of my Father. Then there will be great joy for them in the presence of my Father and in the presence of the holy angels.

The Seven Trumpets, illustrating Rev. 8.1–2, 6, from the Angers Tapestries (1377–82). The prominence of the number seven in the Apocalypse of Thomas reflects the direct influence of the Revelation of John.

the heavenly New Jerusalem, which is described as a city of light (Rev. 21–22). Furthermore, the book's very literal portrayal of bodily resurrection would have been quite unacceptable to Gnostics, and its theology is perhaps best described as a popular form of orthodox Christianity.

The longer Apocalypse of Thomas is in two parts, the second of which corresponds in content to the shorter version. The first part, represented as a letter from Jesus to Thomas, forms a typical apocalyptic review of past and future history, leading up to the final destruction of the world. Again a sevenfold scheme is noticeable: the text relates "the seven signs before the ending of this world" and it culminates in the announcement of seven "woes," recalling a similar literary pattern known in the Bible. This section evidently alludes to real historical events but the language is so cryptic that they are often virtually impossible to identify. One exception is a strange statement about two brothers, the sons of a certain king: "the first is named of the first letter, A, the second of the eighth, H, and the first shall die before the second." This appears to be a clear reference to the Western Roman emperor Arcadius (died 408ce), and his younger brother, the emperor Honorius (died 423ce). This evidence points to the early fifth century ce as the date for the composition of the longer version of the Apocalypse.

THE CHRISTIAN SIBYL

The earliest Sibylline Oracles are compositions of Jewish origin (see pp.100–103) but they were popular among Christians, who also produced their own—partly by adapting the Jewish texts and partly by composing new prophecies. Several sections of the existing Sibylline collection, especially Books 6–8, are entirely, or almost entirely, Christian in origin.

This material is of different dates down to some time in the third century CE. The Christian oracles tend to be longer and more literary than their earlier counterparts, and contain references to the canonical gospels as well as hymns to God or Christ. In the Jewish oracles,

The Sibyl and St. Luke, from the Palazzo dei Priori frescoes (ca. 1498–1500) by Perugino (see p.101).

the end of the world and the inauguration of the final age are brought about by God or a heavenly messianic figure, but in the Christian works they occur through the second coming of Christ, the cosmic Redeemer. In the Christian oracles, the Sibyl foretells Jesus' earthly career as part of a review of history expressed as prophecy, a typical feature of apocalyptic works. Other apocalyptic elements include descriptions of the end of the world, and of the judgment of the wicked. The oracles denounce the usual sins—idolatry, sexual immorality, and love of wealth—but their tone is not markedly ascetic. Martyrs and virgins are accorded honor, but their reward is the same as that of all "who deal justly" and "abstain from adultery." Revelation is to be found in Jesus' earthly life and in the reality of his incarnation and human nature; and salvation consists in the imitation of Christ. This theology is very much that of the mainstream Church, and it is easy to understand the popularity of the oracles among the early Christian theologians, who regularly quote them.

To emphasize Jesus' unique significance, the authors of the Christian Sibylline Oracles employ devices characteristic both of Jewish and Hellenistic literature. Speaking of the Son of God, who will "come to men, clothed in flesh, like mortals on earth," the text states: "Four vowels he has, two the consonants in him, and now will I declare to you also his whole number: eight ones, and to these as many tens, and eight hundreds also his name will show." This is an example of *gematria*, or numerology, revealing the hidden meaning of a word by adding up the numerical value of its letters. In this case the word is "Iesous" (ΙΕΣΟΥΣ), the Greek form of Jesus, which has two consonants and four vowels (the inital "I" counting as a vowel) which in ancient times had the values of 10, 8, 200, 70, 400, and 200. The total of 888 reveals the perfection and completeness of Jesus. Again, there is a poem about the Last Judgment, where the initial letters of the poem's 34 lines reproduce in succession the 34 letters of the Greek title: "Jesus Christ, Son of God, Savior, Cross."

From the Sibylline Oracles, Book 8, lines 299–311

But when all these things of which I have
 spoken are fulfilled,
then for him every law will be dissolved
 which from the beginning
was given in teachings to men, on account of
 a disobedient people.
He will stretch out his hands and measure
 the entire world.
They gave him gall for food and vinegar
 to drink.
They will show forth this table of
inhospitality.
The veil of the Temple will be [torn], and in
 the middle of the day
there will be dark monstrous night for
 three hours.
For no longer with secret law and temple
 must one serve
the phantoms of the world. ...
He will come to Hades announcing hope
 for all
the holy ones, the end of ages and the last day.

DATA

TITLE:
The Sibylline
Oracles
(Books 6–8)

ORIGINAL DATE OF
COMPOSITION:
Before 300CE

ORIGINAL LANGUAGE:
Greek

PROVENANCE:
Syria (Bks 6,7)
Uncertain (Bk 8)

EARLIEST EXTANT MS:
14th cent. CE
(Greek)

CHAPTER 6
LOST LETTERS TO THE FAITHFUL
◆
ABGAR AND JESUS

The apocryphal writings include an exchange of letters between Jesus and King Abgar V Uchama, who ruled the city of Edessa in Syria (present-day Urfa in southeast Turkey) in the early first century CE. The second letter is unique among apocryphal Christian works in being attributed to Jesus himself rather than one of his followers.

The earliest witness for the two letters is the Church historian Eusebius, writing probably ca. 310CE, who claims that he found them in the public records of Edessa and translated them from Syriac. In the first letter, the sick Abgar invites Jesus to come to Edessa and cure him. Jesus replies that he cannot leave Jerusalem until he has fulfilled his destiny, but he promises to send a disciple after the Ascension. Eusebius records that in 28 or 29CE the apostle Thomas duly sent the apostle Thaddaeus to Edessa. Thaddaeus, often identified with the apostle Jude, is mentioned in Matthew and Mark and is described in the letter as one of "the seventy" of Luke 10.1. After healing Abgar and others, Thaddaeus preaches a sermon and the entire city is converted.

The second witness is a Syriac work, The Doctrine of Addai, probably of the fifth century CE. It basically reproduces the material in Eusebius, with expansions and variations. The apostle sent to Abgar is not Thaddaeus but Addai, who in Syriac tradition founded the church at Edessa.

Edessa and the Heretics

The letters no doubt originate in Edessa, where they were well known and preserved, as attested by Eusebius and also the famous pilgrim Egeria, who visited the city in 384CE and was told about the letters by a bishop. The letter from Jesus says that "enemies shall never overcome" the city (see main text), and according to the bishop the letter was read at the city gate to rout enemy armies.

This pious fiction achieved a great reputation as an authentic message from Jesus and it was widely disseminated in a variety of languages. There is no evidence that any of the kings of Edessa were ever Christian. It has been strongly argued that the letters were composed to show that the orthodox version of the faith had been the first to reach Edessa, with a direct pedigree from Jesus himself. The purpose of the letters would be to combat influential heresies such as those of Marcion, Bardaisan, and Mani. One theory is that the letters, at least in their later forms, are aimed especially at Mani (active ca. 250CE), the founder of the widespread Manichean movement, in which Addai (see main text) was greatly revered.

222

It seems likely that he figured in the earliest form of the Abgar legend and that Eusebius changed his name to that of one of the apostles. In the second letter, Jesus says to Abgar, "your town will be blessed and enemies will never overcome it." If this clause, omitted by Eusebius, belonged to the original text, the work would predate 214CE, when Edessa became a Roman colony.

According to legend, Jesus' letter to Abgar was accompanied by the Mandylion, a likeness of his face imprinted on linen. This famous image, which is referred to in the Doctrine of Addai, was "rediscovered" at Edessa in the sixth century CE and provided the model for the classic bearded portraits of Jesus in the art of the Eastern Church (see illustration, below), succeeding the earlier Roman-style clean-shaven Christ. The Mandylion ended up at Constantinople, but disappeared—probably looted by Crusaders—in the early thirteenth century.

DATA

TITLE:
The Letters of
Abgar and Jesus

ORIGINAL DATE OF
COMPOSITION:
1st or 2nd cent. CE?

ORIGINAL LANGUAGE:
Syriac?

PROVENANCE:
Edessa, Syria

EARLIEST EXTANT
MANUSCRIPT:
None

From the Church History of Eusebius

The letter written by the ruler Abgar to Jesus, and sent to him at Jerusalem by the hand of Ananias the courier: "Abgar Uchama the ruler to Jesus the good Savior, who has appeared in the city of Jerusalem, greeting. I have heard of you and of your healings. ... It is for this reason that I write and beseech you to visit me, and heal my affliction. Moreover, I have heard that the Jews murmur against you, and wish to do you injury. Now I have a city, small indeed but noble, and large enough for both of us."

The reply sent by Jesus ... to the ruler Abgar: "Blessed are you, who have believed in me without having seen me. For it is written concerning me, that they who have seen me will not believe in me, and that they who have not seen me shall believe and live. But concerning what you have written to me, that I should come to you, it is necessary that I fulfill here everything for which I was sent, and after this fulfillment be taken up again to him who sent me. And when I am taken up, I will send to you one of my disciples to heal your affliction and give life to you and to those who are with you."

Christ Blessing, a Byzantine icon of ca. 1100CE. This portrait type derives from an image that Jesus is said to have sent to King Abgar (see main text).

THE LETTER TO THE LAODICEANS

Letters modeled on those of the New Testament are not widely represented among the Christian apocryphal texts. Only a small number have survived as separate documents, while some have been incorporated into other writings, such as the so-called "Third Letter to the Corinthians" in the Acts of Paul (see pp.190–191).

However, the Church Fathers mention a number of lost apostolic letters, which suggests that this literary genre was widely employed. Such texts are all written under the assumed name of a great figure of the early Church—a phenomenon also found in the New Testament itself, where the Second Letter of Peter and Paul's Letter to the Hebrews are almost certainly not by the apostles whom they claim as their authors.

Ruins of the ancient city of Laodicea in Asia Minor (present-day Eskihisar, Turkey). It was the site of an early Christian community that is mentioned in Paul's Letter to the Colossians and also in Revelation (Rev. 1.11, 3.14).

The Letter to the Laodiceans was inspired by a verse in Paul's Letter to the Colossians: "When this letter has been read among you, have it read also in the church of the Laodiceans; and see that you read also the letter from Laodicea" (Col. 4.16). This "letter from Laodicea" has not survived and the author aims to fill the gap. The resulting work consists almost entirely of a string of verses taken—with no discernible order or coherence—from Paul's genuine letters. The great majority are from the Letter to the Philippians, perhaps a favorite of the author, while the end of the letter deliberately imitates the verse of Colossians cited above (see extract, below).

It has at times been proposed that Laodiceans was written by a member of the Marcionite sect. The Muratorion Canon (ca. 200CE), an early list of New Testament writings, mentions a Letter to the Laodiceans "forged in Paul's name for the sect of Marcion." Marcion, active in Rome in the mid-second century CE, was excommunicated by the Roman church for rejecting the Hebrew Bible and its God and teaching that the Gospel was fully understood only by Paul. The Letter to the Laodiceans opens with an echo of the Letter to the Galatians, in which Paul teaches the obsolescence of the Jewish law. But this in itself is no proof of Marcionite tendencies in the extant Laodicean letter, which displays no trace of Marcionite theology. (Marcion, incidentally, produced the first New Testament canon—it included only Paul's letters and an edited form of Luke—and founded a church that survived into early medieval times.)

While the letter no doubt deserves the harsh verdict of M. R. James that it is a feebly assembled "canto of Pauline phrases," it is of interest as representing one class of Christian apocryphal material. Moreover, the work was widely accepted in the Church from the fourth century CE and was included in a large number of Bibles down to the end of the Middle Ages.

The Letter to the Laodiceans

1. Paul, an apostle not of men and not through man, but through Jesus Christ, to the brethren who are in Laodicea. 2. Grace to you and peace from God the Father and the Lord Jesus Christ. 3. I thank Christ in all my prayer that you are steadfast in him and persevering in his works, in expectation of the promise for the day of judgment. 4. And may you not be deceived by the vain talk of some people who tell you tales that they may lead you away from the truth of the gospel which is proclaimed by me. ... 10. Therefore, beloved, as you have heard in my presence, so hold fast and do in the fear of God, and eternal life will be your portion. 11. For it is God who works in you. 12. And do without hesitation what you do. 13. And for the rest, beloved, rejoice in Christ and beware of those who are out for sordid gain. 14. May all of your requests be manifest before God, and [may you] be steadfast in the mind of Christ. 15. And what is pure, true, proper, just, and lovely, do. 16. And what you have heard and received, hold in your heart and peace will be with you. ... 18. The saints salute you. 19. The grace of the Lord Jesus Christ be with your spirit. 20. And see that this letter is read to the Colossians and that of the Colossians among you.

DATA

TITLE:
The Letter to the Laodiceans

ORIGINAL DATE OF COMPOSITION:
Uncertain

ORIGINAL LANGUAGE:
Latin

PROVENANCE:
Rome?

EARLIEST EXTANT MANUSCRIPT:
6th cent. CE (Latin)

PAUL AND SENECA

The Roman philosopher Seneca (4BCE/1CE–65CE) was renowned in antiquity as a thinker of the Stoic school, as a prolific, brilliant writer and rhetorician and, until his downfall, as an influential minister of the emperor Nero (ruled 54–69CE). All these aspects are reflected in the fourteen letters which claim to be the correspondence between Seneca and his contemporary, the apostle Paul.

The earliest mention of the letters is by Jerome (ca. 342–420CE)—who wrote probably not long after they were actually written—and they were universally regarded as genuine until the end of the Middle Ages. No doubt the main purpose of the letters was to show the greatest philosopher of his day as receptive to the faith preached by Paul. In the last letter, which forms the climax to the collection, Paul praises Seneca as one in whose "reflection things have been revealed … which the Deity has granted only to a few." He has already come to realize "that the observances of the Gentiles and the Jews are to be avoided" and now Paul appeals to him: "Make yourself a new herald of Christ Jesus." The letters contain many expressions of mutual esteem and suggest that Seneca wished to produce a Latin version of Paul's writings that would join the great literature of the age. Seneca is somewhat critical of the Greek style of Galatians and 1 and 2 Corinthians and he sends Paul "a book on 'verbosity,'" perhaps as a broad hint.

As a whole, the correspondence has been dismissed as showing no interest in the genuine religious and philosophical ideas of the two men. But this was not the author's concern and the fame his work attained indicates his success in achieving his object.

The Letters and Rome in Seneca's Time

The letters of Paul and Seneca display quite accurate knowledge of the Roman philosopher and his times. It mentions his friend Lucilius and a garden in Rome which had once belonged to the historian Sallust. Several letters are precisely dated by naming the two consuls (Rome's highest officials, elected annually) in office at the time. A vivid account of the great fire of Rome in 64CE and of Nero's subsequent persecution of Christians and Jews probably derives from a lost historical source. The letters draw upon the well-known fact of Seneca's influence at the imperial court, as when he writes that he had read some of Paul's letters to Nero and received a favorable reaction. But Nero was a notorious figure among Christians and Paul tells Seneca that what he has done is a waste of time and asks him not to repeat it. Paul is also worried in case the empress Poppaea takes offense at the apostle's departure "from the ancient rites and beliefs" of Judaism. His concern reflects a tradition that Poppaea was attracted to Judaism.

The Fire of Rome, July 18th, 64AD, by Hubert Robert (1733–1808). The emperor Nero's persecution of Jews and Christians exploited popular rumors that they had started the conflagration that destroyed much of Rome.

The Correspondence of Paul and Seneca: From Letter 11

Greeting my dearest Paul! Do you think that I am not saddened and distressed that capital punishment is still visited upon your [people's] innocence? And also that all the populace judges you people so hard-hearted and so ready for any crime, believing that whatever happens amiss in the city is done by you? But let us bear with equanimity ... until invincible good fortune makes an end of evils. The time of the ancients suffered the Macedonian, the son of Philip, the Cyruses, Darius, and Dionysius, our own time also [Caligula], men whose every wish was law. It is clear at whose hands the city of Rome so often suffers burning. But if human humility could declare what is the cause of it, and in this darkness was free to speak with impunity, then all would see everything. Christians and Jews are indeed executed as fire-raisers, as a matter of common custom. ... In six days 132 palaces, 4,000 apartment blocks were burned; the seventh brought a pause. I wish you good health, brother. Given on March 28th in the consulship of Frugi and Bassus [64CE].

DATA

TITLE: The Correspondence of Seneca and Paul

ORIGINAL DATE OF COMPOSITION: 4th cent. CE

ORIGINAL LANGUAGE: Latin

PROVENANCE: Rome?

EARLIEST EXTANT MANUSCRIPT: 9th cent. CE (Latin)

THE LETTER OF PSEUDO-TITUS

The letter "on the state of chastity" claiming to be by Titus, the disciple of Paul, is a curious document that exists in a single eighth-century Latin manuscript discovered only in 1896 and published in full in 1925. The attribution to Titus and the description of the work as a letter are only found in the title and the concluding lines: Titus is not mentioned in the main body of the work, nor does it belong to the letter genre.

The ascription to Titus may have been motivated by statements in the Letter to Titus in the New Testament about the need "to renounce worldly passions" and "to live lives that are self-controlled, upright, and godly." These themes are prominent in Pseudo-Titus, which praises virginity and chastity and denounces those tempted to abandon their vows of celibacy. The work is apparently addressed primarily to "those who are not defiled with women, whom

Ruins of the church of St. Titus at Gortyna, Crete, reputedly founded by Paul's disciple Titus, the first bishop of Crete. He is mentioned several times in Paul's letters and was the recipient of the Letter to Titus.

Priscillianism

Priscillian was the head of a strongly ascetic Christian group in Spain in the late fourth century CE. Its adherents practiced what is known as "spiritual marriage," by which men and women lived together but refrained from sex. This custom was obviously open to abuse and many scholars believe that Pseudo-Titus's denunciations are aimed specifically at such abuses within the Priscillianist movement. Certainly the author appears to hold that even a desire to cohabit constitutes a departure from the celibate ideal. But whether the work can be so precisely linked with Priscillianism, and thus to a particular period and region, is uncertain. Perhaps all that can be said is that Pseudo-Titus is a highly individual rhetorical exercise by a writer who employs all the resources at his disposal to convey an enthusiasm for the life of celibacy, which the writer sees as essential for salvation.

the Lord calls an angelic host" and "those who have not abandoned themselves to men, whom he calls virgins." These groups are ceaselessly rebuked for lapsing into carnal ways. However, it would be wrong to think of people who lived apart from other Christians, and who might be compared to monks and nuns. Rather, a celibate existence was incumbent on all those in the Christian circles which the writer has in view (see box, above). This is shown by his frequent quotations from the apocryphal acts of Andrew, Peter, and John, where conversion to Christianity involves strict asceticism and even the dissolution of existing marriages.

The language of the "letter" is pompous and verbose. As well as citing the apocryphal acts, the work also reproduces some otherwise unknown sayings of Jesus and the apostles. In support of his arguments the author employs a wealth of freely translated biblical quotations.

From the Letter of Pseudo-Titus

The prophecy of the Lord through Ezekiel has finally come to fulfillment: "My house," he says, "has for me turned into such dross as brass, iron, tin, lead, in the midst of silver." Into such a mixture have you turned. For in the state of the ascetic, which is silver, there have emerged in the end alloys of different sorts, bad ingredients. ... The iron signifies the hardness of the heart in which the wisdom of the spiritual mind has taken no root. ... The lead signifies the heaviness of the flesh. ... By this is signified the offense which submerges men in the destruction of death, for the submerging of Pharaoh and his people as lead in the sea according to the account in Scripture was only a sign for us. ... The brass signifies the stench of the sinful flesh, after which the sons of Israel craved in Egypt. ... They are tin who dazzle our eyes with the wisdom of God and who in the matter of chastity exhibit an appearance of polluted silver, but who are in no way of great value in the Church.

DATA

TITLE:
The Letter of
Pseudo-Titus

ORIGINAL DATE OF
COMPOSITION:
5th cent. CE

ORIGINAL LANGUAGE:
Latin

PROVENANCE:
Uncertain. Spain?

EARLIEST EXTANT
MANUSCRIPT:
8th cent. CE (Latin)

THE PREACHINGS OF PETER

Two apocryphal works ascribed to Peter have almost identical titles, but are quite distinct. The Kerygma Petri (Preaching of Peter) is known only from quotations in the writings of Clement of Alexandria. The Kerygmata Petrou (Preachings of Peter), is reconstructed from the Pseudo-Clementines, a collection of Greek writings concerned with the career of St. Clement of Rome, probably from ca. 250CE–ca. 350CE.

The Preachings falls into three parts. It begins with a letter from Peter to James of Jerusalem, the brother of Jesus (see p.141), accompanying "the books of my preachings." This precedes the main section, which consists of teachings and instructions given by Peter. Finally, a narrative relates the reaction of James and the elders of the Jerusalem church.

The Kerygmata throws interesting light on the beliefs and practices of Jewish Christianity, and its desire to enlist the great figure of Peter in its support. The work claims that the "word of truth" was made known in the law of Moses "and was confirmed by our Lord in its everlasting continuance." It goes on to commend the Jewish tradition of biblical interpetation, which seeks "to harmonize the contradictions of the Scriptures, in case one who does not know the traditions is perplexed by the ambiguous utterances of the prophets." No one is permitted "to teach unless he first learn how the Scriptures should be used."

This high evaluation of Jewish interpretative tradition points to the outlook of Jewish Christianity. However, the work claims that this tradition has been corrupted by the Jewish teachers, the scribes and Pharisees, who fail to recognize that, in the course of time, some false passages have intruded into the written law. According to the Preachings, the proper interpretation of Scripture now belongs to a true prophet, Jesus, and those

St. Peter Preaching, by Pedro Serra, probably illustrating Acts 1.15ff. Spanish, second half of the 14th century.

who accept his doctrine "will learn which parts of the Scriptures answer to the truth and which are false." Among the "false" elements are references to the Temple and sacrifices, to kingship and women prophets. The Hebrew Scriptures are central to the author's outlook, and Jesus is the final incarnation of a line of true prophetic witnesses, beginning with Adam. It is said of Jesus, "no other possesses the Spirit but he who from the beginning of the world, changing his forms and his names, runs through universal time, until anointed for his toils by the mercy of God, he comes to his own time and will have rest for ever."

Another sign of Jewish Christianity is the fact that Peter's letter is addressed to James, Jesus' brother. In the New Testament, James appears as the chief representative of Jewish Christianity and he long continued to be venerated in this role within various Christian circles. In the narrative, the books of Peter's teachings are to be handed on only in the church headed by James. The Preachings are also notable for their typical Jewish Christian hostility toward Paul, who appears in the guise of Simon (Magus), the traditional opponent of Peter (see pp.174–8). Peter states that while Paul "came as the first before me to the Gentiles," he, Peter, "came in upon him as light upon darkness, as knowledge upon ignorance, as healing upon sickness." Paul is represented as claiming directly to know Jesus through his experience on the road to Damascus and later visions. Peter disputes the genuineness of visions altogether—for him, the only authentic revelation is the doctrine he received from the historical Jesus (see extract, below).

From the Preachings of Peter (Kerygmata Petrou)

Simon [=Paul] interrupted with the words, "You have stated that you have learned accurately the teaching of your master because you have heard and seen him directly face to face, and that it is not possible for any other to experience the like in a dream or in a vision. I shall show you that this is false. He who hears something directly is by no means certain of what is said. For he must check whether, being a man, he has not been deceived as to what appears to him. On the other hand, [a] vision creates together with the appearance the certainty that one sees something divine." ... Peter replied ... "No one is able to see the incorporeal power of the Son or even of an angel. But he who has a vision should recognize that this is the work of a wicked demon. For to a pious, natural, and pure mind the truth reveals itself; it is not acquired through a dream, but is granted to the good through discernment. For in this way was the Son revealed to me also by the Father. For this reason I know the power of revelation; I have myself learned this from him. ... Can any one be made competent to teach through a vision? And if your opinion is, 'That is possible,' why then did our teacher spend a whole year with us who were awake? ... But if you were visited by him for the space of an hour and were instructed by him and thereby have become an apostle, then proclaim his words, expound what he has taught, be a friend to his apostles and do not contend with me, who am his confidant."

DATA

TITLE:
The Preachings of Peter (Kerygmata Petrou)

ORIGINAL DATE OF COMPOSITION:
ca. 250–ca. 350CE

ORIGINAL LANGUAGE:
Greek

PROVENANCE: Syria?

EARLIEST EXTANT MANUSCRIPT:
5th cent. CE (Syriac)

THE LETTER OF THE APOSTLES

The Letter of the Apostles, which is not mentioned by any ancient author, claims to be a letter from the eleven apostles—the original group, minus Judas Iscariot—to believers in the four quarters of the world. It exists complete in five medieval Ethiopic manuscripts, demonstrating its popularity in the Ethiopian church. There is also a less complete version in Coptic.

Although presented as a letter, the work displays several features of the apocalyptic genre. It takes the form of a series of questions and answers between the disciples and Jesus after the Resurrection and its descriptions of the end of time follow the common apocalyptic pattern. It is written as a reaffirmation of the Gospel in order to combat the teaching of "the false apostles" Simon [Magus] and Cerinthus (see box, p.235), who were regarded as the first Gnostics.

The first of the work's two main sections is largely concerned with the main events in the career of the historical Jesus and their significance. In the episode of the Feeding of the Five Thousand, the disciples ask: "What meaning is there in the five loaves?" and receive the answer that "they are a picture of our faith concerning the great Christianity and that [faith] is in the Father, the ruler of the entire world; and in Jesus Christ our Savior; and in the Holy Spirit, the Paraclete [literally "advocate," or "intercessor"]; and in the holy Church; and in the forgiveness

From the Letter of the Apostles, chapters 13–14

DATA

TITLE:
The Letter of the
Apostles

ORIGINAL DATE OF
COMPOSITION:
ca. 150CE

ORIGINAL LANGUAGE:
Probably Greek

PROVENANCE:
Lower Egypt?

EARLIEST EXTANT
MANUSCRIPT:
4th–5th cent. CE
(Coptic)

What [the Lord] revealed is this ... : "While I was coming from the Father of all, passing by the heavens, wherein I put on the wisdom of the Father and by his power clothed myself in his power, I was like the heavens. And passing by the angels and archangels in their form and as one of them, I passed by the orders, the dominions, and the princes ... And the archangels Michael and Gabriel, Raphael and Uriel followed me until the fifth firmament of heaven, while I appeared as one of them. ...

Then I made the archangels to become distracted with the voice and go up to the altar of the Father and serve the Father in their work until I should return to him. ...

For I became all in all with them. ... Do you know that the angel Gabriel came and brought the message to Mary?" And we said to him: "Yes, O Lord." And he answered and said to us: "Do you not remember that I previously said to you that I became like an angel to the angels?" And we said to him: "Yes, O Lord." And he said to us: "At that time I appeared in the form of the archangel Gabriel to Mary and spoke with her, and her heart received me; she believed and laughed, and I, the Word, went into her and became flesh; and I myself was servant for myself; and in the likeness of an angel, like him will I do, and after it I will go to my Father."

The Descent of the Spirit, by Pieter Coecke van Aelst (1502–50), illustrating the descent of the Holy Spirit upon the Apostles and the Virgin after the Ascension (Acts 2.1–4). The Spirit is represented by a hovering dove.

of sins." This fivefold interpretation resembles the sort of outline of orthodox Catholic faith found in the Christian creeds: belief in the Trinity, the Church, and the remission of sins. The recipients of the letter are commanded to celebrate the remembrance of Christ's death, "which is the Passover" until Jesus comes again, probably a reference to the annual feast of Easter.

The second section of the letter, where the question and answer structure is much more marked, is apocalyptic in character, dealing with the second coming of Jesus and the events of the end of time. The apostles ask Jesus: "In what kind of power and form are you about to come?" The wording of the question suggests that this event is expected in the near future. In reply, Jesus says that he will be carried on "the wings of the clouds in splendor with my cross going on before me." As in other apocalypses, the cross is identified as the sign of the Son of

Christ in Majesty, an Ethiopian manuscript (1632–67). The figure of Christ is surrounded by angels, while below him are the souls of those who have fallen into hell, where the figure of Satan burns.

Man in Matthew 24.30. The apostles go on to ask: "O Lord, how many years yet?" They receive the reply: "When the hundred and fiftieth year is completed, between Pentecost and Passover will the coming of my Father take place." Assuming the author views the Second Coming as imminent, this reply may well date the letter to the mid-second century CE.

Jesus' reference to "the coming of my Father" appears to cause a problem for the apostles, who go on to say: "O Lord, now you said to us, 'I will come,' and then you said 'he who sent me will come.'" In response, Jesus quotes the saying "I am in the Father and the Father in me"(John 10.38, 14.10ff., and else-where) and then expounds its significance more fully: "I am wholly in the Father and the Father in me after his image and after his likeness and after his power and after his perfection and after his light, and I am his perfect word." This is one of the author's main theological concerns: to assert the complete and perfect union, almost to the point of identity, of the Father and the Son.

Several regular apocalyptic features occur in this section, such as a description of the cosmic disasters which will herald the end of the present age, and of the Last Judgment of the righteous and sinners. More importantly for the author, Jesus repeatedly emphasizes the apostles' obligation to preach the gospel of salvation to the whole world, reassuring them that his continued presence will guarantee their success. The work makes it clear that Paul enjoys the same authority as the original apostles (see extract, opposite). Those won over by the apostles are to live lives of strict morality or face stern justice if they fall short. People are responsible for their own actions—as Jesus says: "Every man is given the ability to believe in the light."

The author is also anxious to emphasize the truth of the bodily resurrection of the soul, as opposed to the purely spiritual resurrection advocated by Cerinthus (see box, opposite). Jesus says: "The flesh of every man will rise with his soul alive and his spirit." Thus human beings are one with the Lord in his humanity, as Jesus says: "I have put on your flesh, in which I was born and died and was buried and rose again through my heavenly Father."

From the Letter of the Apostles, chapters 31 and 33

"Look, you will meet a man whose name is Saul, which being interpreted means Paul. He is a Jew, circumcised according to the command of the law, and he will hear my voice from heaven with terror, fear, and trembling; and his eyes will be darkened and by your hand be crossed with spittle. ... Immediately his eyes will be opened ... and he will become strong among the nations and will preach and teach. ... Then will he be hated and delivered into the hand of his enemy, and he will testify before kings, and upon him will come the completion of the testimony to me; because he had persecuted and hated me, he will be converted to me. ... The last of the last will become a preacher to the Gentiles, perfect through the will of my Father." ... And we said: "When, Lord, will we meet that man, and when will you go to your Father?" ... And he answered ... "That man will set out from the land of Cilicia to Damascus in Syria to tear apart the Church which you must create. It is I who will speak to him through you. ... He will be strong in this faith, that the word of the prophet may be fulfilled where it says: 'Behold, out of the land of Syria I will begin to call a new Jerusalem, and I will subdue Zion and it will be captured; and the barren one who has no children will be fruitful and will be called the daughter of my Father, but, to me, my bride....' But that man will I turn aside, that he may not go there and complete his evil plan. And [the] glory of my Father will come in through him. For after I have gone away and remain with my Father, I will speak with him from heaven."

The Letter and the Doctrines of Cerinthus

Cerinthus (active ca. 100CE) held that the world was not created by the supreme Deity and that Jesus was born as an ordinary man who was only united with a divine power at his baptism. This power left him before his Crucifixion, so that there was no physical resurrection of the Savior.

The letter implicitly rejects all these beliefs. Jesus Christ, who "is God and Son of God," is depicted as the agent of creation. An important passage relates how Jesus descends through the heavenly spheres, assuming the forms of the angels and archangels, finally appearing to Mary as Gabriel and entering into her womb to be made flesh, so becoming "servant for myself"—in other words, there is no distinction between the human Jesus and the heavenly Christ (see extract on p.232).

The reality of the Lord's resurrected body is emphasized by a retelling of the famous episode of Doubting Thomas in John's gospel (John 20.24–9). Not only does Thomas put his finger into the wound in Jesus' side, but Peter does the same with the nail wounds and Andrew is asked to observe that Jesus' feet touch the ground—the author quotes an unknown saying of a prophet that "a ghost, a demon, leaves no print on the ground."

That Jesus came to earth in the flesh and truly died and rose again is repeatedly affirmed throughout the work.

GLOSSARY

apocalypse ("revelation") or **apocalyptic** Both terms refer to a type of writing in which cosmic events and phenomena are revealed by God to a wise man through the agency of angels, visions, or dreams. The seer may be transported to the heavens by angels to see at first hand the workings of the cosmos, including the heavenly throne of God and the regions where sinners are punished and the righteous are rewarded. He may also receive a revelation of Israel's history from his own time down to the cataclysmic events of end-time (see below), in which evil is finally destroyed. The most famous Jewish apocalypse is the Book of Daniel in the Bible; others include 1 Enoch, the Apocalypse of Abraham, and the Apocalypse of Zephaniah in the Pseudepigrapha. The most notable Christian apocalypse is Revelation, or the Apocalypse, the New Testament book which gave its name to this type of work.

Apocrypha (1) Old Testament Apocrypha The name given to works included in the Septuagint, the Greek version of the Hebrew Scriptures (see below), but for which the Hebrew originals, where they had existed, were lost. For this reason, among others, these writings—including the books of Judith, Sirach, Tobit, the story of Susanna, and the First and Second Books of the Maccabees—do not form part of the Jewish Bible. In most Christian denominations they possess a quasi-canonical status, and they are often included in editions of the Bible, between the Old and New Testaments. In the Roman Catholic church many of these writings are referred to as "deuterocanonical," that is, secondary to the canon but considered of spiritual value. **(2) New Testament Apocrypha** The term given to the many gospels, acts, and letters written by Christian authors and not included in the canon of the New Testament (see pp.8–9).

apocryphal Of or pertaining to, or derived from, the Apocrypha.

end-time The final age of the world.

eschatological Of or pertaining to the "last things" (the apocalypse, the end of the world, the day of judgment, the dawn of a new age, etc.); from Greek *eskhatos* ("last").

Gnostic Of or pertaining to Gnosticism, a religious movement of the early centuries CE with highly distinctive ideas about the nature of humanity, the divine, and the cosmos. Gnostic Christianity became popular enough to pose a serious threat to the evolving Christian orthodoxy, and it was suppressed as heretical (see pp.156–9).

Hebrew Bible, Hebrew Scriptures The Hebrew writings constituting the Jewish Bible. The Old Testament, the first part of the Christian Bible, consists of the Hebrew Scriptures (ordered differently from the Jewish Bible) with or without the Old Testament Apocrypha (see **Apocrypha (1)**, above), depending on denomination.

Hellenistic Of or pertaining to the period from ca. 300BCE to the beginning of the Roman empire, when Greek language and culture were predominant in the eastern Mediterranean and Near East, as a result of the conquests of Alexander the Great and the empires founded by his successors. Greek remained the most widely spoken language of the region until the coming of Islam in the seventh century CE.

law In this book, the term "law" almost always refers to the Jewish (Mosaic) law, or Torah (see below).

Pentateuch The first five books of the Hebrew Bible: Genesis, Exodus, Leviticus, Numbers, and Deuteronomy. Also referred to as the Torah, the Books of Moses, and the Books of the Law.

Pseudepigrapha Religious writings outside the Jewish and Christian canons, Old Testament Apocrypha, and the corpus of rabbinic works (see pp.6–8).

rabbinic, rabbinical Of or pertaining to the rabbis (Jewish teachers and interpreters of the law) and their teachings.

Septuagint The Greek translation of the Hebrew Bible, probably begun at Alexandria, Egypt, in the third century BCE and used by Greek-speaking Jews in the ancient world. It was later adopted by Christians and it remains the basis of the Old Testament of the Greek Orthodox church. It includes writings omitted from the Jewish canon but possessing a quasi-canonical status among Christians (see **Apocrypha (1)**, above). (See also pp.104–5.)

synoptic gospels (synoptics) The gospels of Matthew, Mark, and Luke. "Synoptic" (Greek *sunoptikos*) literally means "seen together": these three gospels share so many textual similarities that they may be set out in parallel and fruitfully compared.

Talmud The corpus of rabbinic commentary on the Jewish law. There are two versions, one produced in Palestine ca. 400CE (the "Jerusalem" Talmud) and one in Mesopotamia ca. 500CE (the "Babylonian" Talmud).

Temple The Temple of Jerusalem, the focus of Jewish religious life until 70CE. The First Temple was built by King Solomon and destroyed by the Babylonians ca. 587BCE; it was rebuilt following the exile in Babylon and lavishly refurbished by King Herod the Great. This Second Temple, the one Jesus knew, was destroyed by the Romans in 70CE and never rebuilt.

testament A genre of writing purporting to contain the last utterance of a famous figure from Israel's past, such as Adam or Abraham, before his death (see p.40 ff.).

Torah Hebrew, "instruction, direction." In a strict sense, the Torah refers to the Pentateuch (see above), which contain the 633 commandments (*mitzvot*) that form the basis of the Jewish law, believed to have been transmitted by God to Israel through Moses. The written Torah is supplemented by the "oral Torah," various regulations not found in the Bible and codified in the Mishnah and later the Talmud (see above).

ABBREVIATIONS

The following abbreviations are used in this book:

General Abbreviations

BCE	Before the Common Era (the equivalent of BC)
CE	Common Era (the equivalent of AD)
ca.	*circa* (about)
ff.	and following
p./pp.	page/pages

Quotations from the Bible and other Ancient Writings

Books of the Hebrew Scriptures, New Testament, and other writings are often referred to according to the list of short forms and abbreviations below. Short forms are used in the running text. Abbreviations are used in parentheses within the text and in picture captions. Chapter and verse are separated by a period (.) and a sequence is indicated by a dash (–). Thus, Matt. 9.24 = chapter 9, verse 24 of Matthew; Matt. 3.7–10 = chapter 3, verses 7 to 10 of Matthew; Matt. 5–10 = chapters 5 to 10 of Matthew.

Short form	Abbreviation	Short form	Abbreviation
Acts of the Apostles	Acts	1 Kings	1 Kings
Amos	Amos	2 Kings	2 Kings
Baruch	Bar.	Lamentations	Lam.
2 Baruch	2 Bar.	Leviticus	Lev.
3 Baruch	3 Bar.	Luke	Luke
4 Baruch	4 Bar.	1 Maccabees	1 Macc.
Bel and the Dragon	Bel	2 Maccabees	2 Macc.
1 Chronicles	1 Chron.	3 Maccabees	3 Macc.
2 Chronicles	2 Chron.	4 Maccabees	4 Macc.
Colossians	Col.	Malachi	Mal.
1 Corinthians	1 Cor.	Mark	Mark
2 Corinthians	2 Cor.	Matthew	Matt.
Daniel	Dan.	Micah	Mic.
Deuteronomy	Deut.	Nahum	Nah.
Ecclesiastes	Eccles.	Nehemiah	Neh.
1 Enoch	1 En.	Numbers	Num.
2 Enoch	2 En.	Obadiah	Obad.
Ephesians	Eph.	1 Peter	1 Pet.
1 Esdras	1 Esd.	2 Peter	2 Pet.
2 Esdras	2 Esd.	Philippians	Phil.
Esther	Esther	Philemon	Philem.
Exodus	Exod.	Prayer of Azariah and Song of	
Ezekiel	Ezek.	the Three Young Men (Jews)	Song of Thr.
Ezra	Ezra	Prayer of Manasseh	Pr. of Man.
Galatians	Gal.	Proverbs	Prov.
Habakkuk	Hab.	Psalm(s)	Ps(s).
Haggai	Hag.	Psalms of Solomon	Pss. Sol.
Hebrews	Heb.	Revelation	Rev.
Hosea	Hos.	Romans	Rom.
Isaiah	Isa.	Ruth	Ruth
James	James	1 Samuel	1 Sam.
Jeremiah	Jer.	2 Samuel	2 Sam.
Job	Job	Sirach (Ecclesiasticus)	Sir.
Joel	Joel	Song of Solomon	Song of Sol.
John *or* Fourth Gospel	John	Susanna	Sus.
1 John	1 John	1 Thessalonians	1 Thess.
2 John	2 John	2 Thessalonians	2 Thess.
3 John	3 John	1 Timothy	1 Tim.
Jonah	Jon.	2 Timothy	2 Tim.
Joshua	Josh.	Titus	Titus
Jubilees	Jub.	Tobit	Tob.
Jude	Jude	Wisdom of Solomon	Wisd. of Solomon
Judges	Judg.	Zechariah	Zech.
Judith	Jth.	Zephaniah	Zeph.

BIBLIOGRAPHY

THE PSEUDEPIGRAPHA

Charles, R.H., ed. *The Apocrypha and Pseudepigrapha of the Old Testament in English*, vol. 2. Oxford: Clarendon Press, 1913.

Charlesworth, James H., ed. *The Old Testament Pseudepigrapha*, 2 vols. London: Darton, Longman and Todd, 1983.

Charlesworth, James H. *The Pseudepigrapha and Modern Research with a Supplement*. Chico, California: Society of Biblical Literature Septuagint and Cognate Studies Series, no. 75, 1981.

Díez Macho, A., ed. *Apócrifos del Antiguo Testamento*, 4 vols. Madrid: Ediciones Cristiandad, 1982–4.

Dupont-Sommer, André, and Philonenko, Marc, eds. *La Bible: Écrits intertestamentaires*. Paris: Editions Gallimard, 1987.

Eissfeldt, Otto. *The Old Testament: An Introduction*, pp. 571–637. New York and Evanston: Harper and Row, 1965.

Ginzberg, Louis. *The Legends of the Jews*, 7 vols. Philadelphia: Jewish Publication Society of America, 1909.

James, M.R. *The Lost Apocrypha of the Old Testament, their titles and fragments*. London: SPCK Translations of Early Documents, 1920.

Kautzsch, E., ed. *Die Apokryphen und Pseudepigraphen einschliesslich der grossen Qumran-Handschriften*. Heidelberg: Quelle & Meyer, 1971.

Kugel, James L. *Traditions of the Bible*. Cambridge, Massachusetts and London: Harvard University Press, 1998.

Nickelsburg, George W.E. *Jewish Literature between the Bible and the Mishnah*. London: SCM Press, 1981.

Russell, D.S. *The Old Testament Pseudepigrapha: Patriarchs and Prophets in Early Judaism*. London: SCM Press, 1987.

Sparks, H.F.D., ed. *The Apocryphal Old Testament*. Oxford: Clarendon Press, 1984.

Stone, M.E., ed. *Jewish Writings of the Second Temple Period: Apocrypha, Pseudepigrapha, Qumran, Sectarian Writings, Philo, Josephus*. Philadelphia: Fortress Press, 1984.

Stone, M.E. and Bergren, T.A., eds. *Biblical Figures outside the Bible*. Harrisburg, PA: Trinity Press International, 1998.

THE NEW TESTAMENT APOCRYPHA

Amiot, F. *La Bible Apocryphe: Évangiles apocryphes*. Paris: Librairie Arthème Fayard, 1953.

Elliot, J.K. *The Apocryphal New Testament*. Oxford: Oxford University Press, 1993.

James, M.R. *The Apocryphal New Testament*. Oxford: Clarendon Press, 1924.

Layton, Bentley, ed. *The Gnostic Scriptures*. London: SCM Press, 1987.

Pagels, E. *The Gnostic Gospels*. New York: Random House, 1979.

Robinson, J.M., ed. *The Nag Hammadi Library in English*, revised edition. San Francisco: Harper & Row, 1988.

Schneemelcher, Wilhelm, ed. *New Testament Apocrypha*, revised edition, 2 vols. Cambridge: James Clarke & Co., 1991–2.

Voragine, Jacobus de. *Golden Legend*, translated by William Granger Ryan. 2 vols, Princeton: Princeton University Press, 1993.

HISTORICAL BACKGROUND

Baron, Salo W. *A Social and Religious History of the Jews*, 3 vols. New York: Columbia University Press, 1957.

Chadwick, Owen. *A History of Christianity*. London: Weidenfeld and Nicholson, 1995.

Daniélou, J. *Theology of Jewish Christianity*. London: Longman, Darton and Todd, 1964.

Green, V.H.H. *A New History of Christianity*. Oxford: Oxford University Press, 1996.

Schürer, E. *The History of the Jewish People in the Age of Jesus Christ*, revised edition by G. Vermes, F. Millar, M. Black, and M. Goodman, 3 vols. Edinburgh: T. & T. Clark, 1973–87.

INDEX

ACKNOWLEDGMENTS

The publisher would like to thank the following for their kind permission to reproduce the translations and illustrations in this book. Every care has been taken to trace copyright holders. However, if we have omitted anyone, we apologize and will, if informed, make corrections in any future editions.

TEXT CREDITS

Part 1: The "Lost" Hebrew Scriptures (pp.10–127)
Extracts adapted from *The Old Testament Pseudepigrapha*, edited by James H. Charlesworth, copyright © 1983, 1985 by James H. Charlesworth. Used in the U.K. and Commonwealth (excluding Canada) by permission of Darton, Longman and Todd Ltd. Used in the U.S.A. and Canada by permission of Doubleday, a division of Random House, Inc.

Part 2: The "Lost" New Testament (pp.128–235)
Extracts adapted from *New Testament Apocrypha*, revised edition edited by Wilhelm Schneemelcher, copyright © 1990 and 1992 by James Clarke and Co. Ltd. Used in the U.K. and Commonwealth (excluding Canada) by permission of James Clarke and Co. Ltd. Used in the U.S.A. and Canada by permission of Westminster John Knox Press.

PICTURE CREDITS

Abbreviations
AA: Art Archive, London
BAL: Bridgeman Art Library, London
BL: British Library, London
RHPL: Robert Harding Picture Library

1 BL
2 Corbis/Wadsworth Atheneum, Hartford, CT/Francis G. Mayer
7 AKG London/Accademia, Venice/Cameraphoto
10 BL
13 Scala, Florence/St. Mark's, Venice
15 RHPL/BL
16 AKG London/Erich Lessing
19 AA/Dagli Orti
20 BAL
23 BL
25 AKG London/Kunsthistorisches Museum, Vienna/Erich Lessing
27 RHPL/Fred Friberg
31 AA/Dagli Orti
32 Scala, Florence

35 BAL/BL
37 AKG London/Collegiate Church, Klosterneuburg/Erich Lessing
38 AA/Basilica of San Apollinare in Classe, Ravenna/Dagli Orti
41 British Museum, London
42 BL
44 RHPL/David Beatty
47 Corbis/Araldo de Luca
49 AA/Cathedral, Florence/Dagli Orti
50 BAL/Private Collection
53 BAL/Fitzwilliam Museum, University of Cambridge
54 Sonia Halliday Photographs, Weston Turville, Bucks
56 AKG London/Kunsthistorisches Museum, Vienna/Erich Lessing
59 BAL/BL
61 Scala, Florence/Collegiate Church, San Gimignano
62 AA/Egyptian Museum, Turin/A. Dagli Orti
65 AKG London/Staatliche Kunstsammlungen, Kassel
66 Scala, Florence/Sistine Chapel, Vatican
69 Art Resource, New York/The Jewish Museum, New York
70 AKG London/Staatliches Museum, Schwerin
73 AA/Bibliothèque Municipale, Valenciennes/A. Dagli Orti
74 Scala, Florence/Galleria degli Uffizi, Florence
77 Scala, Florence/Accademia, Venice
79 Scala, Florence/Cathedral, Orvieto
80 Scala, Florence/Museu Nacional d'Art de Catalunya, Barcelona
83 AA/Bibliothèque Municipale, Valenciennes/A. Dagli Orti
84 Scala, Florence/Villa dei Misteri, Pompeii
87 AA
88 AKG London/Staatsbibliothek, Preussischer Kulturbesitz, Berlin
90 Scala, Florence/Museo di Roma, Rome
93 AKG London/Bibliothèque Nationale, Paris
95 BAL/Biblioteca Marciana, Venice
96 BAL/Aldeburgh Church, Suffolk
99 AKG London/Erich Lessing
101 Scala, Florence/Galleria Nazionale dell'Umbria, Perugia
102 AA
105 AKG London/Erich Lessing
106 Scala, Florence/Klaus Synagogue, Prague
109 Scala, Florence/San Vitale, Ravenna
110 BAL/The De Morgan Foundation, London
113 Julia Ruxton, London
114 BAL/Catacombs of San Gennaro, Naples
117 BAL/Palazzo Medici-Riccardi, Florence
118 British Museum, London
120 AKG London/Tarek Camoisson
122 Ann and Bury Peerless, Birchington, Kent
125 AA/Musée Condé, Chantilly/Dagli Orti
127 BAL/Vatican Museums and Galleries, Vatican City